W9-BMN-652

A Blessing for the Heart

God's Beautiful Plan for Marital Intimacy

James E. Sheridan

with an introduction by
Barbara Markey, Ph.D.

Marriage Done Right
Adrian, Michigan

NOTICE TO READERS

All scripture quotations, unless otherwise indicated, are taken from the HOLY BIBLE, NEW INTERNATIONAL VERSION®. NIV. ® Copyright © 1973, 1978, 1984 by International Bible Society. Used by permission of Zondervan. All rights reserved.

The "NIV" and "New International Version" trademarks are registered in the United States Patent and Trademark Office by International Bible Society.

All emphasis added to Scripture quotations, by bold print, underline or italics, is the author's.

A Blessing for the Heart
Copyright © 2004 by James E. Sheridan
All rights reserved

Cover photograph © 2004 by Anita Sheridan
All rights reserved

ISBN 0-9758802-0-9

Library of Congress Cataloging-in-Publication Data available on request.

Marriage Done Right
10864 Burton Road
Adrian, MI 49221
517-547-4905
www.marriagedoneright.com

All rights reserved. No part of this publication may be reproduced, stored in a retrieval system or transmitted in any form or by any means – electronic, mechanical, digital, photocopy, recording, or any other – of any nature (except for brief quotations in printed reviews) without the prior written permission of James E. Sheridan.

Style Notice: The constant and repetitive use of duplicate pronouns to indicate a gender-neutral reference (i.e., "he or she," "him and her," "his and hers," etc.) is both wordy and clumsy. It also tends to interfere with the natural flow of the sentence. Therefore, this book uses the masculine pronoun (i.e., he, his or him) in situations in which the context intends a gender-neutral situation, in accordance with traditional rules of English grammar. Whether the masculine pronoun refers to males, in particular, or humanity, in general, should be clear from the context.

When a pronoun is used to refer to God, it is capitalized (i.e., He, His or Him). The only exception is when a quotation from another source uses lower case for a pronoun in reference to God. The modern approach is to use the lower case. This is perfectly acceptable, since neither Hebrew nor Greek had capital letters. The pronoun will be capitalized in this book for two reasons. First, as a personal issue, I wish to accord God all the honor possible. Second, since I will be using the masculine pronoun in gender-neutral settings, which also contain references to God, it will help the reader to know whether the pronoun refers to God or mankind.

References: Bible references are abbreviated, using the standard notations. Thus, "Gen. 2:18" means the Book of Genesis, chapter 2, verse 18. If you have trouble understanding the abbreviations, most Bibles have a table of abbreviations at the front.

Throughout this book, various Hebrew and Greek words are used to help the explanation. In the footnotes you will find references to *Strong's Definitions* and a notation, such as "OT 8085" or "NT 25." *Strong's Definitions* has numbered every word in the Bible as it appears in the original language, no matter how it is translated into English. "OT" means Old Testament and "NT" means New Testament. The number indicates the individual word. Thus, OT 8085 refers to the Hebrew word "*shma*," in the Old Testament, which means both "listen" and "obey." The same number is used no matter how it is translated. Likewise, NT 25 refers to the Greek word "*agape*," in the New Testament, which means "love."

Abbreviations: References are made to the following Bible translations:

ASV	American Standard Version
NIV	New International Version
KJV	King James Version
RSV	Revised Standard Version
NAS	New American Standard
NASU	New American Standard Update
TEV	Today's English Version
TLB	The Living Bible

Dedication

To my wife, Sharron, my source of support, my best editor, my source of inspiration, my *ezer kenegdo*, my Shulamite, and living proof that God loves me.

Acknowledgments

The list of people who aided in this effort is almost endless. Those who spent exceptional time and effort in editing and providing suggestions on content were Kathy Klumpp, Prof. Don Kleinsmith, Anita Sheridan, Rev. John Guthrie, Rev. Michael Goble, Rev. Jeff Meyers, Dr. Barbara Markey, Father Tom Helfrich, Rev. Clark Cothern, Rev. Walt Miller, Char Kamper, Gretchen Warwich, Ph.D., Joyce Faulhaber, M.A., L.L.P.C., and Nathan Klumpp.

I also have had inspiration and encouragement from a wide range of people, including my brother, Dennis, and his wife, Nancy; my sister, Marge Dubuque, and her husband, Tony; the ever encouraging Diane Sollee, founder and director, smartmarriage.com and the Coalition for Marriage, Family and Couples Education; Michael and Harriet McManus, founders of Marriage Savers®; and Rev. Paul Herter and his wife, Carol, and my church family at Hope Lutheran, Adrian, MI, who manage to survive my strange sense of humor.

A special thanks also goes to the congregation at Christ Lutheran Church, Overland Park, KS, who arranged for video-taping the marriage enrichment seminar, on which this book is based. In particular, Denis and Rosemary Clyde, of Christ Lutheran, have provided enormous encouragement and support.

I also wish to thank Rev. Joe Adams, who was the person God used to spark my interest in marriage enrichment and in-depth Bible study.

Finally, I acknowledge God's gift of my parents, James V. and Estelle Sheridan, and the incredible example of love they provided.

Cover design: Anita Sheridan, Los Angeles, CA.
Illustrations: Kathy Johns, Adrian, MI.
Interior design and layout: Lee Lewis, Words Plus Design, Tecumseh, MI.

Contents

Foreword

A marriage therapist will tell you that two of the things most married couples have difficulty talking about well are sex and religion. The more important these topics are to them, the greater risk they feel. Partners are most vulnerable to hurt or to misunderstanding around the issues of sex and religion because these topics are complex, they are personal and they get to the core of each person and of their relationship.

James Sheridan opens wide the doors to conversation on sex and religion. He does not dance around topics. With humor and respect, he drags or cajoles readers right to the heart of the matter. Directly and indirectly he names questions, fears and beliefs. The topics are put out into broad daylight to be explored and discussed.

I believe that this is a great favor to couples. Sexual intimacy is a foundational bonder in a marriage. It provides the glue that both builds and expresses the unique relationship of husband and wife. Lots of factors go into how each member of the couple thinks, feels and responds to sexual intimacy. Background, personality, ability to trust, hopes, and expectations are among the many pieces and parts that play into how the couple puts together a sexual relationship that is life giving…or not. As marriage partners grow more open and trusting in the many facets of their sexual intimacy, they give each other great power to heal or to hurt them. It is an important choice, an act of faith, for two people in a committed relationship to take the risk to build a full, sensual, intimate sexual relationship.

Religion and its day-to-day practice in a lived spirituality provide a couple with a bonder that makes it more possible to risk full sexual intimacy. Religion deals with values, with meaning, and with beliefs about who and how God is. Research done in 1999 on religiosity and marriage by the Center from Marriage and Family at Creighton University demonstrates that religion is either a bonder or a divider in the marriage of a believing couple. A shared spirituality can make it much easier for a couple to enjoy a rich sexual intimacy.

Although he probably could, James Sheridan does not present an encyclopedia on sex and intimacy in the following pages. Instead, he presents a Scriptural basis for sex and intimacy in marriage along with a great many practical suggestions for applying Scriptural principles to everyday married life. Using both his love for and understanding of Scripture and his wide knowledge of human interaction he develops the theme that marital intimacy is a beautiful plan from God. In the process, he also challenges and instructs on a Biblically based approach to marital intimacy that would be helpful for married couples to know and apply in their marriage. At its core, his point is simple: God's plan for marital intimacy is, indeed, "a blessing for the heart" of every marriage.

For some people, *A Blessing for the Heart* will provide a gateway to strengthening both religion and sex as bonders in their marriage relationship. For others, it will affirm with humor and sensitivity what they have always known. It may shock some and it will probably provide a wake-up call for many. When it comes to sex and religion, couples will have something to talk about that will be personal, complex and at the core of their persons and their relationship. It will be an enlightening and entertaining read, which will truly bless the marriages of those who apply its insights.

— Barbara Markey, Ph.D.
Center for Marriage and Family
May 2004

Introduction:

Why Read This Book?

W e spend most of our time in the faith community dancing around the real issue of sex that concerns every married couple: What *can* they do in the privacy of their marriage to make their relationship leap with the joy God has in mind for it? Take a look around you for a moment. On one extreme the world gives us pornography, which sells us the deviant and destructive side of sex. On the other extreme we have lots of books and articles, which tell us what *not* to do, what sexual boundaries we must observe, what sexual harassment policies we need in place and the sexual ethics we need to follow in counseling sessions.

But, there is little available to tell us the positive side of what *is permissible*. God's incredible message about sex and romance in marriage has to be the best-kept secret in religion for the past 1900 years. The purpose of this book is to let out the secret through a comprehensive description of how Scripture depicts sexual intimacy and romance in marriage.

Of course, it's God's Word that defines the good side of sex. The fact is we have an amazingly loving God. It only makes sense that He would tell us the good side of something He invented. Yet, when do

1

we hear this from the church? Rarely. But, it would be a inappropriate to lambast pastors for not regularly preaching and teaching on the subject. Even *assuming* sex is a proper subject for a sermon, most churches act as if a bolt of lightning would toast every member of the congregation if the minister dared to mention it in a sermon. And, if the lightning bolt did not do the job, there would be a large segment of the congregation which would make sure the minister was "fried" anyway. However, there is little need to worry about ministers being turned to "crispy critters." The reality is that so few people, including pastors, are comfortable talking about the intimate area of marriage, especially in a group setting, that the risk of lightning bolts or being fried is quite low.

Historically, this fear of sexual subjects has been nearly comical. It's been said that Jonathan Edwards, a clergyman and one of the most brilliant minds of colonial America, when told by his wife that they were going to have a baby, stood up in his Puritan piety, then told her never to say that to him again. She didn't. They had 12 children.

The extreme reluctance to address the intimate aspects of marriage is difficult to understand in light of Scripture. The Song of Solomon, along with passages in Proverbs and 1 Corinthians, directly addresses the issue. These passages are the word of God, after all. Moreover, we are told that, "All Scripture is God-breathed and is useful for teaching, rebuking, correcting and training in righteousness."[1] Nonetheless, most churches avoid the Song of Solomon in particular, as if hoping it will go away quietly and quit embarrassing everyone.

I have asked nearly 200 ministers whether they have ever led a study on the Song. Barely ten percent have said they had. This attitude prevails despite the availability of some excellent materials on marriage based on the Song.[2] I once presented a Sunday morning Bible study on the Song of Solomon for a large church in Nebraska. Two women in their early eighties sat in the front row. One had been a lifelong member of the congregation. The other was the minister's wife from another church. They were both there because in their combined experience, neither ever had heard a study on the Song of Songs.

This is amazing. Marriage is the foundational human relationship described in Scripture. The last act of creation[3] was the creation of woman out of man, which immediately led to the first wedding. The first blessing to humanity and the first command by God in the Bible were both in the context of marriage.[4] (Most Christians think only of Ten "Commandments." However, the Rabbis of the Rabbinic Period[5] and, even today taught that there were 613.) The first sign by Jesus to show He was the Messiah was in the context of a marriage.[6] When God speaks of His relationship to the church, He often uses the metaphor of marriage.[7] In Malachi 2:13-16, God expresses His extreme displeasure with divorce, concluding with the statement, "I hate divorce." God loves marriage, and a generous dose of affection and sexual interaction is a hallmark of a healthy marriage.

This reluctance to teach from the Song of Songs is all the more amazing since we somehow forget *who* invented sex.

Newsflash: It was God! The last I looked, "God don't make junk." We also forget that the reason sexual perversion (sexual abuse, rape, pornography, etc.) is so abhorrent is that sex, when used as God intended, is so beautiful and God-pleasing. It is the very beauty of healthy sex that makes sexual perversion so detestable.

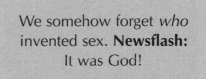

We somehow forget *who* invented sex. **Newsflash: It was God!**

Recently, I took a survey of 100 college students who were asked what they thought the Bible says about sex and romance. One question asked them to describe the "sex/romance life of a couple strictly trying to follow Biblical principles in their marriage." I gave them a dozen descriptive words and phrases from which to choose. The choices ranged from "hot and spicy" to "you mean they actually have sex?" All the negative descriptions were chosen most frequently while all the positive ones were chosen the least. Sadly, the phrase which was selected the least of all was a descriptive phrase that closely paraphrased Scripture.

Newsflash: The modern church is doing a miserable job advertising its own message: God's love for us and His vision of joy and intimacy in marriage.

Newsflash to the faith community: The modern church is doing a miserable job advertising its own message: God's love for us and His vision of joy and intimacy in marriage.

Hosea 4:6 tells us, "My people are destroyed for lack of knowledge."[8] How true! Our society currently is bombarded with sexual messages from Hollywood, television, the print media, and the music industry, all of which purport to present "knowledge." The faith community then wrings its hands, bemoaning how the public follows the lure of misinformation from other sources. All the while the church quietly sits by, neglecting its duty to share the truth about the knowledge it has regarding the profound joy of intimacy intended by God in appropriate sexual relations.

I am neither a theologian nor a marriage counselor. I am a lawyer who has spent the last 25 years serving as a District Court Judge in Michigan. I have taught criminal law and other courses related to the judicial process at the college level for over 27 years. In 1991, I was asked to lead the marriage enrichment program at my home church, Hope Lutheran, Adrian, Michigan. The same year I was asked to lead an evening adult Bible study. The two studies had many overlapping points, especially when studying such portions of Scripture as the Song of Solomon, the first two chapters of Genesis, I Corinthians 7, and Ephesians 5.

Being a trial lawyer by training and a teacher by inclination helped me with both the Bible studies and marriage enrichment. The trial lawyer in me always has wanted to investigate every detail of a subject. Lawyers love reading footnotes and appendices and looking for patterns in information and effective ways of presenting it to a jury. As a teacher, I wanted to know the big picture in order to share it with my audience and be able to put the details into the larger context. Interest and opportunity started a process of discovery.

Over the next several years, I began to recognize a relationship between Scripture, the materials covered in marriage enrichment and the day-to-day cases I was seeing in court. Scripture contains the ultimate description of the model of marriage God desires for us. The more closely couples follow God's model, the more they will experience intimacy and joy in their relationship. The further couples wander from God's model, the more they will have distance and loneliness in their marriage. As distance and loneliness increase for couples who do not follow God's plan, the risk of divorce also increases. When marriages fail, that failure leads to conflict and tends to increase criminal behavior, which, in turn, leads to an increase in the case load in court.

During my years on the trial bench, I have had countless cases in which the breakdown of the marriage was one of the primary factors contributing to criminal behavior. In drinking and driving cases it is a common occurrence for the defense attorney to appear at sentencing and explain, "Judge, my client really is a wonderful guy, but he was completely despondent over his divorce and simply drank too much." Or, "Judge, my client is a wonderful woman, but she's in the middle of a terrible custody battle and she was trying to drown her troubles in too many beers."

Dr. Linda Waite has pointed out that the number of alcohol-related problems double in men and triple in women, when they go from being married to being divorced.[9] The opposite also is true. While divorce tends to cause an increase in alcohol consumption, marriage tends to reduce the use. As Dr. Waite and Maggie Gallagher have noted:

> ...When men marry, they dramatically alter this kind of behavior. This change is not just a statistical artifact of selection – sober-minded men marrying and staying married more often. Instead, the evidence suggests that men actually mend their ways as they first approach and then actually get married.

> Single men who are heading toward marriage, for example, reduce their drinking up to a year before the ceremony. Although they start with the same heavy-drinking patterns as their friends who stay single, by the time they make it to the altar, young men drink much less than they did a year earlier. Meanwhile, their bachelor friends continue to down many more drinks and to experience more symptoms of alcohol problems.

...Marriage actually changes these self-destructive patterns. In the year before marriage, both young men and women smoked less, drank less, snorted less cocaine. Even marijuana use, which tends to drop off after high school, drops two or three times more rapidly among those who marry than among their single counterparts. Meanwhile, their classmates who do not marry increase their use of cocaine and experience more bouts of heavy drinking instead.[10]

It is not limited to alcohol issues. I have had cases in which the attorney explains, "My client is really a fine young man, your Honor. He gets straight A's, and he works at a part-time job. But his parents were divorced when he was nine and ever since he has been jerked between one parent and the other and has not had a stable home for the past ten years. When he broke the window out of the car, it was his anger coming out." Broken homes are a major source of my case load.

Professor James Q. Wilson of U.C.L.A. has observed, "The evidence from a variety of studies is quite clear: even if we hold income and ethnicity constant, children (and especially boys) raised by a single mother are more likely than those raised by two-parents to have difficulty in school, get in trouble with the law and experience emotional and physical problems."[11] A Wisconsin study of juvenile incarceration rates dramatically demonstrates Professor Wilson's point. The rates of incarceration for juvenile delinquents is 12 times higher for children of single, divorced parents than children of two parent families.[12] I rest my case.

The title of this book is *A Blessing for the Heart, God's Beautiful Plan for Marital Intimacy.* Obviously, we do not get directly into the issue of "marital intimacy" in criminal matters in court. However, it is equally obvious that issues involving sex and affection are foundational to husband - wife relations. When they break down, there is a good chance the entire structure will follow. Marriage counselors consistently have told me that almost every marital dispute involves an issue of sex or affection.

The information in this book has been presented for church groups in every major denomination. It has been presented at the

Smart Marriage Conference with marriage counselors and theologians from the major Christian denominations present, as well as at least one Jewish Rabbi. This book has been reviewed by Baptist, United Methodist, Presbyterian, Roman Catholic, Mennonite, and Lutheran ministers. A video presentation on the *Biblical View of Domestic Violence*, some of which material is contained in this work, was reviewed for doctrinal soundness by the Lutheran Church – Missouri Synod in St. Louis. I am satisfied that what you are about to read is Biblically correct information.

This book also has been reviewed by nine women, two of whom have a PhD. Five others have advanced degrees in counseling. For obvious reasons I think "male" better than I think "female." While I am not interested in being politically correct, I am interested in presenting an honest, balanced approach. This required the input of women.

The question remains: Why such a book? There are a number of excellent Christian books on marriage. However, most Christian authors either tend to make a statement, then provide a proof text, or do a verse-by-verse study of a particular set of passages. Both approaches are completely valid and can be very helpful. However, neither provides a comprehensive review of the Biblical approach to intimacy in marriage. There is also a tendency by many Christian authors to skirt the hardest questions and, of those who do address them, most rarely deal with the relevant Biblical principles and passages on a comprehensive basis. Finally, some writers add their opinions where Scripture is silent, without acknowledging the difference. This would have merit, if the opinions were consistent with the larger themes of Scripture. However, that is not always the case.

There are three warnings to those who wish to read further. First, do not expect this book to be politically correct.[13] There has been no intent to follow any particular denominational or popular view. Many liberals and conservatives talk as if they wish to subtract from or add to Scripture. Scripture warns against both.[14] I hope to present a model of thinking and behavior which is Biblically sound. (That is one of the reasons for having this book reviewed by ministers of so many denominations.) God's word is timeless. The divorcing couples with whom I have spoken, both in court and in private practice, have convinced me of a basic point. I never have seen a divorce involving a couple that truly is following the Biblical model of marriage. Indeed, couples that follow God's model are happily married and enjoy a truly passionate and intimate sex and romance life.[15]

Second, the ideas presented in this book are idealistic. They may be things you "can't do." They are simply "too difficult." God's word describes the perfect relationship. The fact that we are limited by our human condition, flawed and sinful as it is, does not mean God should lower His standard to make it easier. Like a coach who describes the perfect play to his team, God describes the perfect marriage to those who would seek it. Falling short of God's model is sin. With God's help, direction, mercy and forgiveness, however, we can heal old wounds, experience new beginnings, and stand up and try again.

> I have never seen a divorce involving a couple that is truly following the Biblical model of marriage.

Remember that with God all things are possible. He will provide us with the strength we need to make the changes we need.[16] We need to pray to Him, then let Him lead and guide us. We all tend to want to put God in a box by telling Him the solution we want.

This brings us to the third and most important warning. As you read through this book you will come across ideas which will conflict with beliefs, attitudes and behaviors you long have clung to as a way of life. Don't simply reject these ideas out of hand or ignore them as irrelevant. Instead, search the Scriptures to determine whether what you are reading is consistent with God's word. Be like the "Bereans (who) were of more noble character than the Thessalonians, for they received the message with great eagerness and examined the Scriptures every day to see if what Paul said was true."[17] Then pray that God will lead you in the direction in which *He* wants you to move, not the direction *you* want. Let His word and the ideas in this book challenge you to confront your own attitudes and behaviors in a God-pleasing way.

I hope you will enjoy this reading. I also hope you will open your heart to try the things that God's word suggests. God really *does* know what He is talking about. Frank Sinatra used to sing, "I Did It *My* Way," as his signature song. I've often wondered why Mr. Sinatra would be proud of a second-rate method of doing things. When we can sing, "I Did It *God's* Way," we truly will have something to sing about with joy. Give it a try. It really does work.

DISCUSSION QUESTIONS

1. Has *your* church ever had an adult Bible study on the Song of Solomon? On the positive aspects of marital sexuality? On God's role for sex in marriage? If so, congratulations. If not, discuss why it has never happened.

2. God invented sex. What are some of the implications of this reality?

3. If God invented sex and sexuality, why do so many people have so many "hangups," even with their own spouses?

4. The text states, "The modern church is doing a miserable job advertising its own message: God's love for us and His vision of joy and intimacy in marriage." Where do most children get their information about marriage and sexuality today? What programs are available in *your* congregation to educate youths and engaged couples about this subject?

5. What problems do you see in your community resulting from the increase in divorce? Out of wedlock births? Absentee fathers? What is *your* church doing about this?

6. Most of us know people who have suffered through a divorce. If you know such a couple, (without naming names) talk about whether both the husband and wife were following the Scriptural model of sacrificial love in their marriage. Were either of them? As you continue through this book, continue to ask this question.

— 1 —

Men and Women:

A Biblical View

I once heard the reason it takes a million sperm to fertilize one egg is that men never ask directions! Men, likewise, often think it is only when things get rough and there are no other options that we should look at the manufacturer's handbook. Indeed, many men act as if real men don't read the instructions!

When it comes to marital relations, the "manufacturer's handbook" is the Bible. God created us, then wrote the book on how we should do things. Sadly, many of us, both men *and* women, don't bother to look at the book even as a last resort when things get rough.

Nonetheless, understanding intimacy in a Biblical marriage[1] begins with understanding how Scripture depicts men and women. Genesis 2:18 gives us much of the explanation:

> The Lord God said, "It is not good that man should
> be alone; I will make him a helper fit for him."[2]

Here God describes both a problem (man's loneliness) and a solution (a "helper fit for him.")

Unfortunately, modern English often uses the word "helper" to imply a "servant" or a minimum-wage worker at an entry level job. We think of a "helper" as a person in a subservient position. A "helper" in our culture is not necessarily someone who is highly respected. Indeed, author John Eldridge comments, "It makes me think of Hamburger Helper."[3] However, that is the early twenty-first century American English meaning of the word "helper." Genesis was written in Hebrew over 3,000 years ago in an ancient, middle-eastern culture. Imagine the problems of doing a literal translation into another language of the phrase: "He had a coat on his tongue and his breath came in short pants." The result would be a ridiculous mental picture. The same problem exists in trying to translate ancient, middle-eastern Hebrew into modern, western English. To have a fair understanding of the words of Scripture, we must look back at what they meant when they were written.

The Hebrew phrase for "helpmate" or "helper fit for" in Genesis is *EZER KENEGDO*. *Ezer* means "help," "a power," or "a force." It can also mean a "lifesaver."[4] An *Ezer* is a helpful, enabling, giving force, one which supports and encourages in a positive way. *"Ezer* signifies a 'giving' quality that woman has always symbolized ... not only as a giver of love, security, encouragement, and advice to her husband, but also as a mother ...."[5]

Ezer also appears in Psalm 46:1, *"God is our* refuge and strength, a very present *help* in trouble."[6] A wife's relationship to her mate has elements reflecting the image of God's relationship to mankind. Just as God is a "help" in trouble, women were created as a "help" to man's trouble with loneliness and life.[7] Just as the Psalmist never would describe God in a subservient role, God does not mean to describe woman as subservient, when He describes her as *"ezer."*

Today we might think of this kind of "helper" as the honored professional who is brought in to complete the team.[8] Someone needing brain surgery would seek the services of the best available surgeon to do the work. The surgeon becomes the "helper." To refer to the surgeon as "subservient" or, somehow, of unequal status with the patient, would be ridiculous.

The second part of the phrase, "kenegdo", implies opposite.[9] The impression is a mirror image, a reflection of, a matching or balancing of something. Hebrew scholar, Dwight A. Pryor,[10] indicates that a better translation for *ezer keneg-do* would be, "a help to match him"; "a help corresponding to him"; "a power which is equal and adequate in every way"; or, "a force to perfectly balance him." When God described woman by the phrase *ezer keneg-do* ("helpmate"), He said she was a balance needed to keep man from being out of balance, a force exactly equal to him and totally adequate to complete him. Indeed, during Biblical times[11] a man was not consid-ered whole if he was not mar-ried; the woman made the man complete.[12]

Figure 1.

To put this in perspective, think of an arch. There is an obvious problem with the arch in Figure 1. It can't stand as it is. To stand it must have an equal but opposite force pushing against it as shown in Figure 2. This is the basic concept of the *ezer kenegdo*: equal opposites that support each other.

IMPLICATIONS OF EZER KENEGDO

There are several implications that follow from God creating men and women to be equal but opposite forces meant to balance each other.

Implication #1: Men and women are intended to be different for a purpose.

Men and women are very different creatures. We think different-ly. We use words differently and in different amounts. The content, style, and structure of our speech are different. Men tend to be more competitive in their conversation, while women tend to be more facil-

Figure 2.

itative.[13] We find different things attractive and are motivated by different stimuli. We are built differently, with different chromosome combinations. Women outlive men by three to four years on average. Women normally have lower basal metabolism and faster heart rates (80, vs 72 for men), and lower blood pressure (about 10 points lower than men). Women have "a shorter head, broader face, less protruding chin, shorter legs, and longer trunk"[14] than men. Women also have a larger stomach, kidneys, liver and appendix, and smaller lungs than men. Men have 50% more muscle mass than women and less water (and correspondingly more red blood cells) in their blood, giving them better endurance at physical labor. And, of course, women menstruate and give birth, and their breasts lactate.

Newsflash for couples: Men and women not only are different, but are intended to be different because the difference serves a purpose. Consider your two hands: similar, but, opposite. The usefulness of our hands would be very limited if they were identical. God intended

> Men and women are *intended* to be different. The differences serve a purpose.

men and women to be different so each can do things the other cannot.

Typically, when we learn that two things are "different," someone wants to know "which is better." We seem to assume that difference requires inequality.

Newsflash for couples: Difference does NOT imply lack of equality. It does not take a math genius to realize that $5 + 5 = 2 + 8$ is correct. But the left side of the equation has two identical numbers, while the right side has two different numbers. Moreover, the left side has two odd numbers, while the right has of two even numbers! Still, the two sides are of exactly the same value, because the differences add up to the same *total* value.

The equality of man and woman is spelled out clearly in Scripture. Genesis 1:27 tells us that *both* were created in God's own image. "**...In the image of God he created him; male and female he created them.**"[15]

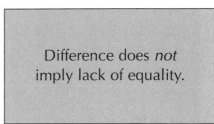

Difference does *not* imply lack of equality.

Galatians 3:26-28 adds that as we stand before God we all are spiritually equal, and there is "neither ... male nor female..." for we "are all one in Christ Jesus." God described all the rest of His creation as "good."[16] It was not until both man and woman were created that God considered His work as "very good."[17]

Implication #2: Men and women are to learn from each other to create total intimacy.

Men and women are meant to learn to understand each other and to create complete intimacy out of their differences. Since the sexes are opposites who support each other, they have to learn about each other. Husbands and wives cannot hold up each other, if they don't know where the other is, or in what direction the other is leaning. The more husbands and wives know about each other as opposites, the better they can maintain balance.

We are to learn about God who provides spiritual support, and likewise, we are to learn about the *kenegdo* (opposite) that God has put into our lives as our support. Hosea 6:6 tells us,

> For I desire steadfast love and not sacrifice, the **knowledge** of God, rather than burnt offerings.[18]

The same concept appears in Genesis 4:1,

> Now Adam **knew** Eve his wife, and she conceived and bore Cain, ...[19]

The words for "knowledge" (da'at) and "knew" (ya'daa) both come from the same root: "to know."

In English we think of "knowledge" in the sense of knowing facts. This comes from the Greek concept of "data." The Hebrew concept of "knowledge" (da'at) is different. It implies an intimate relationship. If you "know" a fact in a Biblical sense, it is part of your being, part of the motivating force of your life. It is not simply a piece of "data" you have tucked away in some brain cell for later use. John Eldridge catches the essence of Biblical knowledge when he tells men, "A woman doesn't want to be related to with formulas, and she certainly doesn't want to be treated like a project that has answers to it. She doesn't want to be solved; she wants to be *known*."[20]

By using the same word in Hosea and Genesis, Scripture is saying that God wants to have a profoundly close relationship with His people; and, likewise, He wants husbands and wives to have a profoundly close relationship with each other. Physical, emotional and spiritual intimacy are the cement that binds the opposite parts together to make one, unified, strengthened whole, the "two" into "one."

Scripture also demonstrates *how* we are to reach this intimacy in marriage by showing how God wants to be close to us, and to have us close to Him. First, Leviticus 26:11 states that God wants to make His "abode" with us.[21] In the same way, husband and wife are to spend time together, live together, and share their life experiences together.

Second, each of us also is to "cleave" to our spouse, just as we are to "cleave" to God. In Genesis 2:24 God tells us,

> Therefore shall a man leave his father and his mother,
> and ... **cleave** unto his wife: and they shall be one ...[22]

Unfortunately, the word for "cleave," *dabaq* (da'-vak), translates to English as a static state of being. *Dabaq,* however, is a highly dynamic verb, implying active and continuous movement, chasing after, seeking, pursuing, holding fast, clinging tightly. The same word is used over 50 times in the Old Testament.[23] In each case it describes how we are to "hold fast" or "cleave" to God. How often are we to "hold fast" to God? Twice a year, on Christmas and Easter? Once a month? Every Sunday for an hour or two? Clearly, we are to seek God constantly. *Dabaq,* likewise, is how you and your spouse are to seek after each other: constantly and continuously.

When Scripture speaks of you and your spouse "knowing" each other and, also, seeking, pursuing and holding fast to each other, the words "know" (yadaa) and "pursue" (dabaq) have broad meanings. We are to know and pursue our spouses emotionally, intellectually, and spiritually. We are to know their dreams, fears, hopes, hurts and desires. The sexual aspect is part, but only one minor part, of the knowledge and pursuit. Knowing and pursuing *the other person* is not knowledge or pursuit for *self*-gratification. It is learning more about and pursuing the other for the sake of strengthening the relationship. Christianity is a dynamic, personal relationship with a living and loving God. Marriage is meant to be a dynamic, personal relationship with a loving spouse.

Sadly, many men quit romancing their wives once the honeymoon is over. Instead, they treat taking a wife like bagging a deer. You shoot the deer,

> Sadly, many men quit romancing their wives once the honeymoon is over.

drag it home, mount its head on the wall and you're done. It would be silly to shoot the same deer twice. Likewise, once you've "caught" (or would it be "bagged"?) your woman, the chase is over. Why catch her more than once? It's a waste of time.

Newsflash to husbands: Women are *not* deer, but they are to be held *dear* continuously. We are to keep chasing, pursuing, wooing, courting, and learning about our wives throughout our marriages so that emotional, intellectual and spiritual closeness becomes ever more intimate. From a Biblical perspective, the *courtship* we are accustomed to is merely the warm up for the *real* chase. The "cleaving" described in Genesis 2:24 is *after* the couple is married, after the husband has already left his father and mother. This model is seen in Isaac's marriage to Rebekah. He never had met his bride before the marriage; yet, we are told, "Isaac brought her into the tent of his mother Sarah, and he married Rebekah. So she became his wife, and he loved her..."[24] The rabbis of Biblical times pointed out that Isaac *first* married Rebekah, *then* loved her.

Gentlemen, the ringing of the wedding bells is the signal to "start your engines!" The race is about to begin. All the revving of your engines that you've done while dating is little more than noise. The wedding is the time to start moving. When you finally say, "I do," *that* is when you should start "doing." That is when the chase for your wife actually starts, and when you are to start "dabaqqing" your wife. The chase is to continue throughout the marriage.

Implication #3: We are to love our spouse completely.

Each side of the *ezer kenegdo* must love the other side completely. Imagine the arch in Figure 2, if one side only partially supports the other. Disaster is inevitable.

The Bible tells us to love the LORD with all our heart, soul and strength (Deut 6:5) and our neighbor as ourselves (Lev 19:18), and that on these two commands rest all the law and the prophets (Matt 22:37 – 40). The first is the "vertical" love between God and humanity. The second is the "horizontal" love between "neighbors" (Figure 3). If you are to love your "neighbor as yourself," who could be a closer "neighbor" than the person with whom you share your life, your bed and your body?

Implication #4: There can be no barriers or spaces between husband and wife.

Using the example of the arch again, suppose the two sides are built so there is a "space" between them. The thought is silly because the space will cause both sides to crash.

We are to know our spouse so that there are no barriers or spaces between us. In Genesis 2:25 we read, "And they were both naked, the man and his wife, and were not ashamed."[25] This passage has tremendous meaning for married couples in two areas of marriage.

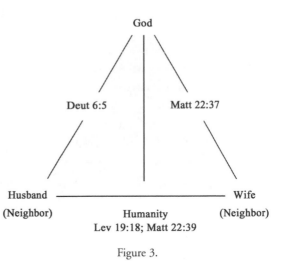

Figure 3.

A. The "no barrier" meaning in the physical aspects of marriage

First, the passage obviously relates to physical nakedness. Yet, there are many marriages in which the husband and wife rarely, if ever, see each other nude. Most men are visual creatures. They enjoy seeing their wives without clothes. Women who deny their husbands this joy are limiting the pleasures God has in mind for marriage. Likewise, there are many women who take pleasure in seeing their husband's body and should not be deprived of that joy.

B. The "no barrier" meaning in the emotional aspects of marriage

Second, verse 25 also refers to emotional nakedness. Just as physical barriers can prevent two from becoming one, so can emotional barriers. Indeed, emotional barriers tend to cause the worse problems. This is easy to demonstrate. While most people in our culture prefer not to physically undress in front of strangers, they would be even more reluctant to *emotionally* undress. Consider the idea of having to stand in front of a group and tell everyone *everything* about yourself. EVERYTHING! This includes telling every lie, hatred, prejudice, desire, foible, idiosyncracy, lust, fear or dream. It includes everything you've ever done wrong or not done that you should have done; every-thing that might not be wrong, but you would not want others to know about. In other words, strip naked *emotionally*. Emotionally undressing in front of others would be terrifying to most people. Yet, to have "oneness" in marriage, we need to be able to do just that with our spouses.

To have "oneness," there can be no separations. The word "one" in Genesis 2:24, *echad*, is the same word used to describe the oneness of God[26]. It is the same concept that Jesus uses when He says "I and my Father are one."[27] There can be no "oneness" when there is emotional distance or physical barriers separating the two parts.

THE EFFECTS OF THESE IMPLICATIONS ON MARRIAGE

Our being equal, but opposite, has three primary effects on marriage. **First, communication is essential.** You cannot know your spouse without talking. God shares who He is with us through His word. You bare your soul to Him through the words of your prayers. Likewise, it is through the words you share with your spouse that allows your spouse into the inner sanctum of your heart and lets him know who you are.

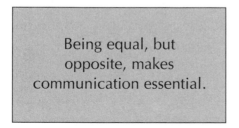

Being equal, but opposite, makes communication essential.

But talking is only half of communication. It also requires listening. There are five primary "filters"[28] that get in the way of effective listening:

- inattention (e.g. trying to talk while the TV is on or having a conversation and reading a magazine at the same time)
- emotions (e.g. anger, sadness, etc.)
- beliefs, expectations and motivations (e.g. hearing what we expect to hear, whether it is actually said or not)
- communication styles (people who use a lot of words often have difficulty understanding people who use only a few.)

• self-protection (e.g., not revealing our real feelings or concerns out of fear of rejection)

The Bible tells us, "Everyone should be quick to listen, (and) slow to speak..."[29] Sadly, most of us are quick to speak and slow to listen. We cannot gain entry into the inner sanctum of our spouses' hearts, when we do not listen.

Second, disagreements between husband and wife are inevitable, necessary, and desirable. *Inevitable* because man and woman are opposite forces that support each other. If two people are "pushing" in opposite directions, however, differences of opinion are bound to happen. *Necessary* because if two people are "pushing" in opposite directions, of necessity, they will end up with differences of opinion. If either stops "pushing," both will fall. *Desirable* because it is the different perceptions of our spouses, when added to our own, that gives us a more complete picture of life. Some disagreements can be resolved, others cannot. Respect, understanding and the recognition that the relationship is more important than any disagreement are the keys to a strong marriage.

Unfortunately, the human mind tends to assume that such differences are either bad, and, thus, something to be avoided, or a sign of conflict, and thus something to win. Neither assumption is correct. Disagreements between spouses are not necessarily bad. They might be God's wake up call that we do not have an exclusive corner on all the insights and wisdom of the world. Disagreements give us an opportunity to listen and learn. Disagreements also are not a necessary sign of conflict. They only become conflicts if the husband and wife choose to let them turn into conflict.

Avoiding disagreements, in effect, says you have nothing to offer, that your spouse is always correct and never needs any contribution from you. You give in and seek peace at all costs. But, this also means that you are not holding up your end of the balance. There are times your spouse is wrong or headed in a direction that could result in future problems. If you are not strong enough to withstand the stress associated with confronting the error, in the end you both may fall because you are not holding up your end of the balance. (What will

Figure 4. "I can't handle the pressure! I have to get out of here."

happen to the two sides of the arch in Figure 4, if one side "leaves" because it thinks it has nothing to contribute, or cannot stand the stress of disagreement?) Of course, your spouse has the same obligation to resist being taken in the wrong direction, if you start pushing too hard.

Newsflash to couples: The fact that we disagree with our spouses does not mean we are necessarily right. Frequently it means we both need each other's input. We need to talk through the matter in love. God put our spouses in our lives to add color and depth to the world we see that would be missing without them.[30]

An obvious question: How do you know who's right and who's wrong? The answer is you may never know. Moreover, it is possible that neither of you is "wrong," but only expressing differences in preference or perspective.[31] Here, again, keep firmly in mind that the issue is not as important as your relationship.

The other extreme (trying "to win") assumes your spouse has nothing to offer, or, worse yet, places your spouse in competition with you. Trying to "win" often leads to an attitude of "I *must* win." What is best for the marriage becomes irrelevant. All that is important is *winning* and *proving* that *I'm* right. This attitude quickly is followed by a mind set that "*I* don't have to listen to *you*!" When that thinking starts,

Figure 5. "If only I can get rid of this opposition, I will be happy."

anything your spouse has to offer becomes little more than an irritating roadblock, arbitrarily thrown in your path of self-righteous self-indulgence.

The attitude of trying "to win" means we are trying to defeat the very force God put in our lives to hold us up. Ironically, the more we succeed at "winning," the more damage we do to ourselves. (What would happen in Figure 5, if one side succeeds in destroying his "opposition"?) If we continue to "win," in the end the prize, at best, will be a dysfunctional marriage; or, at worst, the devastating consequence of divorce.

Newsflash to couples: Marriage is *not* a competition. It is a team sport. The husband and wife comprise the players on the *same* team. Our oppositeness is God's plan to provide reinforcement in our lives and versatility to our team. The pitcher and catcher in baseball have opposite jobs, but they are on the same team. Husbands and wives, despite their oppositeness, should not treat each other as the opposition. The whole idea of "winning" when

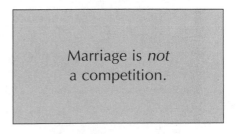

Marriage is *not*
a competition.

dealing with disagreements with our spouses must become foreign to our thinking.

I once spoke with a husband and wife who use sticky notes when they have a disagreement. They each get a sticky note, write on it "I AM NOT YOUR ENEMY," stick the note on their own forehead, then continue the conversation. They explained that the notes help them keep focused on the problem, and realize that the problem is not the other person.

The third effect that our being equal, but opposite, has on marriage involves romance and sex. Every husband and wife who have been married for over a month can count on one reality: There *will* be disagreements in their married life involving sex and romance. In the area of intimacy, all the hormonal differences between men and women and the different nature of what stimulates them become magnified. The differences involve everything from frequency to variety. These differences are part of God's plan.

> In God's plan for mankind, the most desirable act is an act of love.

But, why would God make us so different? As Professor Henry Higgins lamented in *My Fair Lady,* "Why can't a woman be more like a man?"[32] The answer is obvious. God isn't that stupid! It is through our differences that we gain strength and learn to love.

In God's plan for mankind, the most desirable act is an act of love. Yet, love cannot exist where there are no differences. Differences, in turn, inevitably mean that acts of love will always involve elements of sacrifice. Adults and children see the world differently. It is when I sacrifice my time and pride to get down on the floor to play a child's board game with my four year old that love is in action. Both of us end up feeling joy, although the nature of the joy felt by my child will not be the same I feel. Likewise, men and women will feel joy differently when they surrender their pride and get down to the business of giving to each other. There would be no real sacrifice if both you and your spouse always wanted to do the identical thing at the identical time. It is the sacrifice of giving that gives love meaning.

THE UNIQUENESS OF MAN AND WOMAN AND GOD'S PART IN THE PLAN OF MARRIAGE

The equality, but difference, of the sexes also is illustrated by the very name in Scripture for man and woman. In Hebrew man is *ish* and woman is *ishshah*. *Ishshah* is simply the feminized version of *ish*.[33] It implies difference, but not different quality or value. The Hebrew spelling for these words are:

Man	Ish	שׁ	י	א
		Shin	Yod	Aleph
Woman	Ishshah	ה	שׁ	א
		Heh	Shin	Aleph

The rabbis[34] of Biblical times looked at the individual letters of words and came to several conclusions. Hebrew reads right to left, so the first letter (Aleph א) is the same and in the same location in both names, indicating that man and woman are one-third identical. The Shin (שׁ) is in both names but in different locations, indicating that man and woman are one third similar, but opposite. The Heh (ה) and Yod (י) are totally different and in different locations, indicating that man and woman are one third completely dissimilar.

Men and women reflect this pattern. Parts of men and women are identical. We have many of the same primary organs (heart, lungs, liver, teeth, kidneys, etc.); share the same blood types (A, AB, B, O); and can share values, visions and core beliefs such as religion, and how to raise children. Parts of us also are similar, but opposite. We both have sexual organs but their oppositeness is what make them work. We both share certain hormones (testosterone and estrogen) but in opposite ratios. Finally, there is a part of us that is simply different. Women tend to be relationship-oriented. Men tend to be task-oriented. It is this sameness, similarity, oppositeness and uniqueness that every husband and wife should celebrate and recognize as part of God's plan.

The rabbis also noted that the dissimilar letters (Heh ה and Yod י), when put together produce a hard "Yah" sound, as is found at the end of Isaiah, Jeremiah, Hezekiah, and Zechariah. "Yah" is short hand for the name of God in the Old Testament: Yahweh. The rabbis reasoned that taking the differences between man (the Yod י) and woman (the Heh ה), putting them together in love, and binding them together in marriage results in the closest image of God we can have in this world, and bears God's own name. This makes sense in light of Genesis 1:27. If *both* man *and* woman are created in God's image, and God is love,[35] then putting man and woman together in a loving relationship presents the best image of God we can see in this world.

The rabbis further noted that if the Yod (י) and Heh (ה) are taken out of *ish* and *ishshah* both are left with the same remaining letters: אש (Shin / Aleph). In Hebrew this spells *esh*, which is the word for fire. The conclusion: If God is taken out of man and woman, all that remains are two fires, and when they clash, each fire will consume the other, in the end.[36]

How true this is! Over and over in court I have seen the hatred and acrimony spewing forth as men and women, who once swore their love for each other, shoot barrages of fireballs at each other in their private war of mutual self-destruction. God is not in their relationship. The parties have locked the door to Him[37] long ago, and are now in a fight to the emotional death.

But what about the "good divorce" we occasionally hear about, in which one side is "happy" it's "finally over"? Even when the acrimony has been held to a minimum, the devastating hurt remains.

In reality, there is no such thing as a "good" divorce; there are only divorces that are "less bad." Consider this thought: If we see a "good" movie, we will want to see it again sometime. If we find a "good" vacation spot, we will want to return to enjoy it once more. If we read a "good" book, we will recommend it to friends. Yet, after more than 30 years in the field of law, I have yet to see a single situation in which either party to a divorce says, "By golly, that divorce was so good, I think I'll get married again just so I can get divorced again ... and in the mean time I'll recommend to all my friends that they marry so they, too, can get divorced." This never happens because no one has a "good" divorce.[38]

ADDING THE ELEMENTS OF RESPECT AND LOVE

Respect and love must be added to our attributes of equality and oppositeness to have a successful marriage. Respect for your spouse should be obvious. The person you vowed to "love till death do us part," is created in the image of God. That person is of such enormous value that God was willing to send His only Son to die on the cross on his[39] behalf. And, if that weren't enough, you specifically are told to respect your spouse. Ephesians 5:33 instructs wives to respect their husbands. 1 Peter 3:7 instructs husbands to respect their wives. 1 Peter 2:17 tells us to respect everyone.[40]

If God places such high esteem on you and your spouse and commands each of us to do the same, it is the height of arrogance to refuse His command. The disobedience to God which underlies the disrespect you show your spouse, in effect, tells the all-knowing, all-powerful, almighty Creator of the universe that *you* think *He* messed up and, in fact, your spouse is not worthy of *your* respect, despite His conclusion to the contrary.

Clearly, some people have committed acts that undermine respect, such as adultery, alcoholism, drug abuse, gambling addiction, and physical or emotional abuse. In the face of such behavior, love may require extreme action, including cutting off the relationship until there is repentance. God loves us, but He does not tolerate sin. Likewise, He does not want us to tolerate flagrant sin. He wants the best for us, and always seeks our repentance. He also wants us to want the best for each other, and wants us to pray that those who sin will repent.

We also need to respect God's plan to have someone different from ourselves in our lives. Genesis 2:18 says:

> *The LORD God said,* "It is not good for the man to be alone. I will make a *helper* suitable for him." (Emphasis supplied.)

It was *God* who identified the problem. It was *God* who created the solution, the *ezer kenegdo,* with its equality and oppositeness. Failure to respect your spouse is failure to respect God.

The respect you show your spouse and God's plan for your spouse and you should be a celebration. We have been given a magnificent

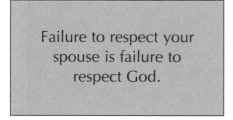

Failure to respect your spouse is failure to respect God.

gift. God is a God of love and life. The gift of one's spouse is meant to bring love and life to us. And, it does! Married people as a group live longer than singles; have healthier lives; have greater wealth, and a fuller, more satisfying sex life.[41] In the face of such a gift, how could we *not* celebrate?

The guiding principle for celebrating that respect is love. Scripture tells us love should be the overriding principle guiding all our actions. God is a God of perfect love, which He shows us through His mercy, grace, forgiveness, loving faithfulness, and uplifting strength. God's essence of love comes through loud and clear.[42]

- "The LORD is slow to anger, abounding in love and forgiving sin and rebellion."
- "Because of the LORD's great love we are not consumed, for his compassions never fail. They are new every morning; great is your faithfulness."
- "Whoever does not love does not know God, because God is love."[43]

It is equally clear that God expects us to love others.

- "Do not seek revenge or bear a grudge against one of your people, but love your neighbor as yourself. I am the LORD."
- "A new command I give you: Love one another. As I have loved you, so you must love one another. By this all men will know that you are my disciples, if you love one another."

• "Dear friends, let us love one another, for love comes from God. Everyone who loves has been born of God and knows God. Whoever does not love does not know God, because God is love."[44]

Jesus once agreed with an expert in the religious law that the greatest command in Scripture is "love your neighbor as yourself." The expert then asked, "who is my neighbor?" In response Jesus told the parable of "The Good Samaritan."[45] The Samaritans were the most hated people in Israel. If a Jew had to travel from Galilee to Jerusalem and the road took him through a Samaritan village, he would walk around the village, even if the longer route took several extra days. Yet, Jesus describes the Samaritan as the "good neighbor." The point was simple and obvious. If the most hated person you can think of is your neighbor, then *everyone* is your neighbor. The application to marriage is equally simple and obvious. If the most hated person you can think of is your neighbor and someone you are to love, then the person you have vowed before God to love, the person with whom you share your bed, is even more "your neighbor."

There are several Greek words in the New Testament[46] that we sometimes translate as love: *agape, phileo,* and *epithumia.*[47] *Agape* is an all-giving, all-forgiving, sacrificial form of love. *Phileo* is a form of love that includes the love between parents and children, between very close friends, and the love of symbols of status. *Epithumia* is a passionate love of things or activities, which can be either completely appropriate or totally wrong. It is often translated as "lust" or "desire." While the other aspects of love should not be ignored, *agape* must be considered first, last and always. *Agape* is the principle that holds a marriage together and keeps it stable. *Agape* is a decision of the mind. It is a calculated decision to love even in the face of rejection. It loves the unlovable. It is unconditional, unchanging, inexhaustible. It is the kind of love each of us receives from God. It is the nature of His love that caused Him to send His Son and lead His Son to die for us.[48] It is also the love we are to show everyone,[49] especially our spouses.[50]

When *agape* is the central focus of our relationship in marriage, all our words and actions will be to uplift our spouses. As Paul wrote,

Do not let any unwholesome talk come out of your mouths, *but only what is helpful for building others up according to their needs, that it may benefit those who listen. … Be kind and compassionate to one another,* forgiving each other, just as in Christ God forgave you.[51] (Emphasis added.)

Tragically, we often spend much of our energy tearing down the very person we should be building up. Indeed, research shows that we are much kinder to those with whom we work and complete strangers than those we say we love.[52] If Christians are to give any meaning at all to their faith, the starting point is to show the love of God to our spouses.

A FINAL THOUGHT ON GOD'S BLESSINGS OR: "BUT, WHAT IF I DON'T WANT ALL THIS ONENESS AND LOVE STUFF?"

So far I've given you the good news. The bad news is the answer to this question: "What if I don't want all this oneness and love stuff in my marriage?" A principle consistently presented throughout Scripture is that God is a God of perfect love, but He is also a God of perfect justice. If we are to receive His blessings, we must do all we can to follow His law. Will we do it perfectly *every* time? Of course not! Indeed, will we *ever* do it perfectly? Absolutely not! To the extent we fall short (i.e., sin), we must turn from the path we are on (i.e., repent), ask God's forgiveness and try even harder to do it right the next time. With God's help, we eventually will move closer ... even though we never will reach perfection in this life.

The word modern Christians translate as "law" in Hebrew is *torah*. *Torah*, however, is better translated as "teachings."[53] We see this in such passages[54] as:

- "But his delight is in the law of the LORD, and on his law he meditates day and night. He is like a tree planted by streams of

water, which yields its fruit in season and whose leaf does not
wither."
• "Your word is a lamp to my feet and a light for my path."

It is hard to "delight" in studying a bunch of technical rules or
view them as "a light" by which to live. But, God's *torah*, His "teachings," are teachings of life. And, to the extent we follow them, we come
closer to the joys and blessings He has in mind for our lives.

This is where things get really tough. God expects obedience if we
are to receive His blessings. Obedience is a major theme of Scripture
and is found throughout the Gospels.[55] In Luke 6:46 Jesus asked,
"Why do you call me 'Lord, Lord,' and not do what I tell you?" Good
question! *If* Jesus is Lord of our lives, *if* God rules over our actions,
then our actions should reflect God's teachings. If Jesus is *not* Lord of
our lives, not the one in charge of our actions, then it is patronizing
and insulting to call Him Lord.[56]

The need to obey also appears regularly in the Old Testament.
God told Moses to instruct the people, "Now *if you obey* me fully and
keep my covenant, then out of all nations you will be my treasured
possession."[57] Note the conditional statement. *Before* the blessing
there *must* be obedience.

In Deuteronomy 6:4 we read, "Hear, O Israel: The LORD our
God, the LORD is one." The word we translate "hear" is *shma*, which
means to listen. But *shma* is emphatic and means to "listen up!" It is a
directive. It can also mean to "obey."[58] In Hebrew thinking, obedience
and listening are inseparably tied together. If you truly "hear," you will
"obey." If you obey, you have heard. If you do not obey, you did not
hear.

A mother with small children might say, "Johnny, it's time to go
to bed. Turn off the TV." Ten minutes later she returns and Johnny
still is watching the TV. She says, "Didn't you hear me?" Johnny
replies, "Sure, Mom, I heard you," his eyes still glued to the screen. In
Hebrew thinking, Johnny hasn't heard anything. He may have taken in
the words and been able to recite them back like a tape-recorder. But,
since he has not obeyed, he still has not heard.

God's law and justice, together with His love and mercy, and the degree to which they are tied to our obedience are spelled out clearly in Isaiah 1:18-20:

> "Come now, let us reason together," says the LORD. "Though your sins are like scarlet, they shall be as white as snow; though they are red as crimson, they shall be like wool. *If you are willing <u>and</u> obedient,* you will eat the best from the land; but *if you resist and rebel,* you will be devoured by the sword." For the mouth of the LORD has spoken. (Emphasis supplied.)

In marriage God lets us eat the best, *if* we are obedient. If you resist His word and rebel against His teachings, you will be devoured in battle with your spouse. Galatians 5:15 makes the same point: "If you keep on biting and devouring each other, watch out or you will be destroyed by each other."

The relationship between obedience to the command and receiving the blessing starts early in Scripture. The first command in Scripture is found in Genesis 1:28 (RSV): "And, God blessed them and said to them, 'Be fruitful and multiply ...'". The word for "said" is a directive, not simply a suggestion God would like us to follow, if it is convenient for us.[59] The command, however, is directly tied to the other verb in the passage, "blessed." If we want the blessing, we must obey the command. If we do not have the blessing of love and peace in our marital relationships, it is because we are not following God's teachings of life. We have no basis on which to complain. We have the choice between living our marriage His way or living our marriage our way. If we chose our way, we will receive the inevitable result of less joy and satisfaction than if we followed God's way. If we don't like those results, it is time to change to God's way. And with God's way, He is there waiting with open arms, offering both His blessing and His forgiveness. Isn't it wonderful to have such a loving God?

An Unfortunate Reality: People tend to look at problems and focus on what the *other* person did wrong. It is always easier to talk about our spouse's errors than to talk about our own. This human characteristic comes out early in Scripture. In Genesis 3, after the fall, when God confronted Adam and Eve, Adam blamed the entire episode on "the woman you gave me."[60] It was the woman's fault for creating the problem and God's fault for creating the woman. Adam was blameless. Eve then passed the blame to the serpent. She, too, was blameless.

God, of course, would have nothing to do with such nonsense. He passed judgment and cursed all three: the serpent, Eve, and Adam.

Newsflash for couples: When we are involved in a marriage that is less than ideal, we should acknowledge our own responsibility and change ourselves.

Jesus addressed the issue of avoiding blame in Matthew 7:3-5:

> Why do you look at the speck of sawdust in your brother's eye and pay no attention to the plank in your own eye? How can you say to your brother, "Let me take the speck out of your eye," when all the time there is a plank in your own eye? You hypocrite, first take the plank out of your own eye, and then you will see clearly to remove the speck from your brother's eye.

The same issue is addressed in 1 John 1:8-10:

> If we claim to be without sin, we deceive ourselves and the truth is not in us. If we confess our sins, he is faithful and just and will forgive us our sins and purify us from all unrighteousness. If we claim we have not sinned, we make him out to be a liar and his word has no place in our lives.

Michelle Warner Davis, in *Changing Her Man, Without His Even Knowing It,* speaks to women who want their husbands to do things differently. Her advice to wives on how to change their husbands is simple. The wife must change her own behavior. This advice applies equally to men *and* women. Get your own act together and your spouse likely will change, too.[61]

As you read this book, do not look for things your spouse should be doing differently. Instead, look for what *you* should change in *your own* life. Unquestionably, there are situations in which one spouse is primarily or even exclusively "at fault." However, *you* are the only one *you* can change. Before talking to your spouse about the difficulty, talk to God about what *you* need to change.

SO, WHAT'S THE POINT?

God has a wonderful plan in mind for marriage. It is filled with intimacy and unity. It is a dynamic system of love, with both husband and wife filling equal, but different roles, each designed to support the other. *If* we obey God's word and follow his direction for marriage, we will experience incredible joy in a lifetime relationship. But this raises obvious questions. While this is a nice plan as a general overview, how are we to live it on a day-to-day basis? What are the specific things husbands and wives are to do? In other words, what does a God-pleasing marriage look like on a day-to-day basis? Chapter 2 begins to answer these questions.

DISCUSSION QUESTIONS

1. If men and women are created equal and both in the image of God, what implication does this have for married couples?

2. What is the implication of your spouse being your "balance"?

3. Does *knowing* that men and women were intended by God to be completely different make any difference in your dealings with your spouse?

4. On a practical level (the day-to-day of real life) what are some things spouses can do to get to know a person intimately who is so very different from each other?

5. What are the day-to-day problems that get in the way of intimate knowledge?

6. What are some cultural problems that create road blocks to such intimacy?

7. If disagreements are not necessarily to be avoided, what is the basic attitude we need to take when we find ourselves not agreeing?

8. When you are in a disagreement, is there anything you can do to identify and resolve the problem?

9. What difference does it make if a couple believes God is a real, active, living part of their marriage? How will that affect their attitudes toward each other?

10. Do you know any couples who have gone through a nasty divorce? How does the image of "two consuming fires destroying each other" fit with such situations?

11. How many people in the modern church are aware that Scripture encourages a continuous, active, passionate relationship in marriage? Were you?

12. How important is respect to a solid marriage?

13. God loves us and He *expects* us to show love to each other. Consider:

Lev. 19:18	Hosea 6:6	Isaiah 1:17
Micah 6:8	Matt. 22:36-40	John 13:34-35
Romans 13:9-11	Cor. 13:13	Gal. 5:14
1 John 4:7-8		

What is the implication of God telling us to love each other so often? What does each of the following mean in the day-to-day ups and downs of real life relationships? Sacrificial love (agape)? Unconditional love? All forgiving love?

14. Christians often speak of God's love, which is a good thing. How often do we speak of our need to obey His word? How important is obedience, if we are to receive His blessings?

15. How does Eph. 4:29 relate to all this?

— 2 —

Lessons From the Song of Solomon

Mutual Strokes Make Happy Folks

> *Geoffrey swept Pamela into his arms, crushing her heaving breasts against his muscular chest. "Pamela," he whispered, passionately, "I have longed for this moment, since the day I left for the war. My life only has meaning because of you. Your love carried me through every day I was gone. The prison, the escape through the swamp, I could never have done it without the image of you always before me." Pamela pulled his head to hers and kissed him, her lips pressing against his as their hearts pounded as one and their souls merged.*

Have you ever noticed that every paperback romance sold in drug stores eventually has a passage like this? Sometimes it's John and Amy, or Frederick and Angela, but the result is always the same: they meet; they don't like each other; they get to know each other; they fall in love; they break up; they fall in love again, then get married. The romantic comedies in the movies follow the same formula. The assumed ending is the same as in all fairy tales: "... and they lived happily ever after." No one has to do anything to keep the relationship strong; it all comes "naturally." So much for fantasy.[1]

The greatest story of love and passion, longing and romance, however, is far more realistic. It is honest and direct. It starts with the young love of courtship and ends with the mature love of marriage. It is in Scripture, the Song of Solomon. The Song was considered so graphic from Biblical times into the early twentieth century that reading it was reserved for married couples. Today it is a book every married couple not only should read, but study. The Song of Solomon begins with the statement, "The Song of Songs." Hebrew repeats a word or phrase to give emphasis. The title, "Song of Songs," means it was best of the best, the best song of the 1,005 songs Solomon wrote.[2]

The Song is a poem in the form of a dialogue, primarily between a man and a woman, with an occasional observation by God. Being poetry, many references were meant to paint broad, colorful pictures filled with allusions to the culture in which it was written, rather than to be taken literally.[3]

The Song contains a number of lessons for husbands, wives and couples. The next few chapters will look at these lessons, then bring the concepts together to show how they affect the intimate side of marriage.

Solomon's beloved will be called Shulamite. She is not actually named in the poem, but referred to as "the Shulamite,"[4] apparently a name of endearment, which is simply the feminine version of Solomon.[5]

LESSON #1 FOR HUSBANDS: BE HIGHLY COMPLIMENTARY TO YOUR WIFE

Solomon is highly complimentary to his bride throughout the Song, but in terms that sound strange when we read them today. He begins this pattern in Chapter 1:9: " I liken you, my darling, to a mare harnessed to one of the chariots of Pharaoh." If a man compared his wife to a horse today in our Western culture, he would be in the "doghouse" for weeks. But this was written over 2500 years ago in Middle Eastern culture, when the comparison was a compliment.[6] In this passage Solomon was comparing Shulamite to a particular horse, the mare pulling Pharaoh's chariot. Generally, mares did not pull chariots. That was the work of stallions. But, on ceremonial occasions, Pharaoh would have the finest mare in all Egypt pull his chariot. Tradition has it that the mare was pure white and completely without blemish. The other chariots in the parade were pulled by stallions.

Shulamite was not being compared to just any mare, but to the most perfect mare in Egypt. Since Egypt was famous for raising fine horses, that was quite a compliment. Moreover, the mare pulling Pharaoh's chariot was the only mare in the parade. The other chariots were pulled by stallions, which would want to follow the beautiful mare. In other words, this is the mare *every* stallion is following. Put into modern English, Solomon was saying she was the most beautiful woman in the world, and every man who saw her was bound to follow after her with his eyes.

Solomon continued the praise:

> How beautiful you are, my darling!
> Oh, how beautiful!
> Your eyes are doves. (Song 1:15)

The repeated phrase ("How beautiful ... how beautiful") was for emphasis, indicating that in his eyes she was really, *really* beautiful, the most beautiful woman in the world.

Solomon compared her eyes to doves. The eyes often are said to be the windows of the soul. When Solomon looked into her soul he saw doves. Then, as now, doves were a sign of peace and tranquility. Indeed, her name, Shulamite, is a play on the root word *shalom*, which means peace.[7] When he looked into her eyes, he felt peace. Solomon had turned this part of her personality into a pet name.

My job as a trial judge can be very stressful. Hearing a case with two argumentative attorneys, who constantly snipe at each other and let their venom spill over at the witnesses and me, is emotionally exhausting. It is like refereeing a grudge match between pitbulls. Worse yet, being a public official means every decision might end up on the front page of the newspaper, and not always in the most favorable light. When I go home, I look for peace, a sanctuary from the battles of the world. Most men feel they work in an environment like this, whether a factory worker, a store clerk, a janitor or a bank president. Solomon found such peace in the eyes of Shulamite, and told her how grateful he was.

Solomon again called her a dove and commented on her beauty in Chapter 2:13b - 14, but, added two points. First, he called her, "My dove in the clefts of the rock, in the hiding places on the mountainside ...", referring to her quiet and unassuming nature. Then he continued, "...let me hear your voice; for your voice is sweet...," complimenting her on the sound of her voice and what she had to say.

The structure of the Song has an interesting feature. In the dialogue between Solomon and Shulamite, she spoke about two thirds of the words. Women generally use more words than men, and would love to hear their husbands say, "I love to hear the sound of your voice and what you say is important to me. I love to listen to you." Granted, this is not a "guy type thing" to say. However, simply being listened to is a compliment for which many women long.

The Song has three long passages of flowery compliments from Solomon to Shulamite.[8] Chapter 4:1 begins with a repetition of the compliment given in Song 1:15, telling her she is really beautiful and her eyes are like doves. Solomon then spent the rest of verses 1 through 15 going into great detail describing every aspect of her beauty. He said:

- **Her hair** was long and flowing like what one saw from a distance while watching a herd of goats descending Mount Gilead. "With the sun ... reflecting off the herds, (it) is a beautiful sight – almost hypnotic."[9] Solomon was captivated by its loveliness, repeating the same thought in Chapter 6:5.
- **Her teeth** were perfectly white, and none was missing[10] (Also 6:6).
- **Her lips** were like scarlet ribbons (4:3) and as sweet as a honeycomb (4:11).
- **Her mouth** was lovely (4:3) and her tongue was sweet like honey (4:11).

- **Her temples** were like "halves of a pomegranate." Pomegranates were among the fruits considered to be aphrodisiacs. Solomon was saying that the sides of her face are not only smooth and round, but also deeply alluring (Also 6:7).
- **Her neck** was a beautiful symbol of the strength of her integrity.[11]
- **Her breasts** were like twin fawns of a gazelle which browse among the lilies. Fawns are soft and gentle and almost call out to be petted. Being among the lilies appears to refer to Shulamite being a "lily of the valley."[12] (Also 7:3) Later he compares her breasts to "clusters of fruit" (7:7), pleasurable to the taste.
- **Her navel** constantly gave him pleasure. (The word for "navel" may well be a "poetic term for vulva."[13])
- **Her waist**, which he described as "a mound of wheat encircled by lilies," referred to her being fertile for bearing children.
- **Her legs** were like jewels, worked by a craftsman.

Finally, he told her she was, "a garden fountain, a well of flowing water..." (Song 4:15) In Hebrew writing, flowing water is associated with purity and life. In Psalm 1:2–3 the poet compares God's word to a stream of water which gives life. God Himself is referred to as "the spring of living water"[14] and Jesus refers to Himself as the source of "living water."[15] The Lamb of God is said to lead believers to "springs of living water."[16] When Solomon tells Shulamite that she is a "well of flowing water" he is saying that she is full of life and she brings life to him.

After reading this description, you may wonder, what did Shulamite look like? The answer is, except that she had long, flowing hair and all of her teeth, we simply don't know. And, frankly, it's not important. The important question is how *Solomon* saw her. He saw her as the most beautiful woman in the world and he told her so repeatedly in vivid detail.

The wedding night took place at the end of chapter 4, when Shulamite invited him into "her garden." But, that did not stop the compliments. They kept flowing from Solomon in an endless song of praise long after the wedding, throughout their life together.

Newsflash to husbands: Women need to hear honest compliments from you, frequently, throughout your marriage. A sincere compliment is one way women hear you say, "I love you."

> Your wife *needs* to hear that she looks good in a *variety* of different ways.

Husbands often tend to miss this point. If a wife comes in from the garden, sweaty and dirty from work, and asks her husband how she looks, typically, he'll glance at her briefly and say, "Fine." If she gets cleaned up and is ready to go to the grocery store, then asks how she looks, he'll give a quick once over and mutter, "Fine." The next evening if she gets dressed up to go to dinner, then asks how she looks, he'll say, "Fine." A week later, if she gets really dressed up, hair done at a beauty parlor, nails manicured, formal evening gown, make up perfectly done, and comes down stairs making her grand entrance ready to go out, then asks how she looks, he'll reflect for a moment and say, "Fine." This is a disaster!

Newsflash to husbands: Your wife *needs* to hear that she looks good. She *needs* to know you appreciate what she does to look good for *you*. Part of love is meeting the needs of the beloved. Work on your vocabulary. Instead of "fine" when your wife asks (or even better, when she doesn't ask) say:

- "You look *really* good!"
- "You look terrific in that outfit!"
- "You'll be the best looking woman at the party!"
- "My goodness, you're beautiful!"
- "I'm speechless! You look so good I can't describe your beauty!"

Both men and women can learn a great deal by reading magazines designed for their spouses. I occasionally skim through women's periodicals such as *Cosmopolitan*, *Better Homes and Gardens* and *Redbook*.

There is much to learn from the subjects covered and the tone of the coverage.[17] Beauty products, current fashions, and diet programs are the subjects of countless articles and ads. The reason editors and advertisers spend so much money on these matters is they are important to women. That's why women buy these magazines. These companies spend all that attention (and all that money) on the premise that beauty is important to women, because they want a payoff from women. Likewise, husbands need to pay attention to how their wives look and genuinely compliment them whenever possible.

LESSON #1 FOR WIVES: BE HIGHLY COMPLIMENTARY TO YOUR HUSBAND

Shulamite returns Solomon's flattery, compliment for compliment. She begins with her first words in Chapter 1:2b-3:

> your love is more delightful than wine.
> Pleasing is the fragrance of your perfumes;
> your name is like perfume poured out.
> No wonder the maidens love you!

Her comparison of his love being "more delightful than wine" was praise, indeed. Wine makes people mellow. His love did the same to her.

Her statement, "your name is like perfume poured out," was a tremendous compliment that went to the very heart of her relationship with Solomon. A person's name in Biblical times was a description of the essence of who he was. When Moses asked the LORD by what "name" He should be known, the question meant more than simply asking for a title. God responded appropriately. He told Moses, "I AM WHO I AM,"[18] which described His eternal essence. "I AM" is a universal verb of being in Hebrew. It means that God was what He chose to be in the past, He is what He chooses to be in the present, and He will be what He chooses to be in the future. It is an emphatic statement of eternal existence.[19]

The significance of a name can be found elsewhere. Abram's name ("father of many") was changed to Abraham ("father of nations.")[20] The angel of the LORD told Joseph to "give him the name Jesus, because he will save his people from their sins."[21] In Hebrew Jesus is *Yeshua*, which means "savior."[22] Joseph was to call the child "*Savior*" because his essential nature would be "to *save* his people from their sins."

What a compliment Shulamite gave! She was saying that Solomon's essential character was both sweet to her senses, and like an expensive "perfume poured out," sweet to everyone around. She then concluded, "No wonder all the young women around love you!"

Shulamite continued in Chapter 1: 13–14:

> My lover is to me a sachet of myrrh
> resting between my breasts.
> My lover is to me a cluster of henna blossoms
> from the vineyards of En Gedi.

Women of Biblical times often wore a small sachet of fragrant herbs on a necklace between their breasts. She was telling Solomon he added a sweet aroma to her life and she wanted to have him that close to her at all times. After Solomon responded with his declaration of her beauty, she returned the compliment in 1:16: "How handsome you are, my lover! Oh, how charming!" Shulamite was on a roll and she kept it going, next comparing Solomon to "a gazelle or a young stag."[23]

Newsflash to wives: Every husband would like his wife to think of him as a stag! The implications of strength, beauty, and sexual prowess are apparent. You can almost see Solomon burst with pride when he heard these words. You would do well to make *your* husband feel this way, too.

> Every husband would like his wife to think of him as a stag!

Solomon had given a long, detailed, highly complimentary description of Shulamite's beauty. In Chapter 5: 10–16, she answered by describing him. She said:

- **His general physique** was incredible. He was well-built, muscular and radiant. He was better looking than any ten thousand men she had seen.

- **His head** radiated the finest nobility. She said, it "is purest gold." The Hebrew phrase for "purest gold" referred to gold that had withstood the most intense heating to remove even the most minute imperfection and the last trace of any inferior metal. His head did not have the slightest imperfection.

- **His hair** had a pleasant wave and was completely black. There was no gray of an aging man. Solomon was in his prime.

- **His eyes** not only brought her the same peace and tranquility hers did to him (the eyes of a dove) but also the whites of his eyes were pure, not bloodshot nor flawed in any way, and they were perfectly set in his face (like jewels), not sunken or bulging. His pupils were surrounded by pure white, like doves, bathing in milk.

- **His cheeks** were ruddy with the sign of healthiness. This probably referred to a perfectly kept beard which was soft as a bed of flowers.[24]

- **His lips** were beautiful, like red lilies.[25] A young man often would put a bit of perfume in his beard to add to the sweetness of the impression he made on the woman he was courting. The lips would end up with some of the myrrh on them.

- **His arms,** or more probably the lower parts of his arms, including his hands, were covered with gold rings and bracelets. Here again, she was describing his beautiful appearance.

- **His body,** which referred to his mid-section, from the shoulders to the thighs, was in perfect shape. Here Shulamite was complimenting the sculpted shape of a young man in perfect condition who wore the exquisite robes of a king, possibly adorned with precious stones.

- **His legs**, likewise, were perfect in shape, strong and secure, set on "bases," (i.e., shoes or sandals, decorated with gold).
- **His mouth** was the source of beautiful speech, eloquent, charming, kind, uplifting. His words made Shulamite feel truly loved at all times.

Shulamite closed her description of Solomon with an accolade which underscored the intimate nature of their relationship. She referred to him as "my lover, my friend." She did not call him her "husband," a legalistic term describing their social relationship. Instead, she said he was the one with whom she was intimate, both physically and emotionally. Just as he had called her "my sister, my bride," instead of the legalistic title of "wife"; at this point, she was using terms of love, not law.

What did Solomon look like? As with Shulamite, we don't have a clue. What we do know, however, is that she, like Solomon, was extravagant in her praise of him. She kept the compliments going, not just during the courtship, but throughout the marriage.

Newsflash to wives: Husbands like to be complimented as much as you do! When was the last time you told your husband that he's a wonderful man? If it has been more than 24 hours, it has been far too long!

LESSON #1 FOR COUPLES: LET THE COMPLIMENTS FLOW!

The Song of Solomon is a picture, painted by God, of what an ideal relationship looks like in marriage. Throughout the Song there is one obvious omission. There are no put-downs, insults or rude remarks. There are no clever, little jokes told at the expense of the spouse. Instead, every statement is uplifting. Both Solomon and Shulamite refused to let any unwholesome comments come out of their mouths. Instead, they said only what built up the other so it would benefit their beloved.

Paul gave us the same instruction in the New Testament: "Do not let any unwholesome talk come out of your mouths, but only what is helpful for building others up according to their needs, that it may benefit those who listen."[26]

Returning again to Genesis 2:24, we are to cleave after our spouses continuously. Critical comments, insults and rude remarks do not constitute chasing after someone. Such words chase people away.

God's model of marital relations is clear. Love is always affirming. Nonetheless, I have seen countless couples, many who call themselves Christian, in the midst of an on-going cold war. They smile at each other, all the while making one pot shot after another. Sadly, these insults are typically followed by the statement: "Oh, I was only kidding," or "Lighten up! Can't you take a joke?" The Biblical basis for marital relations is uplifting behavior.

It long has been said that for every negative criticism we need 10 compliments. Our minds tend to focus so much on the negative that we need positives repeated regularly to act as a balance. Sadly, many couples use most of their communication to throw barbs at each other. The husband then complains, "She's just not interested in sex anymore"; as the wife laments, "He never brings me flowers anymore." If husbands and wives would spend more time uplifting each other, their spouses might have the emotional strength and desire to be more physically and emotionally intimate.

Solomon's continued use of complimentary statements fits well in a book filled with romantic and sexual themes. Think about it! How many people want to make love with a person who has spent the last three days insulting them? Women need to have a sense of being cared for before they are "in the mood." Men need to feel appreciated and that they are sexually attractive before they get the full benefit of a sexual experience and feel like responding romantically.[27]

Dr. Kevin Layman wrote in *Sex Begins in the Kitchen*[28] that in an ideal marriage "your mate

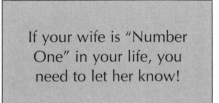

If your wife is "Number One" in your life, you need to let her know!

ought to be the Number One priority in your life; that a good marital relationship is based upon pleasing each other, being sensitive and tuned-in to each other's emotional – as well as sexual – needs." If your wife is "Number One" in your life, you need to let her know! If your husband is your "Number One," you, likewise, need to let him in on it! Compliments must flow in both directions, lots of them. This was the point Solomon addressed in his Song. If you want to have a romantic marriage and be active in the bedroom, you'd better take care of meeting your spouse's needs elsewhere. Sincere compliments are one of the best ways to get started.

DISCUSSION QUESTIONS

1. Why do we need at least 10 compliments to offset a single criticism?

2. We are told to "love your neighbor" (Lev. 19:18; Matt. 22:36-40. Also see: Luke 10:29–37 and John 13:34–35.) Where does your spouse fit into this equation? How does giving compliments fit into this equation?

3. How do we respond romantically and sexually to those who constantly criticize us? To those who insult us? To those who build us up?

4. How often do *you* compliment *your* spouse? How often do you speak with critical words?

5. Try this exercise and talk about it the next time you are discussing this book.

Take a sheet of paper and mark columns for every day of week. At the top of each column write in the number of times you intend to compliment your spouse that day. At the end of the day, write down the actual number of times you *did* compliment your spouse. In light of what Scripture tells each of us, are you living up to the Scriptural model?

Suggestions for Couples:

Go back and read each of the **Newsflash** items. For each **Newsflash for husbands** have the husband read it out loud. Have the wife comment on each **Newsflash for husbands**. Does it apply to her? Would she like her husband to keep this **Newsflash** in mind and apply it to their relationship? Likewise, for each **Newsflash for wives** have the wife read it out loud. Have the husband comment on each **Newsflash for wives**. Does it apply to him? Would he like his wife to keep this **Newsflash** in mind and apply it to their relationship?

＄

— 3 —

Lessons From the Song of Solomon

Appreciation, Protection and the Barbie Doll Syndrome

adies, how many of you would want to have sex with a man, if
you thought he was going to dump you for the "floozie" down
the street first thing tomorrow morning?   Men, how many of
you would feel inclined to be romantic with a woman, if you thought
she was constantly mocking you and laughing contemptuously at
everything you do?

Newsflash for couples: Women need to have a sense of being
cared for and men need to be appreciated.[1]   For women this is especially important in the context of sex.   Women need to feel secure in
their surroundings, their sense of self, and in their relationship with
their husbands, if they are to enjoy sexual relations.   For men, this is
especially important in the context of romance.   If a man does not feel
he is appreciated for who he is, he is not going to feel like being at all
affectionate.

Personal insecurities often result from feeling different, inadequate, or even ugly.   What other people say and do goes a long way
toward whether we believe we fit the norm or meet the standard that
"everyone" else meets.   We cannot control the behavior of others, but,
we can control how we respond to it.   Feelings of inadequacy, which
give rise to a sense of insecurity, are among those controllable respons-

es. The Song of Solomon addresses this issue, both from the perspective of how wives can protect their own self-esteem and how husbands can strengthen their wives' sense of security. A husband who does not try to make his wife feel secure in who she is and in their relationship, is neglecting her in a fundamental area of her world.

Newsflash to husbands: No matter what else is on your "to do" list, meeting your wife's need for security is very near the top of her list.

Men need to feel appreciated. In marriage, the center of the appreciation target for men usually involves appreciating him sexually. Alexandra Penny, in *How To Keep Your Man Monogamous*,[2] related interviews she had with a large number of men, some of whom were faithful to their wives, others who had committed adultery. One interview was particularly insightful. The man had described an event with the "other woman." The author then relays the next part of her interview with him. She writes:

> "Did you consider that 'pure and simple' sex?" I asked.
>
> "Well," he replied, "it's not your everyday bread-and-butter intercourse."
>
> "Could it have been that she knew how to turn you on in a more dramatic way, like hidden tea roses?" I smiled. "Also you said 'She told me all the time she adored having sex with me' – wasn't that a turn on too?"
>
> "Yes, *she made me feel wanted.* My wife wasn't so interested in *me or sex or maybe the two mean the same thing.*" (Italics by Alexandra Penny.)

Many husbands, indeed, do believe that being interested in "me or sex" does mean "the same thing." If a wife is not trying to make her husband feel wanted sexually, she is neglecting him in a fundamental area of his world. Unquestionably, men need to be appreciated and respected in many areas of life, including their work, values and intellect. But, sexual intimacy is one of the key areas for most men.

Newsflash for wives: No matter what else is on your "to do" list, appreciating your husband sexually is right near the top of his list.

A woman's feeling of security in who she is and a man's need to be appreciated as a sexual being, to a large degree, have a common starting point: the wife being sexually attractive. Being sexually attractive, however, has little to do with the superficial passing fads created by Hollywood. It has much more to do with whether she sees herself as sexually attractive. Men need to support their wives in this way. Women have a greater sense of security and a greater capacity to sexually appreciate their husbands if they feel good about themselves. The next five chapters will touch on these issues and how they relate to each other.

LESSON #2 FOR WIVES: ACCEPT THE BEAUTY OF WHO YOU ARE

The opening verses of the Song of Solomon provide a fascinating glimpse into Shulamite's background and her sense of who she was. She said:

> Dark am I, yet lovely,
> O daughters of Jerusalem,
> dark like the tents of Kedar,
> like the tent curtains of Solomon.
> Do not stare at me because I am dark,
> because I am darkened by the sun.
> My mother's sons were angry with me
> and made me take care of the vineyards;
> my own vineyard I have neglected.[3]

Shulamite was a young woman from a rural community living in Jerusalem. Her brothers had been hard on her when she was growing up, forcing her to work in the family vineyard. In those days, however, one important hallmark of beauty for women was to have pasty, white skin. Poor women worked outdoors and did not have time to bathe and oil their bodies. Worse yet, they had a telltale suntan, evidence of their low status in life. Women of wealth spent their days indoors, well shaded.

Shulamite spent a lot of time working outdoors and had a dark suntan. She was forced to neglect her body, which she referred to as "my own vineyard." Simply put, she did not meet the standards of beauty of the time, a major problem among women then, just as it is today.

The modern world has given women a vast new set of ways to feel physically unacceptable. Hollywood and New York advertisers send out thousands of images emphasizing that only very slim women who meet "super model" standards are acceptable. Stories are replete with instances of the media putting pressure on already thin starlets to lose yet more weight, turning a steady stream of actresses into anorexics. And, it is getting worse. In the 1980s the standard sample size for models was a 6 or 8, which is quite thin compared to the average woman. Today, the standard sample size for models has shrunk to a skin and bones size 2 or 4! Many top designers don't even produce clothes in anything larger than a size 8.[4] The message is clear. Real women do not have bodies "good enough" to wear the clothes of "top" designers.

Many women need a reality check. Unlike Shulamite, they find it difficult to accept the beauty God has given them. I often ask couples about a well-known model who has appeared on the cover of several popular magazines. The question I ask is how many women in the world actually look like that in real life? Typically, the answer is "one," the model, in the photograph. The correct answer, however, is none. *No one*, not even the model herself looks like that.

The process of taking professional photos insures the model will look better than she actually does.[5] My daughter, Anita, has worked in the photography business in Los Angeles and has seen the pictures before and after the touch-ups were done. In one instance, the model I used as an example lost a full three inches off her waist and three off her hips, a scar was removed from her leg, and blemishes removed from her face and arms. A photograph of another well-known model was touched up so radically on one occasion that even her navel was erased! During a recent visit, I was shown the original photograph of an ad layout. In the "final" photos, the model had lost some of the thickness under her chin, her chin was shortened, and she had been given a "nose job" to make her look better. Her calves were trimmed down to make her look more "appropriately" thin.

Newsflash to wives: The women to whom most wives compare themselves don't even exist, except in the minds of some photographer and a creative touch-up artist.

> The women to whom most wives compare themselves don't even exist, except in the minds of some photographer and a creative touch-up artist.

Jerusalem set the standard in Solomon's time, not Hollywood. Shulamite, however, refused to accept the artificial standards arbitrarily set by others. The "daughters of Jerusalem" had been talking about her appearance, and she was aware of the gossip. Her reply showed both humility and a deep appreciation for her own worth. She was, indeed, dark like "the tents of Kedar," which were dark due to the black or dark brown goat skins used to make the tent coverings.[6] Still, she knew she was beautiful and compared herself to the beautiful curtains of Solomon's tents. Solomon was one of the richest men in the world.[7] His tents were made of the finest materials, of exquisite workmanship. Shulamite was saying, "It doesn't matter whether I meet the popular standards of beauty. If I meet Solomon's, I am all right." This was not arrogant pride. It was a realistic statement of solid self-confidence.

A wife's inability to appreciate her own looks can be incredibly frustrating for her husband. A man typically sees his wife as uniquely beautiful and often appreciates seeing her in sexy outfits when they are alone together. He goes to a shop that sells sexy lingerie and buys his wife a topless, bottomless, backless, see-through bit of nothing and thinks, "She'll look great!" She receives the gift and thinks, "I'll look ridiculous!" He manages to talk her into trying it on. He thinks, "She *does* look great!" She sees herself in the mirror and *knows* she looks worse than she feared. The wife loses the bit-of-nothing in the back of the bottom dresser drawer, never to be seen again, and she feels good.

The husband, meanwhile, wonders what happened and feels hurt and rejected. Sadly, an opportunity for intimacy has been lost, due to a lack of self-appreciation and understanding.

Even the toys girls play with repeat the message: Little girls should expect to grow up to look like a Barbie Doll, and if they don't, they are not acceptable. I have measured a Barbie Doll.[8] If Barbie's proportions belonged to a real, live woman, who had a waist measurement of 24 inches, the rest of her measurements would be: bust 46 1/3, waist 24, hips 42 1/4. She would also be a whopping 7 feet, 9 inches tall. This, of course, is ridiculous. Yet, there are women who have the thought buried in the backs of their minds that their bodies don't measure up if they don't measure up to Barbie.[9]

No matter what your weight, your husband still may see you as beautiful. It is your husband you are to please, not the "daughters of Hollywood"; just as it was Solomon, not the "daughters of Jerusalem," whom Shulamite sought to please. We need to get our focus back in order if we are to do as God wants us to do.

Men, this is not only your wife's problem. Many women are insecure about their looks. We see our wives in the bedroom and say with a longing look, "My, that's nice!" She sees herself in the mirror and says with a critical tone, "My, I have fat thighs!" I spoke with a woman at our local YMCA a number of years ago who was in remarkably good condition: thin, strong, with a fine athletic figure. We were talking about all the mirrors on walls of the weightlifting room. She surprised me by saying how uncomfortable they made her, because they were a constant reminder of how poor she looked. As a kid, she had always been overweight and extremely self-conscious about her figure. No matter how hard she had worked since, she was never satisfied. A remarkable number of other women make similar remarks. I've read that even super models often focus only on their own flaws. Whether it's their face, hair, nose, lips, skin, breasts, waist, hips, or legs, there is always something wrong. And that's all they see.

Chapter 2 of the Song of Solomon begins with Shulamite's reply to the compliments Solomon lavished upon her. He told her she was the most beautiful woman in the world, the woman every man desires. Her answer in the first verse was simple and straightforward: "I am the rose of Sharon, and the lily of the valleys."[10] "The rose of Sharon" was a wild flower (not a rose in the modern sense but a bulb plant) possibly similar to the narcissus or tulip of today,[11] that grew among the grasses of the Sharon Valley. Though beautiful, it was common.

Shulamite was satisfied with her beauty, but humble. She saw nothing special in it. She wished she had been given the time to tend "her own vineyard," so it would be more refined, less of a "wild flower." It is perfectly all right to recognize that you might look "less wild" if you did not have other responsibilities, such as raising children, household chores and other jobs in and out of the home. It is also perfectly all right to see your beauty as common to all women and nothing to boast about. However, Shulamite still saw herself as beautiful. And that is the point. You also still need to see yourself as beautiful.

The Psalmist praises God in Psalm 139:13–14 with the words:

> For you created my inmost being;
> you knit me together in my mother's womb.
> I praise you because I am fearfully and wonderfully made;
> your works are wonderful,
> I know that full well.

Describing yourself as "*fearfully* and wonderfully made" sounds strange to the modern reader. We tend to think of "fear" as a feeling of dread. The healthy fear referred to in Psalm 139, however, involves "a feeling of reverence, awe, and respect."[12] In fact, it often is used in the Bible for the concept of worship.[13] The Psalmist is saying that we should praise God because we have a feeling of "reverence, awe and respect" for the wonderful job He has done in creating us. Many women would do well to copy in large print the words of Psalm 139:13 – 14 and tape them to their bedroom mirror!

A suggestion for women who feel uncomfortable with their husbands seeing them nude:

1. Find time alone to be in your bedroom, lights on, door locked.
2. Remove all your clothes and stand in front of a full length-mirror.

3. Recite Psalm 139:13 -14 while looking at yourself. Recite it two or three more times, beginning with your head and continue, saying out loud to yourself:
My face is "fearfully and wonderfully made."
My neck is "fearfully and wonderfully made."
My shoulders are "fearfully and wonderfully made."
My arms are "fearfully and wonderfully made."
My breasts are "fearfully and wonderfully made."
My hips are "fearfully and wonderfully made."
Continue listing each part of your body down to your feet.

4. Then pray to God:
"Lord, I praise you for your works are, indeed, wonderful. I am fearfully and wonderfully made. Lord, give me the strength to share this beautiful gift with my husband with a sense of joy and love. Remove any sense of shame or inhibition from me. He is my husband, the one with whom I am to be naked and not ashamed. Thank you, Lord. Amen."

5. Repeat this exercise every day until God gives you the courage to share yourself and your body with your husband in a way that will build intimacy in your relationship.

Some of the women who volunteered to edit this book reported trying this exercise. They said that at first it was very difficult and extremely embarrassing, even though they were alone. It did not make it any easier knowing they were alone *with God.* Yet, they also said it helped after they managed to get past the messages the world has been sending them and into the word God was telling them.

Dr. Tim LaHaye has told women:

> *Chuck your inhibitions.* Though modesty is an admirable virtue in a woman, it is out of place in the bedroom with her husband. The Bible teaches that Adam and Eve in their unfallen state were "naked and not ashamed." (Gen. 2:25) Frankly speaking, that means that even in their nakedness they were uninhibited. It may take time for a chaste woman to shake off the inhibitions of her premarriage days and learn

to be open with her husband – but it is absolutely essential.[14]

He also has suggested to one wife that she "let her husband help her undress and encourage her to relax and enjoy it." When her husband did this, it took a while to feel the joy, because she felt guilty when she found it exciting, but she gradually overcame her acute reticence.[15]

Today too many women have a negative perception of their own looks and it affects their sexual relationships with their spouses. Many husbands welcome their wives' acting or dressing sensually, seeing their wives naked or dressed in sexy outfits just for them; but their wives are held back by their poor self-image or training to be "modest."[16] These women can look to Shulamite and see the lessons she can teach in self-acceptance. They also can read Psalm 139: 13–14 on a regular basis to draw from the power of God's word.

LESSON #2 FOR HUSBANDS: PROTECT YOUR WIFE

Some men see their wives' insecurities as *their* problem. There are two reasons why *her* problem is *his* problem. First, love gives. It is not *God's* problem that *we* sin. Nonetheless, *He* gave *His* only Son for *us*. Love means sacrificing for the beloved. Part of the husband's job, as the *ezer kenegdo* of his wife, is to be her uplifting support. That is love.

The second reason is more basic. Men, let me make it simple: If your beloved isn't secure, she isn't going to be in the mood. And, if she isn't in the mood, then you aren't going to be happy either, because there will be no getting lucky tonight!

When I refer to the need to "protect your wife" and a woman's "feeling of security," men typically think of physical protection. This is part of it. Physical safety is a major issue. In many respects, however, it is the easy issue for many men.

Newsflash for husbands: Doing the things necessary to protect your wife's sense of who she is sounds like warm fuzzies, not the heroic deeds of a testosterone-charged, adrenaline-driven "manly man."

We men like to conquer mountains and kill dragons, not sit and listen, with an open heart and without criticism. Nonetheless, it is emotional insecurity which often disrupts a woman's view of her life as much as, if not more than, physical threats.

Shulamite's humble equation of herself to other women ("I am the rose of Sharon, and the lily of the valleys") was a good start, but a dangerous end. You can almost see what was going on further back in her mind. "If I'm the same as other women, eventually Solomon will want to check out some other 'lily of the valleys.'" Solomon saw the need to put a protecting arm around her *and* their relationship. He replied, "As the lily among thorns, so is my love among the daughters (of Jerusalem)."[17]

> Emotional insecurity often disrupts a woman's view of her life as much as, if not more than, physical threats.

No wonder Solomon was known for his wisdom! First, he continued his stream of compliments to her. Second, he acknowledged that he understood her concern. He neither minimized it nor ignored it. But he did put it in perspective. Third, he confirmed and affirmed her sense of who she was and allowed her to see herself in a more positive way. She may have been a wild flower, but, oh my, Solomon was saying, what a uniquely wonderful flower she was!

Solomon directly addressed an issue with which many women struggle. How does my husband see me compared to other women? I have had a number of women ask why their husbands like to look at other women.

Newsflash for women: Men are visual creatures and always will enjoy a good view. However, the fact that they enjoy the shape of a well-designed car, a perfectly formed oak tree, the lines of a jet plane, or the shape of a particular woman, doesn't mean they want to marry (much less be in bed with) any of them.[18]

Newsflash for men: Our actions and flippant comments can go a long way toward undermining our wives' self-acceptance. Our calling by God is to create a well-grounded sense of security in our wives.

Solomon did what needed to be done. He assured Shulamite that she was secure in her position as number one in his heart. Every husband needs to ask himself: What am *I* doing to reassure *my* wife?

Unquestionably, Solomon had looked at other women and knew what Shulamite was talking about. However, through his words and his actions he assured her that she was the only flower worth smelling, touching ... and picking.

Ironically, the vast majority of husbands seem glad to tell others how beautiful their wives are. Indeed, at the time many women feel most vulnerable about their looks (when they are pregnant) is when men typically see them as being most beautiful. At our office I once did a quick, totally unscientific survey of women about how they felt when they were in their last months of pregnancy. The answers included: Like "a whale," "a waterlogged elephant" and "a blimp." When I surveyed the men, they saw pregnant women as: "awesome," "beautiful," "brimming with life." "Glowing" was a word I heard constantly.

Newsflash to husbands: A sincere statement to your wife that *she* is the most beautiful woman in *your* world, repeated regularly, will do wonders for her and for the strength of your relationship. She *needs* to have this emotional uplift. It protects her from the negative messages that bombard her on a daily basis. This is not something she merely *likes* to hear. She *must* hear it if she is to keep a proper perspective of who she is.

Compliments have another protecting aspect that applies to both men and women. Scripture tells us to praise God in all things and at all times.[19] If God is so smart, why does He need us to tell Him how great He is? Does God have an unquenchable ego that needs constant feeding? (I've had several atheists ask this question in a tone of mockery.) The answer is simple: *God* does not *need* to hear our praises! *We* do! *We* need to hear *ourselves* say our prayers because *our* words are a constant reminder to *us* of who *we* are and who *God* is and the incredible difference between us. Prayer and praise also help remind us of our dependence on Him.

In marriage, *we need* to hear *ourselves* complimenting our spouse as much as our spouse needs to hear our praise. The act of saying the words reminds *each of us* how important this person is whom God has put into our life. The act of praising our spouse not only puts a protecting arm around our spouse, it puts a ring of protection around our relationship.

The very next verse is Shulamite's response to Solomon's wonderful reassurance.

> Like an apple tree among the trees of the forest
> is my lover among the young men.
> I delight to sit in his shade,
> and his fruit is sweet to my taste.[20]

This is both a compliment and an explanation of how he protected her emotionally and physically.

When Solomon compared Shulamite to all the other women, he found her to be the only flower among the thorns. She replied in kind. An apple tree was cultivated, unlike the wild "trees of the forest." She described Solomon as refined, unlike the other young men she had known. Moreover, Middle Eastern culture of the time considered the apple to be a symbol of erotic love.[21] Thus, he not only was cultivated, he knew how to feed her romantic and emotional needs.

Finally, she delighted "to sit in his shade." He was a source of protection for her from the harsh, scorching sun of the physical world. This is an important comparison. Women want a sense of security and protection, but they don't want it forced upon them. A tree never *requires* anyone to "accept" its shade. It simply "invites" by providing shade as part of its nature. People can come and go as they please. Part of the attraction of Solomon's love was that it protected without condition or suffocation.

Solomon's willingness to act as a source of protection for Shulamite also was illustrated by her willingness to make a request of him in chapter 2, verse 15:

> Catch us the foxes,
> the little foxes,
> that spoil the vineyards,
> for our vineyards are in blossom.[22]

Like most women, Shulamite was sensitive to the needs of the relationship and the problems that might endanger it. The "little foxes" she mentioned are the little problems that crop up in every relationship. Foxes have a habit of taking a small bite out of one piece of fruit, then turning to the next piece for another bite. Soon, the entire vineyard is ruined because every fruit has been nibbled. Small things have a way of doing that. Tiny irritants, the "little foxes" of life, can become major problems if not dealt with.

Shulamite requested Solomon to act because she knew he valued their relationship and would take steps to protect it from outside "nibbling." He already had shown that he listened to her and was attentive to her concerns.[23]

Newsflash for couples: Husbands and wives are the support for each other. If *either* spouse has a deep concern, it should *always* be a concern to the other. If your husband feels pain, you, as his wife, need to feel it, too. If your wife is concerned about a perceived threat to the relationship, you, as her husband, need to start hunting down those "little foxes" before they cause real damage.

> Husbands and wives are the support for each other. If *either* spouse has a deep concern, it should *always* be a concern to the other.

Unfortunately, what our spouses see as danger we often view as "silly overreaction." For example, some married individuals engage in conversations with peers of the opposite sex about very personal matters, including what they enjoy sexually and what their spouse will or will not do romantically. When the other spouse finds out and is angered by the breach of confidence, the response is, "It's not that big a deal. We're just friends talking." The little foxes are loose; the warning has been issued and ignored.

This is the beginning of a high-risk time for the marriage for two reasons. First, the breach of trust often results in the other spouse never again feeling safe sharing his most intimate thoughts. Trust is fragile. Once broken, it is difficult to mend. Second, the act of "sharing" information of a personal nature is an act of bonding with the other person. The co-worker, neighbor or friend now is drawn into your intimate life. You've "undressed" emotionally, and chances of an affair are greatly elevated.

There is a more subtle "little fox" that often is ignored, but which often nibbles relationships to ruin. This is the "little fox" of complaining about the faults, irritating habits, or "unreasonable" demands of your spouse to others of your *own* gender, your "girl friends" or "bowling buddies." After hearing your complaint (and, of course, your spouse never has a chance to give the other side of the story), your friends roll their eyes at the "outrage" you have just described, then agree with you with a round of typical statements:

- "Men are such jerks!"
- "No one should have to put up with that!"
- "I'd never let a woman push *me* around like that!"

These responses often are made by people who are either divorced themselves or in unhappy marriages. They are trying to justify their own decisions to bale out, rather than work on their relationships. They may say they are your "friends," but they are neither your friends nor friends of your marriage. Your complaints have set the "little foxes" free.

God designed man and woman so the two will become "one." Letting a third person (who is not a professional counselor) into the emotional secrets of the marriage is the same as inviting him into the relationship itself.

Sharing the emotional secrets of the marriage with others can involve matters other than sexual issues. They can be as simple as complaining to others about your spouse spending too much time at work or on sports ("All he does is watch football." Or, "All she thinks about is bowling.") or with his buddies. They also include talking with others about how much your spouse drinks or gambles and how it leads to arguments. Seeking specific answers to specific questions *from a qualified source* is different. Unfortunately, people often go beyond seeking specific answers, treating the subject like gossip, with their own spouses as the subjects of the gossip.

The "little foxes" also can be the little irritating habits we all have. How many of us snap gum, pick our teeth in public, are late for appointments, forget wedding anniversaries or birthdays, schedule meetings or other commitments without telling our spouses, squeeze the toothpaste in the middle of the tube, forget to put the toilet seat down, leave the toilet paper roll empty without getting a new roll for the next person, leave dirty clothes laying around instead of putting them in the hamper, or habitually coming home late, all of which drive our spouses "up the wall"? We easily can stand on our "rights" to behave as we do. However, in a love relationship, there are no "rights," only the obligation to give to the other.[24] As Paul wrote, "Let no debt remain outstanding, except the continuing debt to love one another ..."[25] If we become aware that our behavior is bothering our beloved, then Scripture is clear. We need to work on changing what we are doing.

LESSON #2 FOR COUPLES: PROTECT THAT RELATIONSHIP!

Most of us think of protection in terms of physical security. When it comes to relationships, it usually means not letting an interloper lope in. But, the first wall of protection for relationships is our own frame of mind. Wives need to understand who they are and how their husbands see them. Likewise, husbands need to understand the insecurities their wives feel and deal with them quickly.[26] This is a joint effort of mutual support. Husbands and wives need to work on their understanding of being a couple, with love and uplifting support (each acting as the *ezer kenegdo* of the other) being the primary principles of action. Home security should start with protecting the relationship, not with a burglar alarm.

DISCUSSION QUESTIONS

1. We have talked of "women's rights" and "women's liberation" since the 1970s, and issues of women's rights have been debated for at least 100 years before that. How does the concept that the husband should be protective of his wife as found in the Song of Solomon fit with this? Are they consistent or inconsistent?

2. How many women today have good self-images? How many actually like the way they look? This includes face, hair, body, hips, breasts, stomach, skin, legs arms, etc. Why? Is it because of an artificial standard created, even imposed, by someone else, e.g. TV or Hollywood?

3. If men are to protect their wives, what should they be doing regarding their wives' self-esteem? Is protection limited only to physical issues of safety from attack?

4. What should the husband and wife do to help her feel more self-confident, and for him to act in a more protective way?

Suggestions for Couples:

Go back and read each of the **Newsflash** items. For each **Newsflash for husbands** have the husband read it out loud. Have the wife comment on each **Newsflash for husbands**. Does it apply to her? Would she like her husband to keep this **Newsflash** in mind and apply it to their relationship? Likewise, for each **Newsflash for wives** have the wife read it out loud. Have the husband comment on each **Newsflash for wives**. Does it apply to him? Would he like his wife to keep this **Newsflash** in mind and apply it to their relationship?

— 4 —

Lessons From the Song of Solomon
How to Wash Your Left Elbow

How do you wash your left elbow? Obviously, with your right hand. When I was 12 years old, I broke my right wrist. I quickly learned how hard it was to wash my left elbow with only my left hand available.

Meeting needs in marriage is like washing elbows. It takes an opposite, uplifting force, an *ezer kenegdo*, to get the job done. The love husbands and wives show to each other is described as *agape* in the New Testament (Ephesians 5:25) and *'ahab* (aw-hav') in the Old Testament (Proverbs 5:18-19). Both words contain a strong element of sacrifice: the willingness to give to the beloved. Before we can sacrifice in a meaningful way, we must know what our spouses need. The easiest way to learn each other's needs is to listen. This may seem obvious, but people often want to talk (and be listened to) so much that they do not spend time *hearing* what their spouses are saying. One of the greatest sacrifices a husband or wife can give is the sacrifice of his own desire to talk, but instead, simply listen to his spouse. Listening is more than being silent while your spouse makes sounds. It means taking in the words and the feelings behind the statements. If you are concerned about your spouse's needs, you will listen.

LESSON #3 FOR HUSBANDS:
BE CONCERNED ABOUT YOUR WIFE'S NEEDS

The Song of Solomon is quick to recognize the need to meet needs. Many of the needs reviewed in this chapter are variations of themes we already have discussed. The review is to help insure a more complete understanding of the basic ideas.

After the initial verses of chapter 1, Shulamite turned to Solomon and expressed a major concern:[1]

> Tell me, you whom I love, where you graze your flock
> and where you rest your sheep at midday.
> Why should I be like a veiled woman
> beside the flocks of your friends?

It was customary in those times for harlots to veil themselves and go out along the road and in the pastureland to sell themselves.[2] Shulamite was worried about her reputation. She wanted to be with him[3], but did not want to wander aimlessly among the flocks to see whether she could find him, and in the process, be taken for a prostitute. She was open and honest in her expression to let Solomon know her misgivings.

All too often when women express their concerns, their husbands brush them off. We act as if the concern is trivial. "Oh, don't be silly!" We insist, "Why should you care about what other people think?" Or, "Don't be so emotional. Can't you see there's nothing to worry about?" Love, by its very nature, cares about the deep concerns of others. Comments that invalidate concerns fly in the face of Biblical caring.

Solomon answered Shulamite's question directly.[4]

> If you do not know, most beautiful of women,
> follow the tracks of the sheep
> and graze your young goats
> by the tents of the shepherds.

He reaffirmed her position ("most beautiful of women") and gave his reply without belittling the question. This honored her. The word for "honor" in Scripture means to give weight to something. To "dishonor" means to "blow it off," to consider someone of no weight, or inconsequential, to ignore them. Solomon gave weight to Shulamite's concerns.

Scripture presents two issues in this setting back to back,[5] in order to compare and contrast the points. The two issues involve matters of outward appearance and matters of inner character. This is a profoundly important distinction. As God told the prophet Samuel, "The LORD does not look at the things man looks at. Man looks at the outward appearance, but the LORD looks at the heart."[6] Matthew Henry has noted, "Let us reckon that to be true beauty which is within, and judge of men, as far as we are capable, by their minds, not their mien."[7]

When dealing with beauty, the standard is what *your beloved* thinks, when acting in a positive and reassuring way. *Outward* beauty truly is "in the eye of the beholder." When your spouse loves you the way you are, that is all that is important.

On issues of character, however, it is not appropriate to ask someone to take an action that violates his ethical standards or tarnishes his reputation. Whether a person is respected in the community or seen as a threat to others is of great importance. Indeed, the importance of noble character is referred to throughout Scripture.[8] Solomon could have confused the issues and demonstrated an inappropriate attitude by replying, "If we don't care what people think about the current fashion, why should we care about what others think regarding our comings and goings? If '*they*' misunderstand, isn't that *their* problem, not *ours*?" Instead, Solomon was sensitive to the nature of the problem and answered Shulamite in a way that dealt directly with the issue.

Good character is fundamental to the romance and sex life of every husband and wife.[9] You need to watch out for each other to protect the reputation of your spouse's character in the community.

Newsflash for husbands: Your wife is your *ezer kenegdo*, your balance. She is created in the image of God and is here to provide you the support God knows you *need*, although it may not necessarily be what you *want*. Choosing to belittle or ignore your wife's needs as simply "illogical" means you choose to belittle God's solution to the problems of your life. This, in itself, is not logical thinking.

Solomon was concerned about Shulamite's emotional and physical needs as well as her reputation. In chapter two, she said:

> His left arm is under my head,
> and his right arm embraces me.[10]

Solomon did two things: He supported her with his left hand and embraced her with his right. This is a tender picture of support and romance. With his right arm he gave her the physical support she needed.[11] With his left arm, which is closer to his heart, he provided her emotional support and attended to her need for romance. The word used to describe the action of the right arm, however, which was embracing her, *chabaq* (khaw-bak'),[12] implies a loving embrace, a gentle fondling or stroking. Solomon was using his strength to comfort and embrace her, not to "lord it over her." It is no coincidence that this passage immediately follows Shulamite's description of his support for her in verses three through five. He considered meeting *her* needs as one of the primary purposes of *his* life.

The Bible's call for a husband to watch over the needs of his wife is the subject of one of the most challenging passages for men in relation to women in all of the New Testament. "Husbands, love your wives, just as Christ loved the church and gave himself up for her..."[13] Think of the implications! How *did* Christ love the church? He loved it so much He poured His whole life into it and in the end He died for it! Jesus said that the Gentiles lord it over one another. However, He did not come to let others serve Him, but He came to serve others.[14] This could be the worst news of all. Many husbands would die for their wives; just don't ask them to take out the garbage, vacuum the floor, set the dinner table, wash the dishes or change the baby's diaper. It is the little, day-to-day things, the small, undramatic acts of service that are so difficult.

Newsflash for guys: The concept of "die for your wife" includes the little deaths: the deaths of self and selfishness so God can replace them with selfless love and sacrificial giving. The goal of manhood in marriage is not to satisfy the male ego, but to uplift our wives, to the point that they can rejoice and be radiant.[15]

Many men are not willing to become servants to meet the needs of their wives. Yet, this is the standard God sets. Men like the idea of their wives "submitting" to them without remembering that they, likewise, are to submit to their wives.[16] And the nature of the submission is pure service, just as Christ served the church.

Men, you may be wondering: "What does all this have to do with sex?" The answer is coming in chapter 10. The "Law of Sticky Notes" will explain the relationship between serving your wife and sex ... and provide a whole new motivation to understand and provide the service to which Scripture calls you.

A warning to wives: The standard of service God sets for your husband is **not** something you are to remind him about. It is the work of the Holy Spirit, *not* you, to correct him. He needs to worry about correcting *himself* and bringing *himself* into line with what Scripture tells him. Likewise, you worry about correcting *yourself* and bringing *yourself* into line with what Scripture tells wives.[17] God gives both husbands and wives more than enough work to do to last the rest of their lives, without having to work on "fixing" their spouses.[18]

BUT DO I HAVE TO DO THAT, TOO?!?

The single biggest complaint from wives is, "My husband won't talk to me and he doesn't listen when I want to talk to him."

Newsflash for husbands: Women need to connect with people and they do it with words. Not talking to them or listening to them is a form of rejection. The Song of Solomon alludes to this problem. Solomon refers to Shulamite four times as, "my sister, my bride."[19] This is a strange figure of speech, especially since the first three occur on their wedding day and the last occurs right after he has made love to her on their wedding night. Referring to your fiancee and then your wife, with whom you've just had sex, as your "sister" makes little sense in twenty-first century, Western English.

The cultural reference to "my sister, my bride," however, is instructive. Prior to a man's marriage the prevailing social norm was that his sister was the only woman of his own generation with whom he could talk in public or share his deepest feelings. Talking with any other women this way was considered inappropriately forward.

Solomon was telling Shulamite that she was not only the woman with whom he will have sexual relations, i.e. his bride; but she was also the woman with whom he could talk. She was the one to whom he could open his heart and tell anything, anywhere, anytime. She was like his sister.

But, Solomon wanted to do more than talk with her. He wanted to listen to her. He told her:

> ... let me hear your voice;
> for your voice is sweet ...[20]

Now, there was a man who understood women, and how to connect with them emotionally.

Newsflash for husbands: One of women's primary emotional needs is conversation.[21] Conversation is not simply something women *want*, it is something they *need*, and need in large quantities. Dr. Willard F. Harley suggests that women *need* fully 15 hours of intimate conversation with their husbands each week.[22]

> The husband who *both* talks with *and* listens to his wife is a man who truly understands women, and how to connect with them emotionally.

Conversation for most men is not only difficult; it is threatening. Give most men a gun and a knife and tell them to go into battle to protect the family and they're happy. Tell them they face torture and certain death in the process, and they will swallow hard; but they can handle that. However, ask them to talk with their wives about the battle and their feelings about what will happen. Now, that is dangerous ground!

There appears to be a number of reasons for this, three of which are worth mentioning here. First, God seems to have wired men's brains differently than women's. Women's speech centers and emotional centers of the brain have easy access to each other. Men do not have the same neurological connection.[23] Second, men "have stronger, more intense, and likely more unpleasant physiological reactions to conflict with their partners" than do women.[24] Third, both men and women like to think of themselves as competent in what they do. Men, in particular, like to believe they are competent to handle their own lives. Many men feel that if they talk about a problem at work, a fear they have, a concern with which they have been struggling, or a goal they hope to achieve, it is an admission they need help with the issue and are not competent to deal with it on their own.[25] Any conversation that might reveal how a man feels is tough work and risks the pain of conflict with his wife, the pain of admitting incompetence, or, worse yet, the pain of rejection. He wonders, "What if she doesn't love me any more, now that she knows what is going on inside me?"

Newsflash for women: Would *you* look forward to a situation that requires a great deal of emotional work, and it appears the best you can do is lose?

Newsflash for men: The *appearance* that you will lose by revealing your feelings is not a reality if your wife is following Biblical principles. Part of God's plan is to put women into men's lives to act as the uplifters, enablers, and emotional strengtheners. Husbands need to learn to let go and trust that God knows what He's doing. Men *need* the support women can give when they talk with women, and women *need* to have the opportunity to give that support. Granted, this takes work, but the reward is worth it.

Newsflash to women: If your husband opens up to you, recognize the incredible gift he is giving you. Listen to him with a gentle spirit. Respond without criticism or scorn. Hold the information he gives you as the most closely guarded secret you ever will have. Your marriage depends on it.

LESSON #3 FOR WIVES: LEARN TO BE ALLURING

An alluring woman is tempting, charming, enticing. That describes Shulamite. She starts off early in the poem, "Let him kiss me with the kisses of his mouth."[26] While Scripture frequently speaks of the kiss of friendship,[27] it is apparent that this is a sensuous kiss, [28] which would be more appropriate for lovers. Shulamite was asking Solomon to show his affection for her in a physical way. Later, after they were married, this enticement to kiss became a full-fledged invitation to make love. On their wedding night she told him:

> Awake, north wind,
> and come, south wind!
> Blow on my garden,
> that its fragrance may spread abroad.
> Let my lover come into his garden
> and taste its choice fruits.[29]

Scripture is incredibly forthright about the alluring nature of the model wife. In our culture we shy away from even talking about it. Shulamite had no such misplaced reticence. She was ready to extend the invitation in terms that could not be misunderstood. But, she also could be subtle. Later in their marriage, she said:

> My lover has gone down to his garden,
> to the beds of spices,
> to browse in the gardens
> and to gather lilies.
> I am my lover's and my lover is mine;
> he browses among the lilies.[30]

There is little doubt as to her meaning. She already had described herself as the "lily of the valleys"(Song 2:1) and later Solomon told her:

> Your waist is a mound of wheat
> encircled by lilies.[31]

Her body was the bed of lilies, and inviting Solomon to "browse among the lilies" was a direct invitation for him to enjoy her body.

We all have watched herds of animals browsing in the pasture, even if only on television. The image is important. A grazing animal takes its time, slowly working its way across the field, inspecting the area as it goes. Touching here, nibbling there as it moves along at a leisurely pace. It is at peace as it feeds itself to contentment. Shulamite was inviting Solomon to take a long, slow, sensual trip over her entire body, caressing here, kissing there, feeding his passions as he moved from one part of her to another.

Women in our culture long have been told, "Good girls don't do *that*," when it comes to sexual matters. They are told they should never intentionally try to entice a man. Unfortunately, this often has resulted in one of two extremes. Some women rebel, knowing that being attractive and enjoying beauty is part of being female. They dress in provocative ways, wearing low cut tops, short shorts, and skin tight outfits. They want to entice every man in sight. The other extreme is the woman who is so caught up in inhibitions that she cannot wear what is commonly considered moderately attractive within our culture. Everything is bland and dowdy. They don't want to entice *any* man, even their own husbands, even in the privacy of their own homes.

We need to look at how Shulamite handled the matter. Unquestionably, Shulamite was a teasing, enticing, alluring woman. But, it is important to remember the context of every single instance of her activity. It *all* was directed to her beloved, Solomon. Moreover, *every* occasion on which she invited him to fully enjoy her body occurred *after* the marriage. She was not making sexy comments to other men or dressing in such a way as to catch their eyes. But, when it came to her beloved, all the rules went out the window. With him she could be seductive without any limitations, reservations or inhibitions.

LESSON #3 FOR COUPLES:
MEET THE NEEDS OF YOUR SPOUSE!

The principle of meeting the needs of your spouse is profoundly important to married couples. We have become a nation obsessed with personal rights over the past 40 years. We forget that with all rights there must be counterbalancing responsibilities. To insist on "my rights" without being responsible for their effect on others is the mark of a tyrannical despot, not the mark of a loving Christian. Nonetheless, we have been told that what is "important" is that *I* want *my* rights, and it really doesn't matter what happens to *you*. During these decades we have heard, "Look out for number one"; "Greed is good"; and "If you don't take care of yourself, who will?"

This attitude also is reflected in our modern popular music. One of Elvis Presley's early hits was *Love Me Tender*. We sat mesmerized as Elvis crooned, "Love me tender, love me true, all my dreams fulfill..." To "love me" meant the other person should fulfill "all *my* dreams." If the beloved fell short of that, the love was gone. Worse yet, the notion that *I* have a responsibility to fulfill any of *your* dreams is never even mentioned in the song. Andrew Fletcher, a Scottish political thinker of the eighteenth-century, once noted, "Give me the making of the songs of a nation and I care not who writes its laws." [32] How true. Sadly, our culture has bought into this upside down thinking, since this song and others like it came out in the 1950s and '60s.

This obsession with "rights," the need to be "number one" and the stubborn insistence that "all my dreams" be fulfilled does not agree with the Biblical concept of marriage, or its associated intimate romance and sex life. Love is sacrificial. It gives without counting cost or comparing the score.[33] John 3:16 tells us, "For God so loved the world that he *gave his one and only Son,* that whoever believes in him shall not perish but have eternal life." (Emphasis added.) It does *NOT* read: "For God so loved the world that He *considered giving* His only begotten Son, *on condition* that His Son's rights would be fully protected and, even then, only if God got something really good, or perhaps better, in return."

The fundamental nature of the relationship between husband and wife requires love, not rights, if couples are to have the blessing of love and intimacy God desires for marriage.[34] The concepts of *rights* and *love* are completely at odds. Rights are centered on self. Love is centered on selflessness. Rights are to be enforced. Love means we surrender. Rights allow us to control others. Love compels us to serve others. Rights create obligations for others to give to us. Love creates an obligation for us to give to others.[35] As Paul said in Romans 13:8, "Let no debt remain outstanding, except the continuing debt to love one another ..."

Christ teaches those who follow Him to serve others. His last great teaching session with His disciples before His death was at the Last Supper. John 13 opens by telling of Jesus removing His garments and washing the feet of His followers. In Biblical times only a servant would remove his garments to ready himself for work. Moreover, the job of washing the feet of the family and guests was done by the lowest slave in the household.[36]

Watching Jesus humble Himself this way was so shocking that Peter could not deal with it. At first he refused to allow Jesus to wash his feet. When it was over, Jesus explained what had happened:

> Now that I, your Lord and Teacher, have washed your feet, you also should wash one another's feet. I have set you an example that you should do as I have done for you.[37]

Christians are to follow Christ's example by serving. A slave, especially the lowest of slaves, does not demand rights. It is through service on this level that we are to demonstrate our love for our spouses.

The Tough Question: What does your spouse need that you don't want to do? How do you justify not doing it? Is it by redefining the need so it becomes something she only "wants," not needs? Or, do you describe what he wants as too "silly" or "weird" or even "disgusting" to take seriously? Or, do you insist it is below your "dignity?" At the Last Supper, Jesus used the example of the worst job done by the lowest slave when He washed the disciples' feet. Early in His ministry He said, "A student is not above his teacher, but everyone who is fully trained will be like his teacher."[38] At the end of His ministry, He was telling us that the teacher acts like a slave.

The slave does not have the luxury of ignoring his master because what is being asked for, in the slave's opinion, is "only" a *want* not a *need.* Likewise, the slave cannot dismiss a request because it seems "silly."

The Tougher Question: If the teacher is like a slave and "everyone who is fully trained will be like his teacher," what does that make you? Tougher answer: A slave! This is the point of Paul's comments in 1 Corinthians 7:3-4:

> The husband should fulfill his marital duty to his wife, and likewise the wife to her husband. The wife's body does not belong to her alone but also to her husband. In the same way, the husband's body does not belong to him alone but also to his wife.

Paul also tells us, "Submit to one another out of reverence for Christ." [39]

The Toughest Question: Are you willing to act as the lowest slave when it comes to your spouse's needs? If not, you are failing to follow Christ's command and need to evaluate whether Jesus truly is Lord of your life.[40] If you are not doing what He tells you, don't complain that you are not receiving the blessings God promises will result from an intimate, loving relationship. Obedience is the key to receiving blessings. Isaiah puts this forcefully:

> If you are willing and obedient,
> you will eat the best from the land;
> but if you resist and rebel,
> you will be devoured by the sword.[41]

Willing obedience to God's word is the path to the best of marriage.

Remember, however, God is a loving God, not an IRS agent in the sky, ready to zap us at the smallest error. Moreover, He never would direct us to do something that is not in our best interest. When we try to meet His impossibly high standard of servanthood, He is ready to give us an incredibly great blessing in return. However, the blessing will be what we *need,* not necessarily what we *want.*

Obedience results in blessings because God's word is the word of life. It is like life-giving water that causes us to grow and flourish.[42] The concept of service bringing blessings, however, is not a new teaching with Christianity. Alfred Edersheim, a Jewish scholar who converted to Christianity and wrote extensively during the middle 1800s, noted an ancient legend:

> A certain wise woman said to her daughter before her marriage: "My child, stand before thy husband and minister to him. If thou wilt act as his maiden he will be thy slave, and honour thee as his mistress; but if thou exalt thyself against him, he will be thy master, and thou shalt become vile in his eyes, like one of the maidservants."[43]

Likewise, there is an ancient Chinese proverb:

> If you seek joy for an hour, take a nap.
> If you seek joy for a day, go fishing.
> If you seek joy for a month, take a trip.
> If you seek joy for a year, get married.
> If you seek joy for a lifetime, learn to serve others.

To this Chinese proverb I would add *Sheridan's Corollary:*

> If you seek joy *in marriage* for a lifetime, learn to serve your spouse.

Studies show that married couples have a more active sex life when the husband helps his wife with the day-to-day chores.[44] This is as surprising as sunrise.

Newsflash for husbands: Women enjoy being cared for. They like the idea that others are thinking of them and volunteering to help them. This is not an attack on their sense of competency. (Have you ever wondered why your wife likes you to help her on with her coat? Or to hold the door open for her? She obviously is capable of doing it for herself. She enjoys it, because when you help her in this way it means you are thinking of her and believe she is of value.) When you help her with little things around the house, such as keeping things picked up, taking out the trash or helping with the dishes, two things happen. First, she feels more connected to you because you have just come to her aid. Second, it gives her less to do and so she is less tired at the end of the day.

Newsflash for husbands: Women who feel cared for and are not tired generally are more sexually interested than women who feel taken advantage of or are physically exhausted.

Newsflash for wives: If you want your husband to be more affectionate, then you should address his needs. Husbands and wives are to be loving servants to each other.

Warning to husbands and wives: We are talking about obedience to God's word and cause and effect, not manipulation. If the motivation behind your kindness is nothing more than self-satisfaction, then it is not love. Love acts without the expectation of return. The motivation behind love is the desire to give, not to get. Love is sacrificial, not a method of "purchasing" desired actions from your spouse. A husband who only shows kindnesses to his wife to improve his chances of having sex has turned the relationship into a barter system, not a love system. Likewise, a wife who "gives sex" as a "reward" or to "soften up" her husband on some issue has missed the point. *All* the kindnesses in marriage are to be shown out of a sense of love, not for the "purpose" of getting more sex or receiving more affection.

> If the motivation behind your kindness is nothing more than self-satisfaction, then it is not love. Love acts without the expectation of return.

Love does not manipulate. However, it does have a natural tendency to encourage a loving response. This is cause and effect. If I fertilize and water the flowers in my garden, I am not trying to "manipulate" them into blooming. Depending on weather and soil conditions, they may not bloom, despite my efforts. However, fertilizing and watering them does tend to create an environment conducive to more blossoms. Likewise, showing behavior that your spouse appreciates is more likely to engender a loving response than is negative behavior.

No matter what area of marriage is considered, intimate or otherwise, God commands us to show love to our spouses. If we obey, He will bless our efforts. If we do not obey, we should not expect the blessing.

DISCUSSION QUESTIONS

1. Why does love require that we look after the needs of others over our own needs?

2. Realistically, how easy is it for us to meet our own emotional needs? Is it even possible?

3. What is the difference between the events of Song of Solomon 1:5–6 and 1:7–8?

4. Why does Scripture rebuff criticism of Shulamite's looks, but support her concern about how her standard of morality is perceived? If we are not to "worry about what other people think" on one issue, why not on both?

5. Song 1:2, 4:16 and 6:2-3 all are invitations by the wife to her husband. How would most men feel if their wives acted like this most of the time? Why *don't* most wives?

Suggestions for Couples:

Go back and read each of the **Newsflash** items. For each **Newsflash for husbands** have the husband read it out loud. Have the wife comment on each **Newsflash for husbands**. Does it apply to her? Would she like her husband to keep this **Newsflash** in mind and apply it to their relationship? Likewise, for each **Newsflash for wives** have the wife read it out loud. Have the husband comment on each **Newsflash for wives**. Does it apply to him? Would he like his wife to keep this **Newsflash** in mind and apply it to their relationship?

Lessons From the Song of Solomon
Romance and Honest Desires

When I was a kid living on the east side of Detroit, my folks would take us to Jefferson Beach, an amusement park about a half hour drive away. Jefferson Beach had the typical assortment of rides such as the ferris wheel and a roller coaster. My favorite amusement, however, was the fun house. In one section of the fun house, the floor seemed to move up and down and shuttle back and forth, forward and back, and tilt on angles in random movements. The trick was to try to keep your balance and walk from the door at one corner of the room to the other door at the opposite corner without falling down. Needless to say, it took all my concentration. The very idea of trying to think about something else or solving some other problem at the same time would have been ridiculous.

The stability of the foundation of every couple's romance life will determine in large degree what else can go on. If the floor is unstable, husbands and wives will spend so much time and energy trying to keep their balance, that they will have little left over for romance or sex.

The foundational floor of a couple's intimate life is built on the actions of the husband and wife. It is essential that husbands help create the proper environment so their wives can feel comfortable enough to reveal their needs and desires. Likewise, before husbands can feel comfortable revealing their needs and showing affection, it is essential that wives help create the proper environment. A foundation in a building is built brick by brick. The foundation of a relationship is built action by action, word by word. This leads us to the actions and words every husband and wife need to display habitually if the foundation of their intimate life is going to be stable.

LESSON #4 FOR HUSBANDS: LAY ON THE ROMANCE

Solomon's courtship of Shulamite must have been awesome to behold. She was a country girl of modest means who had been made to work as a laborer in the fields by her family. He was the most powerful king of the times, a man whose immense wealth was legendary.[1] Yet, he courted her as if she were a princess and he the commoner. It was not until the day of their wedding that he came for her in all the royal formality of king.[2] In Song 2:8–9, she described him approaching her home during the courtship:

> Listen! My lover!
> Look! Here he comes,
> leaping across the mountains,
> bounding over the hills.
> My lover is like a gazelle or a young stag.
> Look! There he stands behind our wall,
> gazing through the windows,
> peering through the lattice.

What an image! This would be enough to make any woman feel special. He was coming to her. His attitude was of a lover in pursuit of his beloved, not a king claiming his rights. He came to her "... leaping across the mountains, bounding over the hills ... like a gazelle or a young stag." We easily can picture the image of love in bloom as he approached with his chest puffed out, his head held high, a definite bounce in his step. He was in love, and didn't care whether the entire world knew about it.

Moreover, he was treating her as an equal. She was not an object to be bought or manipulated. She was some*one* to be courted. In too many cultures, including our own, we often treat those of the opposite sex as if they are inferior. We frequently speak of "male chauvinism"; but women, too, often assume an air of superiority in their attitudes toward men.[3] Despite their obvious difference in status, Solomon did not act that way. Love never takes the attitude of superiority. Christ, the perfect model of love, left his domain as Son of God in heaven to take on the role of a servant.[4] If we talk of love, we cannot, at the same time, talk of superiority.

Solomon continues his courting by "gazing through the windows, peering through the lattice." In modern language this gives the impression of a peeping tom. In ancient times, however, families often owned homes with a courtyard in the front. A wall was built around the courtyard, with a lattice above the wall, which formed windows. A young man would stand by patiently hoping for a glimpse of his beloved. Solomon was courting her as a respectful suitor, and looking "... through the windows – at one time through this one, at another through that one – that he might see her and feast his eyes on her."[5] This was a very romantic gesture. Shulamite loved it.

Shulamite continued her statement by adding:

> My lover spoke and said to me,
> "Arise, my darling,
> my beautiful one, and come with me.
> See! The winter is past;
> the rains are over and gone.
> Flowers appear on the earth;
> the season of singing has come,
> the cooing of doves
> is heard in our land.
> The fig tree forms its early fruit;
> the blossoming vines spread their fragrance.
> Arise, come, my darling;
> my beautiful one, come with me."[6]

It was spring. Shulamite apparently lived in the northern mountainous part of Israel. Travel through this area was difficult during the winter rains. Solomon had waited months to see her, and the waiting was over.[7] He called his "beautiful one" to come with him, that they might go out and renew their relationship.

The entire scene was overlaid with romantic images that Solomon wove for her. He called her his "beautiful one," and then, as if in comparison, he described the beauty around him: the flowers and their fragrance; the doves, a sign of peacefulness; the fig trees and the vines, traditional symbols of peaceful and prosperous times.[8] Many women would love to have their husbands see them in such a warm light and add the extra dose of sweetness to their relationships with such flowery compliments.

The next time Solomon appeared at Shulamite's door it was with even more fanfare.

> Who is this coming up from the desert
> like a column of smoke,
> perfumed with myrrh and incense
> made from all the spices of the merchant?
> Look! It is Solomon's carriage,
> escorted by sixty warriors,
> the noblest of Israel,
> all of them wearing the sword,
> all experienced in battle,
> each with his sword at his side,
> prepared for the terrors of the night.
> King Solomon made for himself the carriage;
> he made it of wood from Lebanon.
> Its posts he made of silver, its base of gold.
> Its seat was upholstered with purple,
> its interior lovingly inlaid
> by the daughters of Jerusalem.
> Come out, you daughters of Zion,
> and look at King Solomon wearing the crown,
> the crown with which his mother crowned him

on the day of his wedding,
the day his heart rejoiced.[9]

He was coming after her to be his bride, with full pomp and ceremony. As he did during the courtship, he came with an attitude of respect, showing that Shulamite was the most special woman in the world to him.

> Your wife needs to be romanced continuously if the relationship is to grow.

Newsflash for men: Solomon has presented the essence of romance through his behavior. Romance makes a woman feel special, that she is the most important person in your world. Your wife needs to be romanced continuously if the relationship is to grow.[10]

LESSON #4 FOR WIVES: BE FORTHRIGHT IN YOUR DESIRES

Just as Solomon knew how to woo Shulamite, Shulamite knew where Solomon lived and how to get to his innermost being.

News flash to women: Most men like to think of themselves as studs. We all want to be the hero of the story. But even more, we want to be the hero women lust after. At the end of the day, however, it is not really "women" we want to lust after us, it is "*our* woman." Men see a great deal of life in sexual terms. We tend to assume that women think the same way. Just as husbands are aroused by the sight of their wives, we would like our wives to be aroused by the sight of us.

Shulamite understood this. She made the first of two telling statements early in the Song:

> Strengthen me with raisins,
> refresh me with apples,
> for I am faint with love.[11]

Raisins and apples were considered aphrodisiacs in Solomon's time. If Shulamite was "faint with love," i.e., lovesick, and in need of strengthening, why would she ask for an aphrodisiac? In other words, "If Shulamite's cry was to be understood literally, one might ... doubt the correctness of the text; for 'love – sickness, even in the age of passion and sentimentality, was not to be cured with roses and apples.'"[12] The observation misses the point. She *was* lovesick and *did not* want to be cured! She wanted it to continue! She was telling Solomon he was the source of her sensual pleasure and did not want the feeling to end.

She added:

> Until the day breaks
> and the shadows flee,
> turn, my lover,
> and be like a gazelle
> or like a young stag
> on the rugged hills.[13]

She was encouraging Solomon to be a "like a young stag." I have asked groups of men how many of them would like their wives to see them as "young stags" and urge them to act that way? The knowing smiles and the raised hands have shown unanimous agreement.

Newsflash to women: Husbands really like their wives seeing them as stags.

Shulamite's desire for Solomon did not wane after they were married.[14] Later she told him:

> Husbands really like
> their wives seeing
> them as stags.

> Let us go early to the vineyards
> to see if the vines have budded,
> if their blossoms have opened,
> and if the pomegranates are in bloom –
> there I will give you my love.

The mandrakes send out their fragrance,
and at our door is every delicacy,
both new and old,
that I have stored up for you, my lover.

Two things about this invitation would cause any husband to remember it with a smile for the rest of his life. First, she invited him out to the garden for a round of intimate passion. Husbands tend to initiate sex most of the time. It is an incredible compliment to a man, however, for his wife occasionally to be the one to initiate intimacy. Not only is there the promise of sex, but she is saying that he is so exciting she can't wait for them to get started.

Second, Shulamite had planned this outing for some time. She told Solomon of the "delicacies ... (she had) ... stored up for" him. He had been a source of romantic inspiration, and she had collected things to make their time together all the more sensual.

Newsflash for wives: Husbands want to be your source of strength. They also *need* to be appreciated and recognized as being sexually attractive. Many wives think it is "wrong" or "inappropriate" to be so direct. Instead, they think it is "right" to act coy and pretend they have no sexual interests. These beliefs date back to the centuries when the church taught that sex itself was totally inappropriate for public discussion, but proper only for procreation.

> Husbands want to be the source of their wives' strength. They also *need* to be appreciated and recognized as sexually attractive.

During the past several decades we have seen a slow realization that these teachings were not Biblically based. During these years, writers in the secular world have gone so far as to say, "A woman who has given herself permission to enjoy sex is the one who can truly please her husband."[15] But, why should any woman have to "give *herself* permission?" God, the almighty, all-knowing, eternal God of perfect love, *already* has given you permission! Indeed, He has *directed* women to have sexual relations with their husbands *and* to *enjoy* it![16]

In light of Scripture, telling a woman to "give herself permission" borders on the silly. Imagine a general in the military ordering a private to sit down at a feast and to enjoy himself. How much sense would it make for the private to think to himself: "I wonder if I really should do this? Sure, the general has *ordered* me to do it, but, do *I* feel it is *right* for me? Should *I* give *myself* permission?" The thought is ridiculous! The top authority in the private's life has just issued a command. There is nothing left to think about. Ladies, if you've been concerned about this, remember that God has commanded you to enjoy, so stop holding back and quit fretting!

Sadly, we tend to assume that "commands" and "obedience" always involve doing something difficult, something we don't want to do, or something very unpleasant. But, our God is a God of love. He gives life and gives it abundantly.[17] It only makes sense that He also would make part of that abundant life enjoyable, and command us to do some things we might enjoy.

LESSON #4 FOR COUPLES: SERVANTHOOD ISN'T JUST THEORY; IT'S DOING!

I already have pointed out that Christ calls for obedience, and obedience is servanthood[18] acted out in love. Now, for the hard part: *doing it!* We all enjoy the warm fuzzies of Christianity: God's forgiveness, mercy and grace, His gift to us of life abundant here and life eternal hereafter. But those are all God's doing. When it gets to what *we*, as believers, should be doing – obeying God – that is another matter. Obedience requires growing and stretching in areas of our lives we desperately want left untouched and unchanged.

Men generally feel a sense of immediacy in the need for sexual fulfillment, and they have a difficult time understanding why women do not feel the same way. By nature men do not want to be patient with their wives. We feel the desire, and want to act on it *now!* Why do women take so long?

Women, on the other hand, tend to like the slow buildup, the long romantic evening, then the soft, gentle pleasure of sexual stimulation. By nature they want to move slowly and enjoy every nuance of the moment. There is no reason to hurry. Why are men in such a rush?

In God's plan, the answer to both questions is simple. Love requires difference if it is to exist. It requires looking beyond your own needs to see the needs of the one you love, and meeting those needs in a way that satisfies your beloved. Women are called to learn to accommodate the immediacy men feel, and men are called to accommodate the slow tenderness women require.

Consider a simple example. A husband and wife want to see a movie together. They check the local movie theater, which has 16 screens. As they peruse the list of movies, both realize there is only one in which the husband is interested; and, likewise, only one the wife wishes to see. Happily, it happens to be the same movie. This is good fortune, but has little to do with love.

It is only when each wants to see a *different* movie that there is an opportunity to show love. They don't have time to see both, so they only have four choices: see his, see hers, see neither, or each go to a movie alone. The last choice defeats the goal of seeing a movie together to have a shared experience. The choice of seeing neither and staying home is likely to lead only to frustration and distance. By working through the problem to a mutual agreement which strengthens the relationship, we have the possibility of exercising love.

God is fundamentally "other" than we are.[19] He is eternal; we are finite. He is all knowing; we have limited knowledge. He sees the infinite future. We cannot see tomorrow. He is perfect love. We are fundamentally selfish. He is perfect justice. We are fundamentally self-centered in our imperfect justice. He is patient in His dealings with us, hoping that in the end all mankind will turn to Him. We are impatient, insisting on instant "justice" as we comprehend it. It is that difference that provides a context for developing love. Love is defined by God treating us with faithfulness and grace, mercy and forgiveness; and by us accepting Him in faith and obedience.

Reconciling differences is the context in which love is defined in every relationship. But, love is *doing*, not merely a mental process of thinking nice thoughts about someone. The Song of Solomon addresses this challenge. Husbands are called upon to do the difficult: to be slow and gentle, soft and tender, affectionate and romantic. Wives, likewise,

> Reconciling differences is the context in which love is defined in every relationship.

are called upon to do the difficult: to be forthright in their sexuality and inviting to their husbands, direct and assertive in their sexuality. If this sounds like you are here to serve your spouse, you've got it right. In the end, love is service. In fact, until we learn servanthood, we have not learned what Christianity is all about.[20]

The process and the results are illustrated in the Song with the wedding night[21] and the events that follow. The long courtship was over. Solomon had complimented Shulamite on the fact that she had maintained her virginity.[22] The time to "arouse" and "awaken love" finally had arrived.[23] Shulamite directly invited Solomon to possess her sexually. She said:

> Awake, north wind,
> and come, south wind!
> Blow on my garden,
> that its fragrance may spread abroad.
> Let my lover come into his garden
> and taste its choice fruits.[24]

I once presented this material to a women's social sorority. I had one of the women read this passage. I asked whether anyone knew to what the "garden" referred. At first there were a series of blank looks. Then, one by one, the women blushed. Finally, one said, "It *can't* mean *that!*" Her "garden," of course, was her body and "its choice fruits" were her breasts and pubic area. Several women expressed shock that the Bible would speak of such things and with such graphic description. They also were amazed that Shulamite ever would be so straight forward in expressing her desire for sexual relations. (One woman explained that she had attended a private religious school through high

school and none of the teachers ever had pointed out this passage.[25])
But, if God invented sex, why can't we talk about it and enjoy it?

The dialogue in the Song continued with Solomon's reply:

> I have come into my garden, my sister, my bride;
> I have gathered my myrrh with my spice.
> I have eaten my honeycomb and my honey;
> I have drunk my wine and my milk.[26]

Solomon was expressing his overwhelming joy at the sexual intimacy he had just experienced.

The passage continues with verses 2 - 6 [27] with an abrupt change of scene to an event which apparently took place sometime (months, perhaps even years) later.[28] Solomon had been out working late into the night. His head was wet with dew. Shulamite was in bed. He knocked on her door, apparently to share a time of sexual intimacy with her. Shulamite's answer (5: 3) was a study in rejection.[29] She said she had taken off her robe, and did not want to bother putting it back on. Worse yet, she added, she did not want to get her feet dirty again by walking from the bed to the door.

In that culture the king and queen had separate bed chambers, with a private passageway between the two. The door could be latched from the inside to prevent the other person from gaining entry, as Shulamite apparently had done. Solomon put his hand through the latch opening in hopes of getting in. But, the door was locked.

In a modern lingo, Solomon had asked Shulamite whether she was in the mood. Shulamite, in effect, answered that she had a headache and, besides, she had to organize her sock drawer. The excuses were patently frivolous, bordering on an insult. In the formal language of Biblical scholars, "she does not meet his love with an equal requital. She is unwilling for his sake to put herself to trouble, or to do that which is disagreeable to her."[30]

Solomon was flatly rejected by the woman he loved. He had addressed her in words of tender caring and she responded with rude coldness. What should he do? In modern terms we might ask, "What would Jesus do?" What does love require *anyone* to do when faced with rejection?

Shulamite finally rose and went to open the door. She put her hand on the latch and found it covered with liquid myrrh, which immediately covered her hand. Myrrh was an expensive perfume. Leaving myrrh as a gift was a sign of great love and honor.[31] A man would leave a few drops of myrrh on the latch of his beloved's door, so when she opened it the next day she would find his fragrant message of love. It was a message that would stay on her hand throughout the day, reminding her of his love. Though Solomon was rejected, "he has left this token of his unchanged love."[32] Wow! This man had it right!

When married couples interact, they often "react" to each other. The word, "react," comes from the concept of "re-enacting." To *react* means, literally, to *re-enact* what the other person has done. If your spouse acts rudely, to *react* means you will act rudely in response. Reacting to love means you will act lovingly, too. The Scriptural model for married couples does not call for "reacting." We are to act with love at all times. Here Solomon showed us how. When he was rejected in an insulting manner, he responded (not "reacted") with a sign of love and affection.

Newsflash to husbands: Women aren't perfect! (But then, neither are we.) They have their bad days. (And so do we.) It is clear from the passage that Shulamite loved Solomon. She repeatedly referred to him as "my lover," told us her "heart began to pound for him" and her "heart sank at his departure." But, loving someone does not mean we won't hurt the person. In fact, while the nature of perfect love is not to hurt, the nature of imperfect mankind is to hurt.

When rejected, God calls on us to respond with signs of love. Solomon did not force his way into Shulamite's bed. He did not argue with her. He did not whine or beg. He did not demand his "rights." He made his request known, and when she rejected it, he told her in no uncertain terms that he loved her anyway.

> When rejected, God calls on us to respond with signs of love.

The response to Solomon's act of love was immediate. She opened the door, but he was not there. She called for him, but he did not answer. He was gone. She searched for him, but could not find him. She ran into trouble with the people she found. Those she met asked, in an apparent tone of smugness, "How is your beloved better than others?"[33] Yet, the question had a certain logic to it. If her beloved was "better than others," why had she spurned him? Shulamite answered in a long statement of incredible praise for the very man she just had rejected so rudely.[34] Her praise makes sense in light of the gracious act of love he had shown in the face of her act of rejection.

What would have happened if he had *reacted* to her in anger, i.e., *reenacted* her rudeness? Division and distance would have been created in their relationship. Instead, his response of love led her to seek him out, in the end, and shower him with praise and respect. This is a sign of strength in the relationship. Paul repeated this instruction by saying each husband, "must love his wife ... , and the wife must respect her husband."[35]

Newsflash to couples: Your relationship will be stronger if you stop *reacting*, i.e., *reenacting* the hurts and sins of your spouse. God's way is full of blessings. Try it. It works. It is the best way to build a strong foundation for your relationship, one act of love at a time.

DISCUSSION QUESTIONS

1. How do these three topics fit together, i.e., patience, romance and honest desires?

2. Solomon was showing a great deal of flourish in his courting of Shulamite (Song 2:8 - 13 and 3:6 - 11). How many women would like to have this kind of attention, even if it was only on an occasional basis? How many on a regular basis?

   - Bringing home cut flowers? (What type of flower?)
   - Being carried off on a surprise weekend?
   - Doing something on the spur of the moment?
   - Taking long walks together?
   - Taking a walk in the rain?

3. Solomon refers to his wife as "my sister, my bride" four times (Song 4:9, 10, 12 and 5:1). It was pointed out that the phrase means he thinks of her not only as his lover and wife, but also someone with whom he can talk to freely about his deepest feelings. How important is it for women to have their husbands talk with them as if they are "my sister, my bride"?

4. Shulamite is forthright about her desires for sexual intimacy with Solomon. This is more than being alluring; she is absolutely straight forward. (Ask a woman in the group to read Song 1:2, 1:4; 4:16 and 7:12 -13, in a seductive tone of voice. If you are a husband and wife reading this together, have the wife read the passages seductively.) How many men would like their wives to be that inviting? Why would God make this a constant theme throughout the Song of Solomon?

5. How would most men respond to such forthright statements by their wives?

Suggestions for Couples:

Go back and read each of the **Newsflash** items. For each **Newsflash for husbands** have the husband read it out loud. Have the wife comment on each **Newsflash for husbands**. Does it apply to her? Would she like her husband to keep this **Newsflash** in mind and apply it to their relationship? Likewise, for each **Newsflash for wives** have the wife read it out loud. Have the husband comment on each **Newsflash for wives**. Does it apply to him? Would he like his wife to keep this **Newsflash** in mind and apply it to their relationship?

Lessons From the Song of Solomon

"Who Ya Gonna Trust
When Times Get Tough?"

I once had a defendant before me on a drunk-driving case. He wanted to be released on a $100 bond while awaiting trial. As I was
going through the file to get what information I could to make the
decision, I noticed that he was from another state and had been arrested in our county about eight years earlier, also for drunk driving. In
that case he posted a $500 bond, but never showed up. I then discov-
ered that about five years later he again was driving through our county, and again was arrested for drunk driving, along with contempt of
court for not appearing on the first case. Again he posted a bond, this
time $1,000. Again, he did not show up. Now he was in court for what
was actually the third drunk-driving charge, with the other two still
pending. Amazingly, he wanted me to release him again on only $100
bond. I told him that he had taught us a lesson: Do not trust him.

He looked at me with big, puppy dog eyes, pleading with me,
promising in the most sincere tone, that *this* time he would be back on
his own. *This* time, I could trust him. (I couldn't help but wonder
whether somehow I accidentally had tattooed the word "stupid" across
my forehead.) There was no way was I going to trust him again. He
had broken faith in his relationship with the court, and I had to deal
with that reality. When times get tough, when tough decisions have to

> All relationships require trust; but the more intimate the relationship, the more trust is required.

be made, the person you trust always will be the person who has acted in a trustworthy way. I set the bond at $50,000. He stayed in jail.[1]

Trust and other issues of ethics and character may seem like a strange topic in a book on romance and sex. But the two areas are integrally related. All relationships require trust; but the more intimate the relationship, the more trust is required. Trust is even more important in marriage than in the court room because the relationship is so much more intimate.[2]

By its very nature, the intimacy of marriage calls on us to undress both emotionally and physically before our spouses. She wants him to

> Romance and sex require closeness. Closeness requires vulnerability. Vulnerability requires trust.

tell her the secrets of his heart and to bare his soul so she can be close to him emotionally. He wants her to bare her body and expose herself sexually to his every desire, so he can feel close to her physically. He will not want to tell her anything, however, if he is concerned that she

may not be there two weeks later or worries that she might "share" his deepest feelings with all her friends. She will be equally unwilling to risk opening herself up sexually to new ideas if she fears he will be gone tomorrow, or may be bragging about what they've done together with his buddies at work. Romance and sex require closeness. Closeness requires vulnerability. Vulnerability requires trust.

LESSON #5 FOR HUSBANDS *AND* WIVES: IF YOU WANT TO BE TRUSTED WITH A GIFT, YOU MUST BE WORTHY OF THE TRUST

The issue of ethics is a repeated theme of the Song of Solomon, played out in several different strains. We already have seen how Solomon was commended for the purity of his "name."[3] Likewise, we have seen how Shulamite was concerned that people did not think she was a prostitute when she visited Solomon by the way she approached his tent.[4]

Song 2:7 takes us deeper into the ethical thinking of Shulamite. She was not simply concerned about her reputation, she wanted to live a life worthy of a good reputation. She said,

> Daughters of Jerusalem, I charge you, ... do not arouse or awaken love until it so desires.

This statement, which Shulamite repeated twice in the Song,[5] was a warning not to awaken the passions of love until it is appropriate in God's scheme of things. As has been noted, this is an "... earnest warning against wantonly exciting love in themselves ... till God Himself awakens it, and heart finds itself in sympathy with heart."[6]

Shulamite was a woman of high moral standards. She was reminding herself and others that sexual promiscuity is totally inappropriate. There are two conditions to be met before it is right to "awaken" the passions of sexual desire. First, it must be right with God. Scripture makes it clear that it is only right in God's eyes when a man and a woman are in a permanent, committed, loving, legally recognized, publically acknowledged relationship, i.e. marriage.[7] Second, if sexual passion is to be *love*, as opposed to *lust*, it needs to have a *heart* with which it can share, not just a body.

Sadly, modern Western English uses the euphemism "making love" for sexual intercourse. Whether it is sex in marriage, adultery, fornication or even prostitution, if it is consensual, it somehow becomes "making love." Sex by itself, however, does not "make" love. It may provide a passing pleasure and it can "make" babies, but it does not *make love* where love does not already exist. Scripture recognizes this and tells us that sexual passions should have a context of love. Sex is

> Sex is meant to be the celebration of an existing love within a committed relationship.

meant to be the celebration of an existing love within a committed relationship, not the means of forming a new love relationship.

Shulamite understood this, and had the moral fortitude to wait. She would not engage in premarital sex, and encouraged others to abstain, as well.

This point is emphasized in the last chapter of the Song of Solomon. Shulamite's older brothers are introduced briefly (by way of a flashback to when she was young), to remind us of a statement they made:

> We have a young sister,
> and her breasts are not yet grown.
> What shall we do for our sister
> for the day she is spoken for?
> If she is a wall,
> we will build towers of silver on her.
> If she is a door,
> we will enclose her with panels of cedar.[8]

She responded in the next verse:

> I am a wall,
> and my breasts are like towers.
> Thus I have become in his eyes
> like one bringing contentment.

The wall to which her brothers referred symbolized strength of character, not easily moved, nor open to every advance or effort at seduction. If Shulamite showed steadfast morality, her brothers would be able to honor her, "build towers of silver on her." But if she were the moral equivalent of a door, easily opened and accessible to all who wished to enter her garden, then they would have to do what was necessary to protect her (if needed, "enclose her with panels of cedar") for her wedding day.

Her answer is like a two-by-four across the head to modern morality, which says anything goes. She was a wall! And, not only a wall, but a wall with towers. Towers were located along the wall of fortified cities, typically on the corners, where the watchmen of a city stood to look for danger. They were a sign of strength. Her breasts were "like towers." In this simile, her breasts are like the towers of a wall, which would be the first thing seen at a distance by anyone approaching, friend or enemy alike. However, like the tower of a fortress, they were not easily put into the hands of those who were not welcome. Only her husband would be welcome beyond the wall and able to have free access to the towers. The result of her high standards of sexual morality was that she brought contentment or "peace"[9] to her husband.

Ironically, modern Western culture insists that sexual promiscuity is something that "kids will engage in anyway," and that it is something to deal with by simply teaching "safe sex."[10] We then bemoan the problems of AIDS and other sexually transmitted diseases, while all the time denying that the same sexual promiscuity we encourage is the cause. Shulamite's answer was simple: Don't mess around with sex outside of marriage, then you can bring your spouse peace of mind that there will be no STD's in your future relationship.

Solomon praised Shulamite's strength of character earlier in the poem. He told her,

> Your neck is like the tower of David,
> built with elegance;
> on it hang a thousand shields,
> all of them shields of warriors.

He also said, "Your neck is like an ivory tower."[11]

These passages are filled with poetic images from Biblical times. The neck was considered the center of a person's character. God described the Children of Israel as having a "stiff neck,"[12] while we would say they were stubborn. "Stiff-necked" meant their character was set, hard to change, difficult to turn. Shulamite's character was not stiff, in the sense of unmovable; rather, it was "like a tower," a source of protection. Indeed, it had the strength of a "thousand warriors." In those days, warriors hung their shields on the tower or the city wall as a warning to enemies that the city was well defended.[13] Shulamite's character was so strong it was as if her morality was protected by a thousand warriors.

Shulamite was not a woman with whom to trifle. She was totally committed to her husband and her family. She was solidly based in solid values and not about to be swayed by every change in fashion or popular fad, nor intimidated by the standards of beauty of the time. She also was sexually pure when she married, and by limiting her sexual involvement to her husband, she remained that way. She was loving and generous to those in need. She worked hard and planned for the future. Proverbs 31:10-31 describes her in detail, giving us a graphic picture of her character:

> She is clothed with strength and dignity;
> she can laugh at the days to come.
> She speaks with wisdom,
> and faithful instruction is on her tongue.[14]

Shulamite not only stood firm with her own values, she acted like a watchtower for Solomon. There are people whose self-righteousness can become offensive to others. They are proud of their humility. (My mother used to describe such people as "so heavenly they're of no earthly good.") These individuals often come across as hypocrites because they speak in such lofty terms no one, including themselves, can meet their standards.[15] Shulamite was not likes this; she did not assault others with her character. (Walls and towers are defensive, not aggressive, in nature.) Her character was a thing of beauty, to be respected. Solomon describes it as being "built with elegance," "like an ivory tower," a thing of beauty.

Solomon's attraction to such a woman also said volumes about his character at this time in his life.[16] He, too, had high standards, and wanted to be with a woman who shared them.

Loyalty: A Key to Trustworthiness

The Song of Solomon specifically emphasized loyalty between husband and wife. Shulamite described their relationship,

> My lover is mine and I am his;
> he browses among the lilies.

Later she repeated the same idea,

> I am my lover's and my lover is mine;
> he browses among the lilies.

Still later she added,

> I belong to my lover,
> and his desire is for me.[17]

These were statements of commitment. She and Solomon were in it together for the long haul. Genesis 2:24 tells us that the two shall "become one."[18] They intended to stick it out through thick and thin.

Ecclesiastes also alludes to the importance of loyalty between husband and wife.

> Two are better than one,
> because they have a good return for their work:
> If one falls down,
> his friend can help him up.
> But pity the man who falls
> and has no one to help him up!
> Also, if two lie down together, they will keep warm.
> But how can one keep warm alone?
> Though one may be overpowered,

two can defend themselves.
A cord of three strands is not quickly broken.[19]

God tells us it is not good for people to be alone.[20] A lack of loyalty means one will *not* be around to help if the other falls, or to keep the other warm when it is time to lie down, or to give aid when there is an attack.

This passage repeatedly speaks of "two," yet it closes with the observation that a cord of "three strands" is not easily broken. Why the sudden shift to three? The third strand is God. We all have bad days. I have my share of them. When I come home feeling less than my best, my wife can be there to build me up. If she has had a bad day, I can give her support. But, what happens if we *both* are having a bad day? That is when God can give the special support every couple needs.

Proverbs 5:18 also refers to loyalty between husband and wife, when it tells husbands, "...may you rejoice in *the wife of your youth.*" Malachi 2:14 adds, "...the LORD is acting as the witness between you and *the wife of your youth* ... the wife of your *marriage covenant.*" The passage continues by instructing, "do not break faith with *the wife of your youth.*"[21] (Italics added.) Women who leave their husbands for inconsequential reasons are described in similar terms:

> It will save you also from the adulteress,
> from the wayward wife with her seductive words,
> who has left *the partner of her youth*
> and ignored the *covenant* she made before God."[2]
> (Italics added.)

Although this reference is to the wife, the concept applies equally to men and women.

Scripture repeatedly refers to the spouse "of your youth," the "covenant" of marriage, and God as a "witness" to that covenant. This tells us that God intends marriage to last a lifetime.[23] God's use of the word "covenant" to describe the marriage agreement goes a long way in demonstrating His view of the relationship. A covenant can be described as an agreement with no conditions and no "ifs." Period.

End of discussion. Covenants, in Biblical times, were taken very seriously.[24] Marriages are intended by God to be committed relationships. Commitment requires loyalty.

God is the silent witness and active partner to every marriage. He is the "third strand," the "witness between you and the wife of your youth."[25] He is the one who is present on the wedding night *and every other night of the marriage* to encourage husbands and wives to love and share intimacies with each other.[26] Your covenant is *both* with your spouse *and* with God.

God's involvement in the covenant of marriage is profoundly significant in several respects. Today there are marriages which are little more than form. Some have "vows" to remain married as long as they "love each other." Some states have drive-through wedding chapels, at which people can get married without the "needless inconvenience" of getting out of the car. Many states have no waiting periods between applying for the marriage license and the wedding itself. I have talked with court clerks in these states and they tell me that people getting married while intoxicated to the point of hardly remembering the ceremony is not unheard of. (There are laws that prohibit such marriages, but that does not prevent them from happening.) Weddings take place without a single mention of God.[27] Nonetheless, God still is a witness to all weddings and a breach of the promises made are a breach of our covenant with Him.[28] In fact, church weddings as we know them are relatively recent events. Prior to the middle ages all weddings were civil in nature.[29] All marriages, whether the participants acknowledge it or not, are covenants made in God's presence and couples are bound by the laws and blessings of that covenant.

The importance of strong character and high ethics may sound fine in theory, and most people will agree they will not open up sexually or emotionally to someone they do not trust. Yet, in practice, this is a standard by which it is difficult to live, because we often think of ethical problems as something with which "other people" suffer.

I often have been asked by wives, "How do I get my husband to open up to me?" The problem usually lies with the man who cannot talk about how he feels. Occasionally, however, the problem is with the wife herself. One husband with whom I became acquainted finally gave in to the constant requests of his wife that he tell her what he *really* wanted sexually. He told her. At first, her reaction was silence. Then she exploded, accusing him of being a demented, sexual pervert. Within days she had told several of her friends in vivid detail of the "disgusting" things her husband wanted. That was years earlier. Since then she again has tried to get him to confide in her. The last time he trusted her he was berated by her and publicly humiliated. He never will make the same mistake. Now she is suffering from the distance created by the very wall she built.

Another wife who was frustrated that her husband would not tell her what he wanted was in a marriage which did not have a great deal of money. The wife constantly criticized her husband for being an inadequate provider, despite his working two jobs. (The problem appeared to be more her spending than his earning.) The criticism extended to almost everything else the man did. Nonetheless, she was amazed that her husband steadfastly refused to share his sexual desires and fantasies with her. His reasoning was simple. She belittled everything else he did, why wouldn't she belittle this, too?

Men, don't allow yourselves to become too self-righteous with these two examples. I also have seen marriages in which the husband criticizes everything the wife does, constantly belittling her for every perceived error. He then will go to great lengths to complain that his wife never will "open up" to him.

Newsflash to couples: Asking our spouses to bare their souls, then ridiculing them because of the content of their deepest secrets, or worse yet, revealing them to others, is the fastest way to build walls of separation so high they may be impossible to overcome. When our spouses tell us their secret desires, fears, yearnings or nightmares, we must treat the information as a gift of infinite delicacy and enormous value. It *never* can be shared (with anyone ... ever ... under any circumstances[30]) and always must be handled delicately. Moreover, if we are going to respond at all, it must be in a positive way. If you are bowled over by the information, just smile and say, "OK, ... let me think about that." Then start praying that God will open your heart and lead you where He wants you to go.

Second newsflash to couples: Do not ask a question if you are not prepared to handle the answer. If your spouse has been reluctant to tell you what he really wants, how are you going to respond if the secret is he wants you shave off all your pubic hair? Or he wants you to cut your hair radically short (like Demi Moore in the movie *GI Jane*), or let it grow till it hangs to your waist? Or he wants you to get a tattoo (the permanent kind) of a butterfly on your butt? Or playing out a fantasy (such as playing doctor / patient, or the pirate and captive virgin?) It may be his secret is nothing more extreme than wanting you to wear thong underwear or tint your hair with a touch of red highlights.

It is equally possible for wives to have a secret desire. How are you going to respond if her secret is she wants you to shave *your* pubic hair? Or, tint your hair a different color? Or do weight lifting exercises nude while she watches? Or get a tattoo, or get an ear ring?

Challenge for couples: If you don't want to know your spouse's deepest sexual desire, ask yourself why. Are you afraid of what it might call on *you* to do?

A Second Challenge for couples: If you *do* learn what your spouse's deepest desire is and you absolutely do *not* want to do it, ask yourself why. Then pray that God will lead you to do what He wants, not necessarily what either you *or* your spouse wants.

Third newsflash for couples: Both men and women learn from past experiences. What is the emotional atmosphere *you* have helped create for your spouse? Is it one of safety or one in which your spouse constantly is being attacked? Scripture tells us,

> There is no fear in love. But perfect love drives out fear, because fear has to do with punishment. The one who fears is not made perfect in love.[31]

If your spouse is afraid to tell you the secret of his soul it may be because of fear of punishment from you. It also is possible, however, that your spouse was raised in a home in which every word and every action was a subject of endless criticism. It also may be related to how a friend once reacted to his feelings in the past. Summary rejection or belittling of a person's thoughts amounts to rejecting him personally. Any sign of rejection is something to fear. If your spouse is not opening up, you need to assess honestly how you and others have dealt with the things he has said and done in the past.

This gets back to integrity, honesty, loyalty, and the general issue of character. The Song describes the sharing of incredible intimacy between man and woman. This is the level of intimacy God intends for every marriage. High ethical standards create a context in which complete sharing of emotional intimacy will thrive. Within that context, both the romantic and sexual aspects of love are bound to flourish.

THE HARDEST ASPECT OF CHARACTER: FACING THE DEMON WITHIN

Part of character is the willingness to acknowledge our own problems and summoning the strength to address them. Most people are happy to talk about everyone *else's* problems, but not their own. I see this regularly in court. At sentencing, the defendants often will prattle on endlessly about what the victim, the police, the prosecutor and the probation department all did wrong. These defendants recite endless litanies of how *their* rights have been violated. I have sat through self-righteous speeches lasting up to an hour before I finally ask the defendant whether there was *anything* in *his* life that needed changing. Typically, the answer is "Well, I suppose I'm not perfect." But when I ask for something specific that needs correcting (after all, they were convicted of criminal charges), they cannot think of a single thing.

Likewise, I have talked with married couples and both the husband and the wife can tick off a long list of problems the other has, but neither can think of a single specific thing he should do differently. I have heard such statements as, "Well, I guess I just love him too much." Of course, this is an insult to the word love. It is not possible to "love too much." However, it is possible to show love in the wrong way. Another statement is, "Maybe I'm just too nice to her." These are no more than thinly-disguised, self-serving efforts to appear perfect.

Scripture addresses this issue. Jesus cautioned us about judging others when we are not willing to change our own behavior.

> Why do you look at the speck of sawdust in your brother's eye and pay no attention to the plank in your own eye? How can you say to your brother, "Let

me take the speck out of your eye," when all the time
there is a plank in your own eye? You hypocrite, first
take the plank out of your own eye, and then you will
see clearly to remove the speck from your brother's
eye.[32]

The Apostle John addressed the same point,

If we claim to be without sin, we deceive ourselves
and the truth is not in us. If we confess our sins, he is
faithful and just and will forgive us our sins and puri-
fy us from all unrighteousness. If we claim we have
not sinned, we make him out to be a liar and his word
has no place in our lives.[33]

We "all have sinned and fall short of the glory of God."[34] We love
to go to church and acknowledge our shortcomings in a general way
on Sunday morning, but none of us likes to get down to the nitty grit-
ty of dealing with the specifics. Yet it is the specifics that start to act as
a day-in, day-out grind in any marital relationship.

The Song of Solomon addressed this issue. Shulamite told
Solomon,

Catch for us the foxes,
the little foxes
that ruin the vineyards,
our vineyards that are in bloom.[35]

As mentioned in Chapter 3, the "little foxes" Shulamite was concerned with involve "...the annoyances and cares that may interfere
with and damage their love."[36] Clearly, some of the "little foxes" are
from outside the marriage, but many of the "little foxes" are ones we
bring into the relationship ourselves: our selfishness, prejudices, fears,
inhibitions, and inappropriate expectations. They tend to be of small
concern and cause no real problems at the start of the marriage (like
"little foxes"), but the toll grows as time goes by. The "little foxes" of a
relationship even can look cute at first. If they are not dealt with honestly, they will grow into destructive problems as the years go by.

The "little foxes" come in countless forms, for example:

- Insensitivity and inappropriate teasing.
- Mannerisms which generally are not acceptable, such as picking your nose or scratching your breasts with a pencil in public.
- Slurping your soup, picking your teeth with a fork and other sloppy table manners.
- Being forgetful and regularly breaking appointments without calling to say you won't make it.
- Constantly buying unnecessary things and breaking the budget.
- The inability to apologize.
- Constantly causing you or your spouse to be late for appointments.

The list is endless. Some are simple irritations, others are basic rudeness, still others are major breaches of ethical standards. But they *all* undermine the relationship. They *all* must be addressed.

Shulamite was telling Solomon that they needed to take care of these problems quickly. This takes a strong character and a great deal of personal and intellectual honesty. How many of us are willing to examine:

Our Barriers to Intimacy	How We Hide Behind the Barrier *We* Build
our own selfishness	(If *I* want it, it *must* be important.)
our own inhibitions	(If *I* don't want to do it, there *must* be something wrong with it. It *must* be perverted.)
our own desires	(If *I* want it, it *must* be reasonable.)
our own fears	(If *I* don't want to do it, the risk *must* be unreasonably high.)

Examining ourselves with an eye of cold honesty is the toughest thing to handle. Yet, Shulamite was saying that for the sake of their relationship, for the sake of their marriage, it was a task which had to be accomplished. If the little foxes are not honestly challenged, even the little foxes we think are so cute (because they are *our* own problems), the marriage will not have the beautiful harvest from the vineyard which God has in mind.

DISCUSSION QUESTIONS

1. This theme goes beyond loyalty to other issues of character. It includes such matters as honesty, trustworthiness and integrity. How is character related to issues of romance and sexual desire? There actually is a series of questions raised here.

    • How can you meet the needs of your spouse, if your spouse is not honest in telling you what they are?
    • How willing are you going to be to reveal your deepest secrets if you don't believe your spouse will keep those secrets?
    • How likely are you to reveal these secrets if you are concerned your spouse will belittle you or mock you over them?
    • How "turned on" will you be by someone who constantly lies to you about little things?
    • How willing will you be to plan something special a month from now if you're not sure your spouse will be there two weeks from now?

2. In Song of Solomon 1:3, Shulamite tells us that Solomon's name is well known for his integrity. Is it important that we be proud of our spouse's reputation in the community?

— 7 —

Lessons From the Song of Solomon

Drink Deeply, Lovers!
Love Like There's No Tomorrow

Two years ago my wife and I were visiting our daughter in Los Angeles. The foundation of a large building was being constructed near her home. I couldn't see a thing. When I peeked over the fence surrounding the site, it looked like nothing but a deep hole in the ground with lots of heavy equipment, a bunch of concrete pylons and a couple dozen men putting steel reinforcement rods into place for yet more pylons. Today a beautiful office building is standing on the site. The foundation, built well below ground, fashioned with concrete and steel, was not much to look at during construction, nor even visible after the building was finished. Yet, on it rests everything of value.

The lessons we have reviewed from the Song of Solomon make up most of the foundation for the Biblical view of sex and romance in marriage. Without them, it will be difficult to build a lasting relationship filled with the intimacy most people seek.

One last foundational issue needs to be considered. We've examined several aspects of love and the need to show love in all our words and actions. Before we can show love, however, we need a clear understanding of what love is.

LESSON #6 FOR HUSBANDS *AND* WIVES: LOVE AS IF THERE'S NO TOMORROW!

The final chapter of the Song of Solomon includes a statement that brings together all the themes of the song:

> Place me like a seal over your heart,
> like a seal on your arm;
> for love is as strong as death,
> its jealousy unyielding as the grave.
> It burns like blazing fire,
> like a mighty flame.
> Many waters cannot quench love;
> rivers cannot wash it away.
> If one were to give
> all the wealth of his house for love,
> it would be utterly scorned.[1]

This passage is so fundamental to understanding love that some commentators[2] have referred to it as "the Old Testament counterpart" to Paul's beautiful description of love in 1 Corinthians 13:4-7.

> Love is patient, love is kind. It does not envy, it does not boast, it is not proud. It is not rude, it is not self-seeking, it is not easily angered, it keeps no record of wrongs. Love does not delight in evil but rejoices with the truth. It always protects, always trusts, always hopes, always perseveres.

Solomon describes love[3] as being as "strong as death," "unyielding as the grave." Paul's description of love tells us why love has such strength. Two qualities summarize the entire concept: "Love is *patient*, love is *kind*." The remaining examples show us *how* we are to be patient and kind.[4]

Patience

We've all heard the line, "Lord, give me patience ... and give it to me **NOW**!" It's funny because, in large measure, it's true. Patience is a virtue we admire in others, but which we typically do not demand of ourselves. If *we're* going slowly, and others complain, we insist, "have some patience." If *they're* going slowly, we yell, "hurry up! We're late!"

The words we translate as patience,[5] also mean "slowness to anger" or "forbearance." If you've been married for more than 27 minutes it should be pretty obvious how important this is, because it comes up in at least three ways in every marriage:

- Your spouse asks you to do something you *REALLY* don't want to do, when you *REALLY* don't want to do it. How do you respond?
- Your spouse is doing what you want; but oh, so very, *VERY* slowly. Waiting for him is like watching a glacier move. How do you respond?
- Your spouse has an irritating little habit. Sure, you noticed it before you were married, but back then, when you were on a hormonal high, you thought it was "cute." Now it drives you nuts. How do you respond?

Hopefully, in each of these cases you will respond ... with patience. Or will you?

This is the tough part of Scripture: It tells me to do things I don't want to do. I don't want to have to wait for my wife, or stop what I'm doing to do what my wife wants. I don't want to put up with all her idiosyncracies. (After all, certainly *I* don't have any, each of us tends to think, so why should I put up with hers?) But Scripture tells me I'm supposed to have *patience*. What pain! What suffering! What sacrifice! But that's the whole point. Another perfectly valid way of translating the Hebrew and Greek for "patience" is "longsuffering." This makes sense because *patience* assumes you are suffering!

However, having patience means more than simply suffering. We also are not to be rude while putting up with our spouses. When we are patient we are not to boast about it. Moreover, there is the matter of keeping score of all the times *we* had to be patient with our spouses so we can beat them into submission with the list later. *Having patience* means we are not to keep a record of those times. Finally, being *im*patient also includes always wanting our own way (self-seeking) along with feeling envy when others get their way while *we* have to sit back and wait our turn (which may never come). None of this is easy. But then, love is not easy.

Billy Graham has noted that the Biblical word for patience "speaks of a person's steadfastness under provocation. Inherent in the word is the thought of patiently enduring ill-treatment without anger or thought of retaliation or revenge."[6] Think about it. God wants us to be patient, even when the other person *is* acting like an inconsiderate jerk. In fact, He's *assuming* the other person is acting like a jerk!

God knows He's asking us to suffer when we show patience. But, then, didn't He suffer, dying on the cross for us, putting up with all our foibles and sins, loving us even when *we* are acting like inconsiderate jerks? Jesus commands us to love others as He has loved us.[7] And, love includes being *patient!* This is not a request by Christ. He *commands* us to be patient. It is not a matter of faith; it is a matter of obedience.

Christ demonstrated patience by doing what He didn't want to do, when He didn't want to do it, **because** He loved us.[8] Scripture tells us, "greater love has no man than this: that he lay down his life for his friends."[9] Men, if you want an example of "longsuffering," how about this?

> Greater love has no husband than this, that he goes shopping with his wife ... with a smile on his face.

And, ladies, how about,

> Greater love has no wife, than to let her husband watch that football game without making smart remarks.

Or, let's get really radical,

> Greater love has no husband, than to take the time to listen to his wife and to tell her what is actually on his heart.

Or, how about something really controversial:

> Greater love has no wife, than to put up with her husband and wear that silly, little topless, bottomless, see-through thing he bought for her, ... with a sensuous smile on her face and joy in her heart.

At this point you may want to turn to your spouse and say, "See, you have to be more patient with me! The Bible says so!" Demanding patience from others grows out of impatience in us! Patience is *NOT* something we are to demand of anyone, except ourselves, because Christ commands it of us.

Newsflash to both husbands *and* wives: *Im*patience is sin. It is sin because impatience means NOT being slow to anger or longsuffering. It means NOT acting "Christ-like" and NOT being led by the Holy Spirit. Moreover, the fact that our spouses are impatient is no reason for us not to be patient with their impatience.

This brings us to the delicate subject of forgiveness. *Patience* is *forgiveness* in action, for the dozens of little irritations we constantly are called to put up with. Patience *assumes* our spouses are doing less than perfectly.

> *Patience* is *forgiveness* in action, for the dozens of little irritations we constantly are called to put up with.

Christ expects us to be forgiving.[10] That expectation is so foundational that he says *our* being forgiven is conditioned on *our* showing forgiveness. He taught us to pray, "Forgive us our sins *as we* forgive those who sin against us." And, then He added:

> For if you forgive men when they sin against you,
> your heavenly Father will also forgive you. But if you
> do not forgive men their sins, your Father will not
> forgive your sins.[11]

Newsflash to couples: God will show the same level of patience to us as we show to others, especially our spouses! Think about that as a reality check the next time you feel like you're running out of patience with your spouse.

Having patience not only assumes your spouse has failed, but this is the 100th time in a row he's done the same, dumb thing. Nonetheless, Christ tells us to forgive over and over again, "seventy times seven" times.[12] Before you ignore this as totally unreasonable, keep one thought in mind. Don't you and I keep doing the same dumb things over and over again, then keep going back to God, asking Him to be patient and show forgiveness to us over and over again?[13]

We must not confuse patience with license. God shows us patience, but He still expects us to change. He constantly is calling us through His word and by the Holy Spirt to change. Likewise, when our spouses are patient with us, we never should think it means we are doing fine and can continue doing what we have been doing. Just as we never should take God's patience for granted, we should not take our spouses' for granted. Instead, we should accept that patience as a gift of love, then resolve not to make the same mistake again. By doing that, we respond to the loving gift of patience by showing love in return.

Forgiveness as an attitude of the heart

Forgiveness is an attitude of the heart.[14] It is an attitude of passionately wanting:

- reconciliation with the person who has offended us;
- the offending person to change his ways so there will be no more hurts;
- the offending person to turn to God and truly comprehend what he has done.

Just as patience is forgiveness in action, forgiveness is love in action.

Forgiveness as a system of healing relationships

The word forgiveness refers to two different situations. As an action, forgiveness is what we are to give from our hearts. As a description, we can talk of a "forgiving heart." But, if we talk of the *process* of forgiveness, in other words, the *process* of healing a hurt relationship, we must talk about more than the forgiveness offered by the person who was hurt.

God places very high value on relationships, especially marriage. If there is a break in the relationship, it takes *both* forgiveness *and* repentance to produce complete healing. When Jesus spoke of the process of forgiveness, He was careful to include the dual requirement of both forgiveness and repentance. In Luke 17:3, for example, Jesus stated, "If your brother sins, rebuke him, and *if* he repents, *forgive* him."[15]

Repentance is more than saying you're sorry. It is a process involving three steps. First, there needs to be true sorrow for causing the wrong. This is *not* merely sorrow at being caught. It is sorrow for having done the wrong in the first place. Paul recognized this difference when he wrote, "Godly sorrow brings repentance that leads to salvation, ... but worldly sorrow brings death."[16]

Second, a change of behavior is required. As Paul also noted in describing his preaching, "I preached that they should repent and *turn to God* and *prove their repentance by their deeds.*"[17] Repentance requires a heartfelt effort to change the way we behave.[18] If the wrong is leaving dirty clothes on the floor, it will involve a conscious effort to develop a new habit of putting the clothes in the hamper. If the wrong is adultery, it will mean never, ever having any contact at all with the third party and setting up absolute boundaries to make sure there are no future third parties. If the wrong is an addiction (alcohol, gambling, etc.), repentance will require intensive counseling and a complete change of behavior.

Third, the best possible effort must be made to right the wrong.[19] The nature of the effort will depend on the circumstances. Zacchaeus was a tax collector in Israel. Tax collectors at that time were notorious for cheating people when they assessed taxes. They would assess more than was really due, keeping the difference for themselves. After meeting Jesus, Zacchaeus promised to repent, which meant righting the wrong to the extent he could. Zacchaeus promised to repay everyone he had cheated four times the amount wrongly assessed as a tax. When Jesus was crucified, there were two thieves who also were put to death, one on His right, the other on His left. One of the thieves asked for forgiveness. He was within hours of his own death and hardly able to repay anyone. For the thief on the cross, the best he could do to right the wrong was his public witness of faith.

Our forgiveness *combined with* the repentance of the wrongdoer is the process that heals a hurt relationship. Without repentance, forgiveness (the action) does not mend the relationship. Likewise, without forgiveness, repentance does not provide a complete healing. God wants the whole job done. However, even if there is no repentance, He still wants us to have forgiving hearts.[20]

God wants marriages to succeed. They will not succeed if there is not forgiveness or repentance. In marriage, as in the rest of our lives, God expects us to have forgiving hearts, but He also expects us to repent when we are wrong.

Forgiveness and trust

We should not confuse either patience or forgiveness with trust. As Rev. Rick Warren has explained:

> Many people are reluctant to show mercy because they don't understand the difference between trust and forgiveness. Forgiveness is letting go of the past. Trust has to do with future behavior.
>
> Forgiveness must be immediate, whether or not a person asks for it. Trust must be rebuilt over time. Trust requires a track record. If someone hurts you repeatedly, you are commanded by God to forgive them instantly, but you are not expected to trust them immediately, and you are not expected to continue allowing them to hurt you. They must prove they have changed over time.[21]

> **Patience is the backbone of love.**

Patience is the backbone of love. Patience is a continuous demonstration to our spouses that we really mean it when we say we love them. Patience strengthens any relationship, giving it height and breadth, allowing our love to stand tall through all the years together.

Kindness

Patience demonstrates how love *refrains* from acting *in*appropriately. Kindness shows how love *acts appropriately* when dealing with others. Patience holds back; kindness steps forward. Kindness "rejoices with the truth. It always protects, always trusts, always hopes, always perseveres."[22] Kindness means to be "helpful, friendly, thoughtful and gentle."[23] Kindness involves being courteous so that others can feel happy and comfortable.[24] The concept comes up regularly in Scripture.[25]

We all want others to be kind. God is kind to us. He gives us more than we deserve. (Indeed, only fools ask for what they deserve.) The problem is in *our* showing kindness. Yet, kindness is an essential part of Godly wisdom.

> But the wisdom that comes from heaven is first of all pure; then peace-loving, considerate, submissive, full of mercy and good fruit, impartial and sincere.[26]

Kindness includes doing favors, showing sympathy, being empathetic. The word Paul uses in 1 Corinthians 13 for kindness[27] means to be useful to others or to act benevolently. When we are kind, we look at the world through the eyes of others, see their needs and do our best to meet them. We have a friend at church who is a true "chocoholic." She goes out of her way to bring to church functions homemade desserts that are running over with chocolate. Sadly, I happen to be allergic to chocolate. The same woman also makes a point of bringing a second homemade, chocolate-free dessert. That is an act of kindness. She is seeing the world through my eyes.

We start to see a more complete picture of kindness as Paul provides specific examples. We show kindness when we:

- **Rejoice in the truth.** Your spouse has had a long-standing addiction that you suddenly learn about. He admits the problem, feels very remorseful, and immediately takes steps to deal with the difficulty. You rejoice that the truth now is being dealt with openly and honestly, and you completely support him in his efforts.

- **Protect** our friends from their own foibles *and hold fast* to them without making a big show of the effort.[28] We all have a weird side to our personalities. We all like things at which a lot of people would laugh. Kindness is having that information about people and *not* telling anyone, so as to avoid embarrassing them. As the old saying goes, "A friend is one who sees through your act and still enjoys the show." Likewise, kindness gives aid and support without constantly complaining about how *much* we've had to do, and what a *great* burden it all was.

- **Trust** all things. I constantly am amazed at the number of times people hear a rumor about a friend and jump to the conclusion that the rumor is true. Unfortunately, most "rumors" are actually gossip, and should be cut off without even being heard. Even when dealing with facts, however, kindness puts the best construction on events. It is willing to listen to the facts with an open mind, but be honest enough to recognize the truth when it becomes apparent.[29]

- **Hope** for the best. Being kind means we hope things will turn out well for others, even others we don't like. How often do we hear of someone in trouble, someone we don't like, and deep down hope that they get "what they deserve," at least what they "deserve" from *our* point of view?

- **Persevere** or **endure** to the end for others. This is a matter of tenacious loyalty. But it is honest loyalty. We want the best for our friend, but it must be the best built on truth.

Kindness and patience play out like the positive and negative ends of the same magnet. A few examples will illustrate:

- Your husband wants to watch the football game. You want him to rake the leaves. Patience tells you to put up with it without complaining. Kindness tells you to try to learn about football and offer to make the popcorn for snacks.

- Your wife wants you to go shopping with her to look for a new dress for an upcoming wedding. Patience tells you to go and not fuss after you've gone through 397 dresses and she still wants to try the two malls across town to see what they have. Kindness tells you to offer with a genuine smile to take her back to the first store you were at three hours ago after she tells you she "really liked" the light blue dress she found within the first 10 minutes of the trip.

- Your husband has purchased another topless, bottomless, backless, see-through teddy for you to wear. Patience tells you *not* to tell him that if he likes it so much he can wear it! Kindness tells you to wear it with a seductive smile that lets him know you love him, even though normally you would not be caught dead in such an outfit.

- Your wife has invited a houseful of guests over for a gathering on Saturday evening. She wants you to help her dust, run the vacuum and bring up some extra tables and chairs from the basement to the family room, although the game to decide the Big Ten Championship is about to start. Patience tells you not to get upset at the timing. Kindness tells you to do everything she asks *when* she asks and to offer to do more, even though that means only catching snippets of the game.

The Greek words for "love" most often used in the New Testament, *agape* and *phileo*,[30] are the basic equivalents of the Hebrew word for love used in the Old Testament, *ahab*.[31] These words for love all include fundamental elements: sacrificial patience, kindness and a strong desire to share and be close to those we love. This is the love husbands and wives are to show each other.

BACK TO THE SONG OF SOLOMON

By demonstrating patience and kindness, love produces unyielding feelings and steadfast loyalty, which is "strong as death,... unyielding as the grave" and "burns like a blazing fire" with such heat that "many waters cannot quench (it)."[32] Real love engenders loyalty that is just as unyielding and unstoppable.

We all want to be accepted for who we are. We all crave to belong and to have the people we care for, care for us. When this happens, a love as "strong as death" exists. We see this in husbands and wives willing to die to save their spouses and, in parents, willing to give up everything for their children.

Love is a driving force that causes people to do all sorts of things they otherwise never would consider.[33] It should not be surprising that there is significant evidence that married men earn more than their single counterparts.[34] When men have someone to love and are loved in return, it motivates them to take that extra step to reach beyond themselves to a higher level.

Shulamite asked Solomon to wear his love for her as a seal:

> Place me like a seal over your heart,
> like a seal on your arm.[35]

In ancient times, and even beyond the middle ages, a seal identified ownership and protected against snooping. An intact seal meant the message or container had not been opened by a stranger. Shulamite told Solomon to make her a "seal over [his] heart" (the center of his emotions) and "on [his] arm" (the center of his strength) so they would be known publicly to be hers and something only she could to put to full use. Any man who loves his wife as envisioned by Scripture should feel honored to grant this request.

Love like there's no tomorrow

We all fall into ruts. We become so accustomed to our surroundings that we stop seeing them. It is not until we face a loss that we stop taking the familiar for granted. Marriages also frequently fall into ruts. Unfortunately, Western culture paints the picture of passionate love during the courtship and the honeymoon, and then ... well, things slow down. It's "expected" that passions will cool. The answer Scripture gives is simple: Every day of our lives together husbands and wives are to love each other as if there is no tomorrow.

This message is given with the repetition of a drum beat in Scripture.[36]

- The husband is to "cleave" or "be united" with his wife. The concept (Hebrew: *davaq*) is a constant "chasing after." There are no "ruts."
- Isaac began to love his wife only *after* they were married. Likewise, we are to learn what real love is after we marry.
- Husbands are to be forever infatuated with both the physical and emotional love of their wives.
- The love of husband and wife is stronger than the grave and more forceful than a raging, unquenchable fire.

Quicky Quiz for Couples #1: Are there any passages in Scripture that tell us we to become intoxicated?

There are two situations in which Scripture tells us to become intoxicated. Paul tells us that we are not to become intoxicated with alcohol, but instead we are to be intoxicated with the Holy Spirit.[37] The only other time we are to be intoxicated is with the love of our spouses. On the wedding night in the Song of Solomon, after they have retired to the wedding chamber, Shulamite invites Solomon "to come into his garden and taste its choicest fruits," an offer he gladly accepts.[38] After they have completed their first act of intimacy, God announces the benediction,

> Eat, O friends, and drink;
> drink your fill, O lovers.[39]

What happens when you "drink your fill"? You become intoxicated.

Quicky Quiz for Couples #2: What happens when you become intoxicated?

When you "drink your fill," of wine in this case, you become intoxicated and lose your inhibitions. You do things you normally would not do. You think things you normally wouldn't think. You let yourself go. Here God was telling the bride and groom to become intoxicated by each other's love.

Likewise, Proverbs 5:18-19 tells husbands,

> May your fountain be blessed,
> and may you rejoice in the wife of your youth.
> A loving doe, a graceful deer—
> may her breasts satisfy you always,
> may you ever be captivated by her love.

The Hebrew words for both "satisfy" and "captivated" refer to the effects of intoxication.[40] Husbands are to be intoxicated with the physical love (her breasts) and the emotional love of their wives. Earlier in the Song, Shulamite already has told Solomon that his "love is more delightful than wine."[41] It also is interesting that the situation in the Song is on the wedding night, the first night of the marriage, while the Proverbs passage refers to "the wife of your youth," indicating it is late in the marriage. God wants us to remain intoxicated with the love of our spouses from the beginning to the end.

Reality check for husbands and wives: How do you kiss your spouse? As if you were lovers, intoxicated with love? As if it were the last time you might ever be able to kiss your beloved? Or do you kiss your spouse as you would Aunt Milly at a family reunion: A quick, polite peck out of habit? If the wedding marks the beginning of the courtship, then it also should start the beginning of the passionate kiss, making "The Ten-Second Kiss"[42] a regular part of a couple's relationship. This is no "regular" kiss. It is one filled with passion, taking time (at least 10 seconds) to linger and enjoy.

When I run workshops for marriage enrichment retreats, at every break I have couples "assume the position." That means to hug each other. Then I have them kiss for a full 10 seconds, which I time. By the

> If the wedding marks the beginning of the courtship, then it also should start the beginning of the passionate kiss.

end of the workshop, many couples are "cheating." They are still kissing *after* the 10 seconds is over.

The next time you and your spouse are about to part for the day, or when you first see each other after work, stop and hold each other. Then take a full 10 seconds to kiss and renew your sense of intimacy. Certainly your marriage is worth an extra 20 seconds a day.

Scripture tells married couples to act like lovers, because we *are* lovers, both romantically and sexually. Consider some of the things you did (or wanted to do) while you were still dating:

1. **Have dinner alone as a couple.** Married couples, even those with children, should arrange to have a meal alone at least once every week. It can be breakfast, lunch or dinner, as long as it is not rushed or interrupted, and the two of you are the only ones there.

2. **Run off to be alone with each other.** As soon as the children are old enough to stay overnight with a sitter (certainly by the time they are two), schedule an overnight get-away at a local motel. If money is a problem, find a friend or relative to watch your kids at their house, while you stay home. (The only rooms in the house you can use, however, are the bedroom, bathroom and kitchen. This is *not* a project time. The only "project" to work on is each other and your relationship.)[43] Many couples link up with other couples who have children of approximately the same age to trade weekends.

3. **Dress (or undress) for each other.** When was the last time you slept nude? When was the last time you tried to find something to wear, as you were going out to a movie, that you knew your spouse really liked?

4. **Spend time talking with each other.** Lovers schedule time to talk. They run up big phone bills chatting for hours. When was

the last time you specifically set aside time to talk with your spouse? Women need to have this emotional connection. Men need to fulfill it.

On September 11, 2001, the United States suffered an atrocity at the hands of terrorists with the attacks on the World Trade Center and the Pentagon. During the months that followed, countless interviews were published in which people said they suddenly had a new understanding that life could not be taken for granted. They realized that when they said "good bye" to their loved ones in the morning it could be the last time they would see them. God always has wanted us to have this feeling when we separate from our spouses. That is how love should feel.

Much more will be said on the subject of saying you love your spouse[44] when we return to it in chapters 10 and 11. For now, the question is, what was the last thing you said to *your* spouse? What was your tone of voice? What have you withheld from the person you have vowed to love? Did you show love as if there will be no tomorrow: giving everything, withholding nothing, just as Christ gave everything and withheld nothing on the cross?

DISCUSSION QUESTIONS

1. *Patience* is *forgiveness* in action, for the dozens of little irritations we constantly are called to put up with. Patience *assumes* our spouses are doing less than perfectly. We are to be patient with each other. But how easy is that on a day to day basis?

2. What is the difference between forgiveness and trust? How does this difference affect our dealings with others on a day-to-day basis?

3. Think back to some of the things you and your spouse did while you still were dating that helped to create a bond of love between you. Write a list. Are there any of these activities you could do again, which might help strengthen your marriage?

4. When was the last time you and your spouse had a "Ten Second Kiss?" How often should you? What is stopping you? Develop a plan to get this started again as a regular part of your marriage. AND, if your spouse is nearby, do it NOW!

Suggestions for Couples:

Go back and read each of the **Newsflash** items. For each **Newsflash for husbands** have the husband read it out loud. Have the wife comment on each **Newsflash for husbands**. Does it apply to her? Would she like her husband to keep this **Newsflash** in mind and apply it to their relationship? Likewise, for each **Newsflash for wives** have the wife read it out loud. Have the husband comment on each **Newsflash for wives**. Does it apply to him? Would he like his wife to keep this **Newsflash** in mind and apply it to their relationship?

— 8 —

The Biblical Limits on Sex:

So What Can We Do?

S ex? Christians? Somehow we all "know" the two words don't go together.[1] The only time Christian couples can have sex is after marriage, for the purpose of having children, in the bedroom, with the lights out, the curtains closed and under the covers, using the missionary position, on the third Wednesday of the month, in the midst of a new moon. The wife, obviously dressed in her long, flannel nightgown, momentarily pulls it only far enough out of the way so her husband won't "violate" her modesty by seeing her naked. Neither of them can have any fun ...especially the wife. And such subjects as oral sex or seductive lingerie of the topless, bottomless, backless, see through type ..? Well, any fool "knows" they are sinful, and must never be discussed.[2]

In the programs I have presented, I have been amazed at what couples have told me they can and cannot do sexually within their marriage. Everyone seems to have limits, and, typically,they blame the limits on God.

The desire to place limits on behavior beyond those placed by God has a long history. It started in the Garden of Eden. God told Adam, "you *must not eat* from the tree of the knowledge of good and evil."[3] However, when the serpent asked Eve about the limits God had imposed, she replied, "You *must not eat* fruit from the tree that is in the middle of the garden, *and you must not touch it,* or you will die."[4] The additional limitation, "you must not touch it," was a clear exaggeration of what God had commanded. Misquoting God's word usually makes His commands appear arbitrary and unreasonable. And making His word arbitrary and unreasonable is the first step toward disobedience to God's word.[5] After all, why would any rational human being be forced to follow an "arbitrary and unreasonable" command?

Most Christians do not misquote God's word intentionally. But many of us, as did Eve, like to exaggerate a bit, making things sound "better" (at least to our own ears) or more "emphatic" than they really are.

The desire to exaggerate comes from our desire to set our own limits. It puts us in control. This desire is helped along by our natural tendency to "find" in Scripture exactly what we were looking for when we started. We are not seeking *God's* will. Instead, we are seeking "proof" that God was smart enough to agree with our ideas in the first place.[6] This process gives us power and control. It no longer is someone else saying we can't do something. Now it's *our* idea. But, what is really great is that it is our idea with a twist. We still can turn around and blame God for the very rule that we have "found" in His word.

Setting our own limits on sexual expression also helps us justify both our inhibitions and fears.[7] And who better to blame than God? After all, if *I* tell you "No," you can argue with me. But if *God* tells you "No," what's to talk about? If a woman is extremely modest, telling her that *God* says she should never let her husband see her nude becomes an emotional lifesaver. She never will have to face her inhibitions. *God* has told her it's all right to remain covered; thus, her inhibitions now are justified. What more does she need?

Many limitations not recognized in Scripture are based on cultural norms. In some parts of the world use of nose rings by women is commonplace. In the United States, they can draw stares and looks of disapproval. Yet, there is nothing in Scripture that prohibits them. Indeed, they appear to have been part of accepted customs in Biblical times.[8] I am not for a moment suggesting that women run out and get nose rings! Instead, I am saying that if you don't want to do something, at least be honest enough to admit that it is you, *not* God, who does-n't want it done. Acknowledge that it is *your* fear, inhibition, concern for cost, low hormonal drive, stress, physical exhaustion, or any other personal reason that may apply. At least you'll be honest.

Scripture makes it clear that we are neither to add to nor subtract from God's word. Consider[9]:

- "Do not add to what I command you and do not subtract from it, but keep the commands of the LORD your God that I give you."
- "See that you do all I command you; do not add to it or take away from it."
- "Every word of God is flawless; he is a shield to those who take refuge in him. Do not add to his words, or he will rebuke you and prove you a liar."
- "I warn everyone who hears the words of the prophecy of this book: If anyone adds anything to them, God will add to him the plagues described in this book. And if anyone takes words away from this book of prophecy, God will take away from him his share in the tree of life and in the holy city, which are described in this book."

If God is perfect, all-knowing and all-loving, it is not possible for Him to *both* put a pleasure in front of us *and* also command us to use it unless it is good for us.[10] Our refusal to enjoy His gifts of pleasure, within the limits which *He* sets, is the equivalent of saying that God does not know what is good for us and that we are more aware of our needs than He is. That is an incredibly arrogant position to take. It is sin.[11]

> Refusal to enjoy romance and sexual intimacy in marriage is equivalent to saying God does not know what is good for us.

THREE BASIC PRINCIPLES FOR INTIMACY IN MARRIAGE

The basic principles of Scripture for romance and sex in marriage can be summarized quite simply:

1. God invented romance, sex and marriage.[12]
2. The romance and sex life of a married couple is to be continuous, active and passionate.[13]
3. Romance *and* sexual relations within marriage are specifically commanded by Scripture.[14]

With these principles in mind, the question becomes: What limits does God actually place on the sex lives of couples? There are only five which can be justified by Scripture.

THE BIBLICAL LIMITS ON SEX

#1. It must be a man and a woman who are married to each other.

Adultery (sex between a married person and someone not his spouse) specifically is prohibited by Scripture.[15] Fornication (sex between two people, neither of whom is married to anyone) is also prohibited.[16] Sexual relations between members of the same sex, i.e., homosexuality, also are prohibited.[17] Sexual relations *within* marriage, however, not only are *encouraged* by Scripture; they are *commanded*.[18]

#2. The sexual behavior must be within the privacy of the marriage.

Sexual intimacy is the context in which husbands and wives celebrate the unique oneness of their marriage[19] and produce godly offspring.[20] Sexual intimacy is a time for two becoming one, not the 18 becoming one. As long as the husband and wife are alone, by themselves, with no one effectively being part of their time together, then the two, indeed, are becoming one.

But limiting sex to the privacy of the marriage is not a limit on *where.* May a husband and wife have sex in the bedroom with the door locked, the lights out, the curtains shut tight, and the covers pulled up high? Of course. May they have sex with the door locked, the curtains closed and the lights on? Of course. How about with the door unlocked, if no one will be barging in on them? Of course.

- How about out in the living room, if no one is home? Of course.
- In the kitchen, on the kitchen table? If no one is home, no problem, but try to avoid breaking dishes.
- On the floor under the kitchen table? Fine, if the floor is clean.
- In the laundry room on top of the dryer, while it is running? It may add an interesting rhythm.
- On some secluded beach? Sounds great.
- In the woods, with no one there? Fantastic!

The issue is the *privacy* of the couple, the husband and wife alone together, not the physical location.

#3. The sexual activity must be something both want to do.

Sexual intimacy is an expression of love. Love never can be purchased.[21] Nor does love ever force its own way on others. It is one thing for husbands and wives to ask their spouses to do something sexually. It is altogether different, however, for either to insist on participation in something the other finds uncomfortable. But what should couples do when one spouse wants something and the other does not? That issue will be addressed in chapter 9.

#4. The specific sexual activity must not be inherently dangerous.

The body is the temple of the Holy Spirit within us.[22] Your body is a gift from God. It is not something to be endangered simply for a cheap thrill or a momentary pleasure.

Even if you and your wife agree that it would be great fun to sky dive naked over the Mojave Desert, have sex in midair and neither pull your rip cord until both have had an orgasm, that would not be consistent with Scripture. True, you are married, you are alone and you both want to do it, but it still is too dangerous for your bodies.

In our current culture there is at least one practice that has gained some popularity that violates this principle. This is the practice of tongue piercing. In talking with people who have done this, the typical reason is that it improves stimulation during oral sex. It is something both partners may want to do. Yet, there are some serious medical issues. The piercing cannot be brushed, flossed or adequately rinsed, and, thus, is a breeding ground for bacteria. Dentists point out that individuals with tongue rings have higher rates of gum disease, and that tongue rings chip the enamel on the teeth and bruise the gums .[23]

One additional danger must be recognized: spiritual risks. 1 Corinthians 6:12 refers to the incredible freedom Scripture gives married couples, "Everything is permissible for me." But, the entire passage contains an important caveat:

> "Everything is permissible for me" – but not everything is beneficial. "Everything is permissible for me" – but I will not be mastered by anything.

God gives us sexual pleasure for our pleasure as married couples. It is something to be enjoyed, to strengthen the bonds of intimacy and oneness between husbands and wives. But it is not meant to control us. If we get so wrapped up in sex to the point it is the *only* thing we live for, the *only* thing that gives our lives meaning and purpose, the *only* reason we are attracted to our spouses, the thing we rely on most to lift us up when we are down, then, in effect, sex has become our god and we are forgetting the true God who gave us life and gave us sex as a pleasure in life.

#5. The activity must not violate the law.

We are to obey the civil law. As Paul put it:

> Everyone must submit himself to the governing authorities, for there is no authority except that which God has established. The authorities that exist have

been established by God. Consequently, he who
rebels against the authority is rebelling against what
God has instituted, and those who do so will bring
judgment on themselves.[24]

It would be only a direct conflict between civil law and God's law
that would allow an exception. If the civil authorities outlawed *all* sexual relations of any kind between spouses, that would violate God's
law. Having made this observation, however, it appears extremely
unlikely (if a couple followed the first four principles) that there would
be a violation of the civil law.

Surely, there must be more ... ?

Any sexual activity that meets all five of these conditions is acceptable when observing Biblical principles.[25] This is shocking to many
Christians who have been told that all sorts of sexual practices between
husbands and wives are off limits. In answer to this problem, one
source put it, "Yet when it comes to marriage, the biblical message is
one of freedom rather than restriction. No passage in Old or New
Testaments regulates sexual practices within marriage. Instead, the
Bible affirms the joys and values of human sexuality."[26]

So, sit back. Take a moment. Close your eyes emotionally. (You'll
have to leave them open physically, however, to keep reading.) Think
of the wildest, most extravagant, sexual fantasy you can possibly imagine. Then ask yourself a few questions. Does this fantasy involve only
you and your spouse? Are the two of you alone when the fantasy is
being played out? Is it something both of you want to do? Is it physically dangerous? Is there any civil law being broken? If the answers are
yes, yes, yes, no, no, then go for it! Have a wonderful time, and praise
God for the blessing He has given your marriage.

Is it OK for us to ....?

It is important that some specifics be reviewed at this point to
understand how Biblical principles can be used to determine whether
behavior is appropriate. So, let's get down to basics for a short time to

consider a few of the questions that couples ask during presentations about sexuality in the Christian marriage.

1. "Should women allow their husbands to see them completely nude? Aren't women told to be modest in Scripture?"

A number of women have been plagued by the fear of having their husbands see them completely nude, even in the privacy of their own bedrooms. Many of these women consider their inhibition as being "modest" in the Biblical sense, or have been taught to be extremely modest by their parents. While this tends to be an inhibition more of women than men, there also are husbands who are very uncomfortable with their wives seeing them nude. (While this answer is aimed primarily at wives, it applies to inappropriately modest husbands as well.)

There are a number of problems with this type of modesty in a Christian marriage. First, it is not supported by Scripture. In Genesis 2:25, we are told, "The man and his wife were both naked, and they felt no shame." Some have argued, however, that this was before the fall, and after the fall, not only did Adam and Eve make coverings for themselves[27], but even God made clothing for them from the skins of animals.[28] The context of God's action makes it clear that He was about to put the man and woman out of the Garden, into a harsh world of wind and weather. There is nothing in the context to suggest that God approved of their newfound modesty.

Moreover, other passages of Scripture clearly imply that between husbands and wives each is to have free view of the other's body.

- Proverbs 5:18-19 tells husbands to let "her breasts satisfy you always." A man must see his wife's breasts on a regular basis to be satisfied by them "always."
- In Song of Solomon 4:16, Shulamite invited her husband to "come into his garden and taste its choice fruits." The "garden" is her body. The woman whom Scripture describes as the ideal wife made this invitation. The invitation made sense only if he was able to see the garden into which she was inviting him. Moreover, she described her body as "*his* garden." Limiting his

view of *his* own garden would make a mockery of describing it as something *he* owned.

- 1 Corinthians 7:4 says, "The wife's body does not belong to her alone but also to her husband."[29] If her body belongs to him as much as to her, keeping him from seeing it is keeping him from seeing what he owns.

- Throughout Scripture husbands and wives are described as becoming "one."[30] It seems strange to say that the two are one but that one half of that oneness cannot see what the other half looks like.

- After the fall, we are told, "Now Adam knew Eve his wife, and she conceived ..."[31] The word for "knew," *yaada*, implies a complete, personal knowledge. Indeed, the word often is translated in Genesis as meaning "had intercourse with his wife" (TEV) or "had sexual intercourse with his wife." (TLB) While it is quite possible to have sexual intercourse without seeing the woman completely naked, it is not possible to "know" her completely in every way without seeing her nude.

There are some translations that refer to women being "modest" in the home.[32] However, the Greek word,[33] which is translated as "modest," actually refers to being sober, prudent, or sound of mind.[34] It also can be translated as "propriety" (NIV), "self-control" (NKJV) or "self-restraint" (NAS). It does not refer to physical modesty at all.

The second problem with physical modesty in a Christian marriage is that God wants husbands and wives to be one with each other. Clothing is a barrier to oneness. We have five physical senses. Three of them are blocked by clothing: sight, touch and taste. A fourth, smell, is limited.

Unquestionably, some people (typically, though not always, women) are raised in environments that make them want to hide their bodies, even from their spouses. Their spouses, though wanting to see them nude, out of a sense of gentleness, will not press this issue. Accepting people as they are is an act of love. However, as has been often said, God loves us as we are, but loves us too much to leave us that way. Since modesty is a barrier to the oneness God wants us to have, it is something couples should endeavor to overcome.

I have dealt with a number of couples for whom the wife's modesty is a major issue in their marriage. When we talk about the wife allowing her husband to see her nude, I've been hit with all sorts of statements, including,

- "I thought my husband was supposed to protect me? Doesn't that include my feelings of modesty?"
- "I was raised in a very modest home. It's hard to change. Shouldn't my husband be sensitive to this?"
- "How about *my* needs for privacy and modesty? Isn't *he* supposed to meet *my* needs as much as I am to meet his? Why isn't it *my* turn to have *my* needs met?"
- "I don't 'refuse' to let my husband see me nude. He does two or three times a year."
- "I occasionally run from the bathroom to the bed with nothing on. He gets to see me then. That should be enough."

If we are to be at all honest, we must recognize behavior for what it is. The attitude of inappropriate modesty behind these questions and comments is an attitude of sin. Sin is the failure to follow God's model of action or the path He wants us to take.[35] "One of the main Hebrew words used to describe sin is *het*, which is a term from the world of archery or marksmanship. It means to miss the mark or fall short of a target, in the same way an arrow or sling-stone misses the bull's-eye."[36] Sinning is missing the mark God wants us to hit. God wants intimacy in marriage. God tells us that our bodies belong to our spouses. Withholding ourselves from our spouses is withholding what does not belong to us alone. It is missing the mark God sets for married couples. It is sin.

Moreover, this is a sin that denies God's plan of oneness and creates barriers God never intended. Tim Gardner noted in *Sacred Sex* that "the number-one purpose of sex is neither procreation nor recreation, but *unification*."[37] He added, "The 'Big O' of sex is not orgasm; it's oneness."[38] Oneness is not possible with artificial barriers between husband and wife.

Husbands sometimes have commented that they recognize their wives' modesty and the childhood home life that led to it. These husbands show great patience. Patience, however, should not become permission to sin. Spouses who inappropriately withhold their bodies from the view of their mates need to be confronted in a loving way. *Failing* to confront the sin, in effect, is *approval* of the sin. Scripture warns us, "Rebuke your neighbor frankly so you will not share in his guilt."[39]

2. "I feel like it would be un-Christian to shop at a Fredericks of Hollywood. Can you expand on this? Are sex 'toys' acceptable?"

Shopping at Fredericks of Hollywood or similar stores *with your own spouse* **or** *for your own spouse* **or** *for yourself to wear for your own spouse* is not prohibited by Scripture. There also is no problem with you and your spouse buying something for a friend to enjoy *only* with *his own spouse.* Mankind has been eager to add things to the list of what cannot be done in a Christian marriage. However, Scripture makes it clear that we are neither to add to nor subtract from God's word. The marital bedroom should be like returning to the Garden of Eden. Play. Have fun. Laugh. God intends romance and sex to be fun. There is no need to put artificial limits on marital relations.

Sex toys also are not mentioned in the Bible. There are several references in the Song of Solomon, however, to apples, raisins and pomegranates (Song of Solomon 2:3; 2:5; 7:8 and 7:12), which were considered aphrodisiacs in that culture. These obviously are not "sex toys," but they are aids to sexual pleasure. The general rule remains: Anything not prohibited is acceptable, assuming that both husband and wife wish to use the toy, and it meets the other conditions. If so, have fun.

There is a broader principle at work here. The purpose of sexual relations is both reproduction and enhancement of intimate oneness. If the married couple wants to use a toy or dress up in some enticing outfit (and remember, the wife may like seeing her husband in certain outfits just as much as the husband wants to see her in something special), it is only the two of them in the privacy of their marriage and it is not physically harmful; it is completely acceptable. Indeed, it may create a memory that will last for years and help to cement their relationship for life. Scripture encourages married couples to play and do things that are a "little wild."[40] There is nothing in Scripture that suggests that doing things to nurture the oneness of marriage would not include the use of toys.

3. "What part do visual or mental fantasies play in sex? What's acceptable? What's not? My husband wants to buy an antique doctor's examining table so we can play doctor and patient."

Fantasies played out between husbands and wives are completely acceptable to Scripture, as long as the other conditions are met. Playing an injured Civil War soldier and caring nurse, who fall in love and marry, or a shipwrecked couple on a deserted island, or a cave man with his wife, or any of the other countless fantasies people have can be ways for couples to get to know each other better and to enjoy closeness. What's acceptable and what's not is easy to determine: Does it meet the five limits listed above? If the answer is yes, have fun.

4. "Is oral sex acceptable in marriage?"

Assuming neither husband nor wife is suffering from any diseases of the mouth or the genitals, oral sex is an acceptable activity. Scripture simply does not address the issue. In Song of Solomon 4:16, the wife does tell her husband to "taste" the fruits of her vineyard, i.e. her body. In the next verse, 5:1, the husband replies that he has "eaten" of her sweetness, her "honeycomb" and her "honey." Some authors have suggested that this refers to oral sex. While this is possible, it seems more likely "eating" is simply a poetic reference to being completely involved in an experience, "taking it all in," as it were.[41]

Again, since Scripture does not prohibit oral sex in marriage, it is safe to assume it is permitted. However, there is a more specific reason to believe oral sex is acceptable. One of the primary reasons for sexual interaction is to enhance and reinforce the bonding process between man and woman in marriage. Some individuals consider oral sex to be even more intimate than vaginal intercourse. Many women report they experience more intense orgasms with oral stimulation than through intercourse. Sexual acts done in love that reinforce the love of man and woman are completely consistent with God's plan.

I have asked husbands, "If your wife woke you early and performed oral sex on you, would you leave for work with a smile on your face?" The response was a universal: "Are you kidding? Of course!" I then asked, "Would you think about it again?" Again, the answer was universal: They would think about it all day, that day, the next day, the next week, and for weeks, if not years, to come. They would have warm feelings of love toward their wives and would be in a hurry to get home. Every Christian wife needs to ask herself whether these feelings of love and connection by a husband for his wife are God-pleasing? The answer clearly is yes.

Since oral sex also can be performed by the husband on the wife, the question, likewise, becomes one of providing pleasure and emotional oneness. Every Christian husband needs to ask himself whether these feelings of pleasure and connection felt by a wife for her husband are God-pleasing? Again, the answer clearly is yes.

5. "Is it all right to shave the pubic hair, even if I shave the entire area clean?"

There are people who prefer their spouse's pubic hair either trimmed short, shaved in part, or shaved off completely. Some prefer it removed in part or completely for the visual aspect. Such a preference is not new. It has been said that the ancient Greeks "plucked out their sparse pubic hair because it did not conform to their aesthetic ideals."[42] Others greatly prefer the hair left exactly as it is. Indeed, some prefer to leave the pubic hair at full length and decorate it. During the 16th century it became popular among the upper class in France for women to put ribbons in their pubic hair.[43]

Scripture does not address the issue. The question, therefore, is what the individual married couple prefers. Shaving your pubic hair or leaving it untouched should be a gift of love to your spouse. Shaving your spouse's pubic hair can be an intensely intimate time together, in light of the vulnerability and the level of trust involved.[44]

6. "Is there any position for sexual intercourse or oral sex which is not acceptable?"

If couples want to try it, it is in the privacy of the marriage and it is not physically dangerous, there is no position which is not acceptable. A number of possible positions (some of which require Herculean strength and Olympic agility) are contained in the Kama Sutra.[45]

7. "Is masturbation acceptable for married couples?"

The Biblical view of sexual relations in marriage is for procreation and emotional bonding. It's goal is oneness. Masturbation can be consistent with or completely at odds with the idea of oneness. If one spouse is secretly masturbating alone, especially while fantasizing about someone other than his own spouse, it is, in essence, adultery. It is sin.

However, if the couple is using masturbation to learn about each other, then intimacy is enhanced. The same is true if one of the spouses is ill or injured and he is masturbating[46] the other or using masturbation to provide pleasure to the other. In these instances, intimacy is enhanced, oneness is strengthened and it is appropriate for the married couple.

For couples who have to be separated due to business trips, "telephone sex" can be helpful for maintaining marital closeness. This is simply the process of mutual masturbation while the couple talks softly to each other over the phone. So long as it is within the privacy of the marriage and both want to participate, it is completely consistent with Scriptural principles.

ARE YOU TELLING US THAT WE *SHOULD* ...?

Keep this *firmly* in mind. I am NOT telling, suggesting, encouraging or requiring that married couples *do* any of the specific acts that are described in this book as "permitted." Married couples *are* commanded to seek oneness in marriage. The goal is a romance and sexual life in marriage which leads to total, complete, unrestricted intimacy and oneness. God's word *permits* a wide variety of activities by which couples might attain that goal. However, His word neither *requires* nor *suggests* any of them in particular. Couples are command-ed to show each other affection and sacrificial love, to have romance and passionate sex, and be "naked and not ashamed" in each other's presence. Beyond that, I am *not* suggesting that anyone try acting out fantasies or engaging in oral sex or any of the other activities I've men-tioned! The reason specific activities are mentioned is to give an idea of what is *permissible*, not what is required.

We all are different. Every married couple is wonderfully unique. There are no two alike. What will add to intimacy and oneness in one couple may lead to distance and differences in another. It is up to each husband and wife, as a couple, to determine for themselves what sexu-al practices will add to intimacy and oneness. Therefore, I *am* telling, suggesting and encouraging married couples to do the things that are permitted by God *and* which will add to a sense of oneness in *their own, unique* marriage. While we are not *required* to do any *specific* act, God does tell us to strive toward oneness in marriage.

My parents loved to go out to eat. One of their favorite places was a buffet style restaurant, which had a dozen serving islands, each with dozens of different types of food. Every trip was a grand adventure.

The people who paid to get into the buffet were not *required* to take anything in particular. In fact they didn't have to take anything at all. There were no "food police" telling patrons what they "should" eat. Still, it would have been a shame to pass up all the wonderful dishes and only take one crust of slightly stale bread.

God has set a wonderful buffet banquet of experiences in front of each of us in this world. The finest delicacies are found in the garden of marriage. It would be an unfortunate thing, indeed, if we go through the entire banquet and pick out only one slab of warm, overcooked roast beef and a pile of cold mashed pota-toes to put on our plates. I can picture the moment when God approaches us and says in dis-

> God's word *permits* a wide variety of activities by which couples might attain oneness. However, His word does not *require* any of them in particular.

may, "I put all this here for you, and *that* is *all* you could bring yourself to enjoy. How sad."

Scripture tells us to "Enjoy life with your wife, whom you love."[47] Jesus told His followers that He "came that they may have life, and have it abundantly."[48] Sexual relations are one of the truly beautiful gifts of God to married couples. It is one of the ways we are to enjoy life with our spouses. It is a gift that is part of the abundance that God provides, and which can add a sense of enormous intimacy to couples. In the end, God wants us to partake of it to the fullest. So feel free to enjoy the banquet. Fill your plate! Go back for seconds! Hit the dessert table as often as you like. As He told the bride and the groom on their wedding night, "Eat, O friends, and drink; drink your fill, O lovers."[49] That is what the Master of the banquet desires.

DISCUSSION QUESTIONS

1. What are some of the limits you have heard Scripture places on sexual relations?

2. Why have people put extra limits on sex beyond what Scripture tells us?

3. In Biblical times, the rabbis taught that sin not only included doing the things God told us *not* to do, but *also* included failing to take advantage of the pleasures God has given us to enjoy. Why does this make sense? How is this consistent with a loving God? How does this affect marriage?

4. Review again the Five Limits on Sex that are supported by Scripture:

   • The man and woman are married to each other;
   • The sexual behavior must be within the privacy of the marriage;
   • The activity must be something both want to do;
   • The activity must be something that is neither inherently dangerous nor a risk to the health of either spouse; and
   • The activity is not a violation of civil law.

Brainstorm the idea of all the crazy places married couples could have sex and all the crazy things they could do involving sex. Assuming both husband and wife want to do them, which of these are actually prohibited by Scripture?

5. If Scripture permits such freedom of sexual expression within the confines of marriage, what *does* that say to married couples? What *doesn't* it say?

— 9 —

Dealing With Differences
"You Want to do *WHAT*...?"

Your idea of adventurous sex is leaving the lights on in the bedroom while you make love under the covers. Your husband, however, has just come home with Batman and Catwoman outfits and wants to try some major role playing. Or, your wife wants to try oral sex and you don't. Or, he wants you to shave your pubic hairs and you think he's got to be kidding. Or, she wants you to get a tattoo and you think she's crazy. Or, he wants you to dye your hair blond and you want to stay the dark brown you've always been. Or, she wants you to shave your head, grow a moustache and wear an earring. You like your full head of hair and clean-shaven face. The idea of having your ear pierced sounds crazy. Dilemmas such as these can become stumbling blocks for any marriage. The question becomes, now what? How are differences lovingly resolved so both husband and wife are acting in a way that will bring God's blessing to their marriage.

BASIC PRINCIPLES FROM SCRIPTURE

Scripture gives us three basic principles for dealing with differences.

146

Principle #1. Husbands and wives are made for each other. We are to submit to each other and the body of each belongs in part to the other.

Shulamite graphically illustrated the issue of mutual submission and mutual ownership on two separate occasions in the Song. On the wedding night, when she invited her husband to have sexual relations with her, she chose her words carefully,

> Awake, north wind,
> and come, south wind!
> Blow on *my* garden,
> that its fragrance may spread abroad.
> Let my lover come into *his* garden
> and taste its choice fruits.[1] (Emphasis added)

She first referred to the garden as "*my* garden," then invited her husband to "come into *his* garden." She used two different possessive pronouns because *her* body is both *her* garden and *his* garden!

Later she used a similar metaphor to emphasize her husband's ownership of her body. She said,

> But my own vineyard is mine to give;
> the thousand shekels are for you, O Solomon,
> and two hundred are for those who tend its fruit.[2]

Again, she began by pointing out that her body was "... my own ... mine to give." It was up to *her* to determine who entered her vineyard (i.e. her body) and under what circumstances. Her husband could use it, but *only* if she gave it to him as a gift. Yet, she then continued, without a pause, to add that "the thousand shekels are for" her husband and "two hundred are for" the person who tends her vineyard, i.e. herself. In Solomon's day a thousand shekels was "the owner's share of the vineyard" while the "two hundred" was keeping back "only the bare essentials for the care of the vineyard."[3] In other words, she was again saying *her* body was hers, but was also *his* vineyard.

This is not a one-sided matter, however, in which it is only the wife's body that belongs to the husband. On the contrary, the mutual nature of submission and ownership is established clearly in a number of passages:

- "For this reason a man will leave his father and mother and be united to his wife, and they will become one flesh." Genesis 2:24
- "My lover is mine and I am his ..." Song 2:16
- "I am my lover's and my lover is mine ..." Song 6:3
- "I belong to my lover, and his desire is for me." Song 7:10
- "The husband should fulfill his marital duty to his wife, and likewise the wife to her husband. The wife's body does not belong to her alone but also to her husband. In the same way, the husband's body does not belong to him alone but also to his wife." 1 Cor. 7:3-4
- "Submit to one another out of reverence for Christ." Eph. 5:21

Principle #2. Husbands and wives are to love each other, but love does not demand or force its way on others.

Love gives. It does not demand. "For God so loved the world that He *gave* ..."[4] He did not request anything first. Love serves. It does not force others to serve. "Even the Son of Man did not come to be served, but to serve."[5] While each of us has an ownership interest in the body of our spouse, love prevents us from demanding. We have a claim of right, but love sacrifices; it never insists on its rights.[6]

Principle #3. Love calls each of us to try to grow and to change, to overcome our inhibitions and fears, our habits and self-centered ways, so we can better accommodate the desires of our spouses that are not prohibited by Scripture.

Love constantly calls us to do what we don't want to do. It requires us to leave our comfort zones, and to move out to help those we are to love. Your spouse is the one you vowed to love the most. This is the person for whom you are to change the most.

The old adage that the only person who likes change is a baby with a dirty diaper has a lot of truth. We struggle against change. Yet, when it comes to loving someone, deep, personal change is essential. It is what God calls us to do.

> Love constantly calls us to do what we don't want to do.

THE PROBLEM WITH PRINCIPLES

While these principles help, they do not act as a step-by-step process for coming to a solution. They are too general and sometimes seem inconsistent. If *I* already own *your* body (or am a part owner of it), why do *I* have to grow and change? If I rule over your body, why do I have to submit to you when it comes to the use of your body? And, how can the wife's "garden" belong to both her and her alone, and to her husband at the same time?

The problem with principles has led primarily to three different solutions being proposed over the centuries. Unfortunately, all three are seriously flawed when we compare them to Biblical precepts.

First Flawed Solution: The person who says "Yes" wins.

For centuries the basic attitude was that the husband had an absolute right to have sexual relations with his wife any time he wanted. The wife had no standing in law to complain. Indeed, she had nothing to complain about, since she basically was the property of her husband.[7] Therefore, it was legally impossible for a husband to rape his wife. Only recently has this been changed in Western law.[8]

This attitude, of course, is a statement of power. If I want something, I can have it, regardless of anyone else's thoughts or feelings. There is no relation between this kind of thinking and the love Scripture tells us to show.[9]

Second Flawed Solution: The person who says "No" wins.

More recently we have begun to take the sensitivities of individuals far more seriously. Therefore, we now hear such statements as, "If you hear 'No,' that's the end of it," or, "If you ask your wife to do anything she finds offensive, you never should raise the subject again, since love does not offend."

Unfortunately, this, too, is a solution of power, not love. There is no Scriptural passage supporting the conclusion that simply because a person says "no," he can control others. It may well be that "no" is an appropriate and reasonable answer in some situations in marriage, just as in all other areas of life. It is equally possible, however, that the "no" is inappropriate, unreasonable and little more than a polite way of committing sin. The ability to say "no" is not an automatic release from our obligations to meet the needs of our spouses.

Even the statement that the discussion should end if your spouse finds a suggestion "offensive," is hardly helpful, and certainly not Biblically based.[10] I know several couples in which the wives find *any* nudity, even in the bedroom or *any* sexual intercourse under *any* circumstances, "offensive." They simply do not want to talk about it. The question is *not* whether your *spouse* finds something "offensive." The question is: Does *God* find it offensive?

Third Flawed Solution: Compromise.

Compromise is the most reasonable of the suggestions for dealing with differences, and often it works well. When it does, and it is used appropriately within the context of a loving relationship in marriage, terrific. But there are times when compromise simply does not work. Where is the compromise if your wife wants you to get a tattoo, and you do not? Get half a tattoo? Not likely! There once was a television advertisement showing a couple in a tattoo parlor. The young man was having a heart put on his arm along with, "I love Donna." Unfortunately, he ran out of money and his tattoo ended up: "I love Don." Sometimes doing less than all is worse than doing nothing at all.

I once posed this question to a marriage enrichment group: What if the husband wants his wife to wear a topless, bottomless, backless, see-through bit of nothing from Fredericks of Hollywood and she wants to wear long-sleeved, up-to-the- neck, down-to-the-ankles flannel? How do they compromise? The minister of the church had the answer: Give her the long, flannel nightgown and give him a pair of scissors! When everyone stopped laughing, the general agreement was that, by the time the husband finished with the scissors, the wife would have been better off with Fredericks of Hollywood.

There are fundamental problems with compromise in a Biblically-based marriage. Scripture consistently tells us that our relationships with others are to be based on love.[11] The idea behind the word used for love ("*agape*") is unconditional, unending, limitless, sacrificial loving. It is a form of love that gives without keeping score. When Christ was on the cross, He never looked down and said, "Now just a minute, here. This is too one-sided. I'm doing everything. Let's compromise. You do half and I'll do the other half." He was showing us how we are to show limitless love to our spouses. It was all-giving, sacrificial love, not compromise.

Compromise assumes negotiation. I will give, *if* you will give something in return. If I don't like what you are offering, I may decide not to give what you want. How much I *give* compared to how much I *get* will be determined by relative power and negotiating strength. A "good" compromise is one that meets *my* self-interest. This is not sacrificial love. This is a business arrangement.

Moreover, the word "compromise" does not appear in Scripture.[12] Obviously, there are other words that are not in the Bible, such as "Trinity," which we frequently use in Christianity. However, in cases like the word "Trinity," the concept clearly does appear[13] and we simply are putting a modern label on an ancient concept. It is only the label that is not in Scripture. There is no such concept in the Bible as compromise in the context of loving relationships.[14] God loves us. He expects us to love others. Love sacrifices and tries to meet the needs of others. Period. End of discussion. No compromise!

Here's a radical thought: Why not try a Biblical solution?

If these solutions are fundamentally flawed, how are differences to be resolved? Any solution must be consistent with the three principles set out earlier. Using love as the starting point, there should be four basic principles to any Biblically-based system of dealing with differences.

#1. Both husband and wife must have complete freedom to express their desires and needs without making demands.

Love requires openness. The only way the two can become one is if they know each other. It is no coincidence that the Hebrew euphemism used in Scripture for sexual intercourse is to "know," i.e., the "man knew the woman."[15] There cannot be knowledge if the person to be known is afraid to say what is on his mind, what he wants, what he desires.

Keep in mind that saying *what* you want and explaining *why* you want it are two completely different issues. To resolve differences, it is essential that both husband and wife be able to explain *what* they want, not necessarily *why* they want it.

But why not ask "WHY?"

What is your favorite dessert? Banana cream pie? Moose tracks ice cream? German chocolate cake? Strawberry parfaits? Turtle sundaes?

Why? *Why* do you happen to like the particular dessert you picked? You could answer, "Because it tastes good." But, that begs the question, so I'll ask it again: "*Why* does it taste good?" You can't answer the question because the question is silly. That it tastes good is all the answer there can be.

When your spouse wants to do something romantic or sexual that you may not enjoy, and you ask "why," there is no real way of answering the question. To say that it will feel good or make him feel loved is all the answer there can be. Beyond that, there is no answer, any more than it is possible to explain why I like banana cream pie with whipped cream topping.

Worse yet, the question *why* too easily becomes a means of avoidance. When we ask *why*, what we often are thinking is, I only should have to do things that are reasonable. If you can't give me a reason *why* you want me to do something, *and* have a logical basis for the reason, then it would be *un*reasonable for me to be required to do what you ask. No one ever should have to do anything *un*reasonable. Therefore, if you cannot give a reason *I* accept, *I* don't have to do what you want.

The obvious flaw in this thought process is that love itself is not reasonable. It calls us to give in order to satisfy the needs of the beloved even when those needs seem foreign to our own needs. It was totally unreasonable for Jesus to spend six hours on the cross for us, yet He did. The only thing that drove Him to such an outrageously unreasonable act was His love for us. He obviously had no personal "need" to be crucified, except the need to love us.

Love Involves Intimacy

If there is to be love, there must be openness between husband and wife on the most personal level. Dennis Rainey calls this "transparency."[16] Openness and intimacy not only open the

> Intimacy in marriage requires that husbands and wives feel completely safe to be completely vulnerable with absolute knowledge that they will not be hurt.

mind to let someone else know what we are thinking, they also expose the heart and let others know our vulnerabilities. This carries a risk. Knowledge is power. If I know your vulnerability, I know *both* how to help you *and* how to hurt you. Intimacy in marriage requires that husbands and wives feel completely safe to be completely vulnerable with absolute knowledge that they will not be hurt.

Newsflash to couples: If you receive personal information from your spouse, treat it as a sacred treasure of enormous value.

An expression of desires or needs must NEVER be in the form of a demand.

Demands are not statements of love. As Gary Chapman puts it, "We can request things of each other, but we must never demand anything. Requests give direction to love, but demands stop the flow of love."[17] In fact, demands are signs of attack. They usually originate from fear, anger, selfishness, or a sense of power. God calls us to use a love model. Love never uses fear, anger, selfishness, or power as a basis of action.

The constant and repetitive statement of a need or desire, i.e. nagging, is likewise an attack. Nagging does not represent love.

#2. Both husband and wife must have complete freedom to express their lack of interest, or desire along with their fears and inhibitions.

If there is to be truly intimate communication, both husband and wife must be able to express inhibitions, fears, or just plain lack of interest or desire for a suggested activity just as readily as they are able to express desires. Again, there is no need to explain *why*. It is just as difficult to explain *why* you don't enjoy butter brickle ice cream as it is to explain why you do. Even if your spouse cannot explain *why*, the lack of desire or the inhibition is just as real. Love creates an environment of safety in which we can be vulnerable to express our "yes" *and* equally vulnerable to express our "no."

The ability to express a lack of interest, fear, or inhibition carries with it a need to be responsible. If you don't want to do something, say so. Don't become angry with your spouse for making the request. Simply say *you are* uncomfortable with the idea. Don't say "yes," then conveniently "forget" to follow through, or otherwise sabotage the plan. A false "yes" not only is dishonest, it also creates false expectations. When the expectations are not met, the disappointment will lead to distance, not oneness.

Taking responsibility is honest, healing, and helps create intimacy. Your disagreement is honest because it is true. You don't want to do what is being asked. Your spouse needs to know that. It is healing because it takes the onus off your spouse for making the suggestion. Any disagreement creates a moment of stress in a relationship. An honest statement gently made will heal that stress immediately. It also helps intimacy because you now know each other all the more. Your "no" has revealed a secret part of you, which shows your vulnerability, just as your spouse's request has revealed a secret part of him, which shows his vulnerability.

I once suggested something to my wife. Sharron responded, "I don't feel comfortable with that." Then, she added: "But, that's *my* hangup. I guess I'll have to think about it." Her statement made me love her all the more. She honestly had revealed another part of her innermost self, and had not done it defensively. Her answer avoided any possible tension that might have developed between us.

#3. Husbands and wives are called to have a loving spirit, which will accept even imperfect gifts as gifts of love.

We all are sinners. Everything we do is imperfect. Our gifts to each other often will be less than what is desired. But love intentionally overlooks imperfection and accepts the gift with the spirit with which it was given. This is as true with sexual issues as with Christmas and birthday gifts. Christ tells us that husbands and wives are to love each other, just as He has loved each of us.[18] Since God accepts our imperfect gifts, we, too, are to accept the imperfect gifts of our spouses.

#4. *God* is the ultimate head of the household. He can deal with differences that create distance.

God wants us to have intimacy in our marriages. Differences create areas of distance and division in our married lives. Intimacy requires closeness. There should be no walls, no barriers, no lines of separation. Just as God wants us to know Him completely, He wants us to know our spouses completely. If we realize that God is in control and put our faith in Him, He will help us overcome any distance created by differences.

This means we need to take our differences to God. He is the ultimate healer of all hurts, including hurt relationships. God already knows the problem. We should be praying to Him to give us the solution.

A Biblical Solution to Differences

With this framework in mind, the solution to differences is *not* an event, but *a process* based on this framework. The process can best be understood by applying it to a specific example. For the purpose of this example let us assume the husband, Zach, (who is the "requesting spouse") wants his wife, Betty,[19] (who is the "responding spouse") to wear a completely sheer negligee, cover the bed with rose petals and light the bedroom with a dozen vanilla-scented candles while they leisurely explore each other's bodies as a prelude to having sexual intercourse. We also will assume Betty feels this is a "silly" request and completely rejects the idea. (It just as easily could be the wife making a request that the husband does not like. The same principles would apply.) If Zach and Betty are following the Biblical model, several steps should be taken. After each step the applicable principle outlined above will be noted.

#1. Zach feels completely safe to express his desire or need to Betty. (Principle #1)

#2. Betty feels very uncomfortable with the request (the rose petals will be a lot of cleanup, the candles might set the bedroom on fire, and the negligee will make her feel very self-conscious), but feels perfectly safe to say "No." (Principle #2)

#3. Zach and Betty now have identified a difference. **Both** Zach **and** Betty should be praying for direction and help. (Principle #4) They should be praying separately *and* as a couple, since this is an issue which affects both of them individually and as part of a relationship.

I have run into couples who have had major sexual issues. When I've asked them whether they have prayed about it, I typically get a blank stare followed by a sheepish look, then a mumbled, "Oh, we couldn't tell God about *that!*"

Newsflash to couples: God *already* knows about the problem and has seen the same problem in a thousand other marriages. He simply is waiting for you to bring it to Him. He will not be "embarrassed" by the question! Who do you think invented sex in the first place?

Obviously, couples should be praying continuously throughout their marriages. However, when there is difference on a personal level, we need to redouble our prayers.

#4. Zach accepts the "No," but still feels free to continue to express the desire when appropriate, without nagging or demanding. Over the months and years, occasions naturally will arise when the subject will be a normal part of the conversation. At such times, Zach should let Betty know the issue is still alive. (Principle #1)

Newsflash to the responding spouse: The fact that your spouse has not mentioned the issue in weeks or months does *not* mean it is no longer important. Your spouse simply is trying not to nag.

I have talked with couples in which one spouse is totally frustrated. If an issue is raised with any frequency, the requesting spouse is accused of nagging. "Why are you always on my back?!? Give me a break. I'll think about it," becomes the defensive reaction. If the subject is not mentioned, however, the responding spouse gives a shrug of indifference and says with a slightly self-righteous and extremely defensive tone, "Well, I assumed you'd forgotten about it. It couldn't have been all *that* important; you haven't mentioned it in weeks!" The requesting spouse feels it is a no-win situation, and begins to feel angry.

The misguided belief that lack of nagging means lack of interest is one area in which men tend to be worse then women, although both are capable of being guilty of this fault.

Newsflash to husbands: If your wife is nagging you, *listen* to what she is saying. It is an important matter to her. If she stops nagging and you have *not* taken care of the problem, that is a very bad sign. Most divorces are filed by wives. The classic situation I have seen in court is that the wife has complained about an issue for years without any positive response by her husband. Finally, she stops nagging. He assumes that finally all is well. Actually, all is much worse. Now she is planning her exit from the marriage.

Newsflash to wives: Men tend to "nag" by their actions, while you tend to use words. In the intimate aspects of your marriage your husband might buy you a sexy outfit for your wedding anniversary. You lose it in the back of some closet. He buys you another one for Christmas. You also lose it. He buys you another for Valentine's Day. You tell him, "I wish you'd quit buying me these things! I am *not* going to wear them!" He stops. You think all is well. You have made the same mistake.

Newsflash to couples: The persistent refusal to meet the legitimate needs of your spouse is the opposite equivalent of nagging. As I mentioned earlier, nagging does not represent love. It is a form of attack. However, refusing to meet needs is a form of defensiveness. It creates distance between you and your spouse. It is silently shouting at your spouse, "I do not wish to be close to you. I do not want to be your *ezer kenegdo.*"

#5. Betty asks **herself** and prays about *why* she is saying "no"? (Principle #4) What's wrong with rose petals? Candles can be set up so the risk of fire is very small, can't they? Why is the negligee so threatening?

This is *not* a question Zach is to ever ask Betty if the Biblical model is being followed. Instead, it is a question she is to ask herself. This is a matter of introspection. It also is a subject of regular prayer. Keep in mind, the "no" might well be sin, or it might be simply a matter of taste. This is something she needs to be discussing with God.

Such reasons as, "I don't want to," "I don't like it," "I think it's disgusting," "I don't *have* to do what I don't *want* to do," and "It doesn't turn me on" are not adequate.

Newsflash to couples: Stonewalling your spouse, ignoring the issue, procrastinating, or flatly refusing to pray about it are not acts of love. Love is sacrificial. It always calls on us to do what we don't want to do, to stretch and grow in directions we don't want to go, to open ourselves to ideas we always have rejected ... as long as they are not prohibited by God's word. The fact that we "don't want to do" something, or "don't like it," or even find it "disgusting" is a legitimate starting point. But love never allows it to be the final resting point.

> Stonewalling your spouse, ignoring the issue, procrastinating, or flatly refusing to pray about it are not acts of love.

#6. Zach, likewise, asks ***himself,*** and prays about, why he wants this. Is it really all that important? (Principle #4)

The marriage relationship is more important than any single issue that may separate a husband and wife. Zach needs to reflect upon and pray regularly about the issue to put it into proper perspective. This is a matter of introspection. Keep in mind, the "no" might well be sin, or simply a matter of taste. It also is possible that some request by Zach might be leading toward sin. In that case, Betty's "no" actually is most appropriate. This is something he needs to be talking about with God.

Just as Zach should not ask Betty why she does not want to satisfy the request, Betty should not ask Zach why the request is so important to him. If he made it, that means it is important. That is all the information *she* needs. However, Zach must be searching himself, with God's help, to find out *why* he is raising the issue.

#7. Betty tries harder to meet the request, even if only in part. (Principle #4) Perhaps the rose petals wouldn't be all *that* hard to clean up.

While some requests are not possible to meet half way (such as a tattoo) many others are. The long flannel nightgown can be shortened and the genitals can be kissed even if oral sex is not performed fully. The wife can be nude in the bedroom with only a soft light on, instead of all the lights blazing. (A single colored night light can be very useful as a first step.) The husband can cut his hair progressively shorter, even if it is not completely shaved.

#8. Zach accepts Betty's effort as a fully satisfactory gift from his spouse. (Principle #3) She has made a gift of love and is doing the best she can at the moment.

Watch how parents accept the gifts of love from their children. Stick figure drawings are displayed proudly on refrigerators at home and desks at the office,[20] although Rembrandt and Monet have nothing to fear, since the art work is miserable. **Question for couples:** If the art quality is so poor, why do we value these works of "art" so highly? **Answer for couples:** The gift was given out of love, and it was the best our children could do.

Second question for couples: If we accept gifts of love, which are imperfect from our children, why can't we accept imperfect gifts of love from our spouses? They are gifts of love and the best our spouses can do. We are children of God. None of our gifts to God are very good, adequate or worthwhile,[21] but when they are the best we can do and are given in love, He still accepts them and is overjoyed by them because we are His children. We are called upon to love others just as He loves us.[22]

> If we accept gifts of love, which are imperfect, from our children, why can't we accept imperfect gifts of love from our spouses?

#9. Betty continues to try harder to do even more. Perhaps she can wear a white satin gown. It's not sheer, but it is clinging. Betty also should continue her self-evaluation and regular prayer, while Zach needs to try his best not to demand or nag and to continue to pray regularly, but still be free to clearly state what he actually desires or needs. (Principles #1, #2 & #4)

This is a process, not an event. As the problem is addressed by God's power and the couple's love, strange things will happen. A point of balance may appear which neither the husband nor the wife ever considered, and which would not have been possible through negotiations designed to lead to compromise.

Newsflash to couples: God is smarter than we are. If you present a problem to Him, you'll be amazed at the creative solutions He can come up with.

A model prayer for couples

Here are some prayers you could use as a model for dealing with the issue, when the process is turned over to God:

Prayer for the requesting spouse (Zach in the example.)

> Lord, I thank You for all You have done for me and in my life. I thank You for putting my spouse into my life. I ask that You increase my spouse's desire to do what I would like. I ask that You decrease this desire in me so my spouse will not have to deal with this burden. Lord, above all, I ask that You change both of us so we have the marriage You want us to have so we can reflect Your love in our lives to each other and to the world. Amen.

Prayer for the responding spouse (Betty in the example.)

> Lord, I thank You for all you have done for me and in my life. I thank You for putting my spouse into my life. I ask You to take my fears and inhibitions from me and increase the desire in me so I am able to do what my spouse would like with a sense of joy. I ask that You decrease this desire in my spouse so that it is not a burden to me. Above all, Lord, I ask You to change both of us so we have the marriage You want us to have so we can reflect Your love in our lives to each other and to the world. Amen.

Notice how different this is than compromise. Compromise is finding a mutually acceptable middle ground between two competing positions. Love does not compromise. It gives. It sacrifices. Compromise may leave spouses with feelings of resentment for what they feel they had to "give up."[23] Love causes you to feel the sense of joy the gift gives to your spouse. Compromise is *self*-focused: What do *I* have to give up and what do *I* get in return? Love is *other*-focused: What can I give to *you* to make *your* life better, to be more uplifting to *you*? In the Biblical model, *both* husbands and wives:

- give as much as each can to the other,
- feel the joy their spouses feel from the gift,

- accept their spouses' feelings with love and respect,
- accept their spouses' gift of love as the gift it is, without looking at what is left undone,
- ask God to change them *both* for the improvement of the marriage, and
- look to God, in faith, that He will lead them to where *He* wants them and their marriages to be.

This model of dealing with differences can be used in settings other than those involving sex and romance. Suppose the wife wants her husband to go shopping with her, but he hates to shop? I once posed this to a group of couples. Several of the men groaned at the thought. I reminded them that husbands are to love their wives "as Christ loved the church and gave himself up for it."[24] Then I asked, "Would it be worse to spend six hours on the cross or a few hours shopping with your wife?" One of the men answered, "Can I think about it and get back to you?"

Newsflash for wives: For a lot of men, shopping is a slow, torturous form of death.

Here, too, both husband and wife have to pray for God's help. Both have to ask themselves the same set of questions. However, here the wife has to be willing to accept the incomplete gift. At first, the best the husband may be able to do is drop her off at the parking lot and pick her up hours later. On another trip, he may be able to park and walk into the mall with her as far as the first store. Eventually, by imperceptibly small increments, he may be able to work himself up to actually spend time looking for things in the store. Each step should be accepted by the wife as a wonderful gift.

It helps men in this situation if they can change their mind-set concerning the purpose of the shopping trip. Men tend to hunt, not shop. They have a specific thing in mind they are after before they go to the store. They go, find it, buy it, then leave. They often even take pride in "conquering" the project of getting what they need in the shortest time possible. Women tend to shop. They look at everything in the store and think about how it makes them feel, or wonder how it would make someone they care for feel. This type of exploration is incredibly time consuming. **The shift of purpose for men:** Men, you are *not* going shopping to *buy* something. You go with your wife to *learn* about *who* she is. Shopping is a learning situation, not a buying trip. It is entirely possible that you *may* actually end up buying something, but that is *not* the purpose of the outing.

Now that we have a way of resolving differences, what's next ...?

In chapter 8 we looked at what is *permissible* in marriage. Now we have a model for dealing with differences that may arise when a couple is deciding which of these permissible activities it may choose to do or not to do.[25] Next, we will take a candid look at some of the fundamental differences between men and women that tend to show up in the intimate areas of marriage: a woman's need for affection and a man's need for sexual fulfillment.

DISCUSSION QUESTIONS

1. Consider the types of differences that often arise between husbands and wives over sexual issues, such as frequency of sex, activities to try, where to have sex, and when to have sex. What other differences can be added to this list?

2. Why shouldn't couples simply agree that, "If either of us doesn't want to do something, we don't do it? No questions asked. No argument." If Scripture calls for mutual submission between husbands and wives, why isn't this agreement completely Biblical?

3. When dealing with differences, what are the primary principles we should be following?

4. What is the problem with compromise in these situations?

5. Discuss how each of the four basic elements of the solution identified in this chapter, and listed below, match with the basic Scriptural principles of love and respect, mutual submission, and obedience to God's word:
   A. Freedom for both husband and wife to express desires and needs, no matter how unusual, without making demands.
   B. Freedom for both husband and wife to express fears and inhibitions.
   C. The loving kindness to accept gifts of love, even simple gifts.
   D. The need of both husband and wife to remember that God is the ultimate head of the household and the bedroom.

6. Review the progression for the solution described in this chapter. Does it seem realistic? If it does *not* seem realistic, the appropriate question is, "Is it Biblical?" If it is, the next question becomes: "Have you really tried it, or simply ignored it?"

7. Why are the reasons "I don't want to," "I don't like it," "I think it's disgusting," "It doesn't do anything for me," "It would make me feel uncomfortable," etc., not Biblical? The chapter states that stonewalling your spouse is not love. Why is this true?

8. Review the prayers for both spouses. How do they fit with the Four Basic Principles for a solution and the primary principles from Scripture (listed in Discussion Question 5)? Go through each of the phrases in the prayer and each of the principles individually. Why do both prayers include a petition for God to change the person speaking the prayer?

Suggestions for Couples:

Go back and read each of the **Newsflash** items. For each **Newsflash for husbands** have the husband read it out loud. Have the wife comment on each **Newsflash for husbands**. Does it apply to her? Would she like her husband to keep this **Newsflash** in mind and apply it to their relationship? Likewise, for each **Newsflash for wives** have the wife read it out loud. Have the husband comment on each **Newsflash for wives**. Does it apply to him? Would he like his wife to keep this **Newsflash** in mind and apply it to their relationship?

— 10 —

Women and Affection:

A Quick Study for Men:
Why Your Wife Likes Cut Flowers

There is a simple truth men need to know: Women tend to ooze affection. Most women believe it is their personal obligation to leave little trails of affection behind them everywhere they go, as if they were spreading rose petals of love in the path of life for others to tread upon. Women give affection to their parents, husbands, children, friends, co-workers, neighbors, pets, and plants. They even are affectionate toward their stuffed animals.

When women run out of people to whom they can give affection, they create a new group. There are "secret sister" groups both at where I work and at our church. The women organize to give each other small gifts and send cards periodically throughout the year, but especially on birthdays, anniversaries, Christmas, Thanksgiving, Easter, Memorial Day, Fourth of July, Labor Day, New Year's, and just because. I've never heard of a "secret brother" group started so men could give cute, little gifts to each other.

As a man, I stand in awe of this gift God has given women. My wife can give more affection in a morning by accident than most men can give in a month with concerted effort. And Sharron is not alone. The vast majority of women are like this.

I have done programs at local sororities. When I arrive, the setting always is completely predictable. The house will be in perfect condition. There will be flowers set out; the dining room table will have mints or chocolates in a nice, cut-glass bowl or plate; the silverware will be laid out in a fan design next to the stack of the finest china the hostess owns, and the dessert napkins will be set out in a matching pattern. As for the women themselves, they all will be dressed in very nice outfits, their hair done, nails polished.

If I do a program for a group of men, they will be dressed in their nicer blue jeans. All the plastic ware simply will be thrown in a pile on the kitchen table next to the paper plates, that is if anyone has bothered to take them out of the boxes.

Since women ooze affection, they need regular refills of their affection tanks.[1] They need to receive affection as much as they need to give it to others. Women can receive large doses of affection from friends, neighbors, co-workers and other family members. If they are married, however, the one person to whom each eventually will turn to as her primary source of affection is her husband.

Newsflash to husbands: Any husband who fails to give his wife the affection she needs, leaves a hole in her heart, which cannot be filled by others.

The concept of the husband being the wife's primary source of affection is one of the often overlooked nuances of Ephesians 5:23, "... the husband is the head of the wife as Christ is the head of the church ..." The Greek word for "head,"[2] typically is translated as the head of a person, that thing above your neck with two eyes, two ears, a nose and a mouth.[3] However, the same word can also be translated as "capstone," for example, when Jesus quoted Psalm 118:22-23, "The stone the builders rejected has become the capstone ..."[4] The Hebrew used in Psalm 118:22, which we translate as "capstone,"[5] also refers to "a beginning."[6] Paul, the writer of Ephesians, was well-versed in the Old Testament. It would not be sur-

> Any husband who fails to give his wife the affection she needs, leaves a hole in her heart which cannot be filled by others.

prising to have him refer to the husband as the "beginning" or "the source" or the wife. After all, man was the "source" or the "beginning" from which God took the rib to make woman.[7]

Newsflash to husbands: When you are not the source or "the beginning" point of affection for your wife, you are not meeting your Biblical obligations to her. You are not acting as her "head" or "beginning," as envisioned by Scripture.

WHAT IS AFFECTION TO WOMEN?

From a woman's point of view, affection is a combination of words and actions which demonstrate:

- you're thinking of her regularly;
- you care for what she cares for;
- you accept her as she is; and
- you find her of great value.

Affection is the visible demonstration of love for women. It is a display of gentleness in their lives, which makes life worthwhile.

> Affection is a display of gentleness in a woman's life, which makes life worthwhile.

Women tend to value lots of small signs of affection more than one, big sign. As one popular magazine put it, "What's the sexiest thing a young dad can do for his wife? The dishes."[8] One newspaper columnist wrote, "What makes a man sexy is how he walks when he's carrying the groceries in from the car or how he always says 'Never' when you ask whether you're getting too plump."[9] Dr. James Dobson worded it slightly differently when he agreed with author Kevin Leman, who commented that "the greatest of all aphrodisiacs is for a man to take out the garbage for his wife."[10] From a woman's point of view the logic is simple: One big sign means you have thought of her once. Lots of little signs mean you are thinking of her constantly.[11] It can be called romance, caring, or attentiveness. But, it all adds up to the same thing: affection.

Women see affection to be profoundly important in its own right. It is something that gives life value and meaning. It is something to do when nothing else is going on, because, whether it is given or received, affection brings pleasure.

The female need for affection marks a significant difference between men and women. Women's primary emotional need is affection. Men's primary emotional need is sexual fulfillment (as we will discuss in the next chapter.) This difference has been stated by many authorities[12] over the years.

- "The first thing she can't do without – Affection."[13]
- "The first thing he can't do without – Sexual Fulfillment."[14]
- "The typical wife doesn't understand her husband's deep need for sex any more than the typical husband understands his wife's deep need for affection."[15]
- "… The anatomy of the male ego is critically different from that of the female's – men have certain ego needs and women have others."[16]
- "… For a man, a primitive sense of masculinity is fulfilled through sexuality whereas the primary establishment of femininity lies in her being loved."[17]

God puts this difference quite simply:

> The husband should fulfill his marital duty to his wife, and likewise the wife to her husband. The wife's body does not belong to her alone but also to her husband. In the same way, the husband's body does not belong to him alone but also to his wife. Do not deprive each other except by mutual consent and for a time, so that you may devote yourselves to prayer.[18]

Affection has a powerful symbolic meaning in a woman's life: It represents security, protection, comfort, acceptance, approval, and value.[19] This is important for two reasons:

1. **Newsflash for husbands:** How would *you* feel if you had no sense of security, acceptance, approval or value in your life? Your life would be a disaster.
2. Do a quick review of what the Scripture says in the Song of Solomon about how men are to deal with women: Compliment them; give them a sense of security; accept them for who they are; value them highly; talk with them; leave myrrh on the latch of their door, even when you feel rejected. Sounds like affection, doesn't it?

Husbands who follow the principles of Scripture will be affectionate and their wives will feel truly loved.

The importance of affection in the life of a woman cannot be overestimated. I have asked groups of women how they would like to live for a full year in a world with no affection, none whatsoever! None shown to them and none that they could show to others. Most women respond in horror at the thought. The typical response is that it would be like dying. One woman said it would be like being forced to stand outside for a year of dark nights, in cold weather with drizzling rain, with a coat warm enough to keep you alive, but not heavy enough to keep you warm. You are chilled to the bones, your toes and fingers ache, and there is nothing you can do to find comfort. Such would be a year without affection for women.

I have pressed the issue: How about a month? A week? A day? In each instance, women completely reject the idea of going so long without any affection. When I ask them how often they need affection, they always give the same answer: *CONTINUOUSLY!*

Newsflash for husbands: Women not only *want* affection, they *need* a constant flow of it coming into their lives. Since it is oozing out of them continuously, they need a source that will ooze affection back into them continuously. Otherwise they will dry up and die emotionally. Whether in the form of a hug, a kiss good-bye or hello, or calling her to find out how she is, a woman needs affection in her life.

The husband's importance as the primary source of affection in his wife's life cannot be overstated. A woman can be loved by every other person in the world, but if her husband is treating her cooly, the world still is a miserable place. Scripture tells us that "under three things the earth trembles, under four it cannot bear up." One of them is "an unloved woman who is married."[20] An unloved wife not only is a sad thing to behold, she also can become a source of pain and bitterness to those around her. There is an old saying, "If mamma ain't happy, ain't nobody happy." The fastest way to make mamma unhappy is for her husband not to love her.

Men, this is where we need to step back and look at how we view affection, compared to women. Put bluntly, most men see affection and sex as being substantially synonymous, since in most men's minds affection automatically leads to sex.[21] Women, however, see affection and sex as *potentially* related, but usually completely different subjects. In other words, affection *might* lead to sex, if it involves the right setting under the right circumstances. But, typically, they are not related at all.

To understand the depth of this difference, imagine affection as a room. For women, the room has many doors leading from the main room into a series of very long hallways. (See Figure 6.) Each hallway has a series of doors along both sides, each door leading into an individual room. Each of these smaller rooms represents a person to whom the woman feels a compelling need to give affection. There is a room each for her husband, her parents, her children, aunts and uncles, cousins, friends, neighbors, and anyone else to whom she wants to show a kindness ...which could include anyone. (One woman told me that not only is there an individual room for each person, but each room is individually decorated for that person to make the person feel most comfortable.)

One of the rooms is marked, "Have sex with husband." For most women this is a nice room, one they enjoy visiting. Some women enjoy the visit more than others. But what is important is that there is only one room marked "sex."

The need for affection and the need to show affection to so many people create a highly complex world for women. Every morning

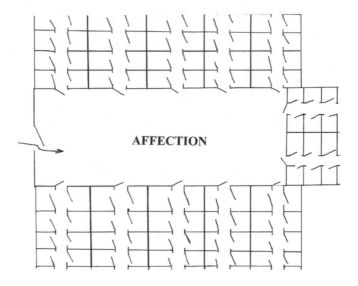

Figure 6.

women wake up with long lists of things they need to do. There are so many people in the world needing their affection, and they have so little time to give it. What are they to do? This brings us to what I call, "The Law of Sticky Notes," a law husbands ignore at their peril.

THE LAW OF STICKY NOTES

Men, when your wife wakes up in the morning she instantly sees the world like a huge note board, at least 50 feet long and eight feet high. The board is covered with hundreds and hundreds of sticky notes. Each note is a reminder of something she needs to do for others. One (that's right, only one) of those sticky notes is marked, "have sex with your husband." She *wants* to be intimate with you, but she also wants to give affection to all those other people who obviously need her kindnesses.

Question for men: since sexual fulfillment is a primary need for most men, how do we get to *that* one sticky note so we will be visiting *the* room marked "sex" as often as possible? There are two basic strategies.

172

Strategy #1: A husband can ignore the sticky notes and want to make love that night anyway. His wife often will be so tired from all her efforts that she will find it difficult to "get in the mood." Or, she may not have had time to get everything done, in which case she still will be thinking about her list when she goes to bed.

Strategy #2: A husband can recognize the obvious. The more sticky notes taken care of, the fewer will remain at the end of the day to cover the one marked "sex." Moreover, if the husband *helps* his wife with some of her sticky notes, not only will there be fewer to hide the one marked "sex," but she will not be as tired from all her efforts.

It should be no surprise that research indicates that husbands who help their wives with chores have a better sex life than husbands who give no help.[22] I have seen this in my own marriage. Several years ago I was out mowing the lawn when a friend of my son stopped by. He asked the generic question, "What cha doin'?"

I answered, "Seducing Sharron."

He looked surprised. "It doesn't *look* like you're seducing her."

I then explained about The Law of Sticky Notes and that mowing the lawn was on her note board for the day.

He wanted to know what a mowed lawn had to do with giving affection to other people. I explained, "It shows affection to everyone who drives by. The world they see looks better." Later that afternoon I was changing some light bulbs that had burned out. He asked me the same question. I gave the same answer.

"Another sticky note?" he asked.

"You've got it," I answered.

Did it pay off? In the vernacular of some men, I did, indeed, "get lucky." But it is not "luck" when something happens that is a natural result of specific behavior. A woman needs to know her husband loves her and cares for her before she can enjoy sex. The more she knows he loves her and cares for her, the more likely she is to want to share sex and do the things her husband would like to do. The more her husband helps with sticky notes, the more likely it is that she will be in the mood. It is not inevitable. There are other factors, including the time of the month and her overall physical health. But it is more likely.

Keep in mind that attitude is everything. Helping with the sticky notes is *not* a matter of "manipulation," or "purchasing" a sexual payoff. The truth is I would have mowed the lawn and changed the light bulbs even if there had been no chance for sex that night. Love gives unconditionally; it does not give in trade. The husband's attitude is to be one of sacrificial love, not manipulation or working trades of one service for another. However, the truth remains that a natural result of love is that it motivates others. A husband's sacrificial love will tend to motivate his wife to want to be intimate with him.

Taking care of sticky notes for your wife not only saves her time and gets her chores off her mind, it is also a sign of affection for her, since it recognizes as important what she sees as important. Affection is foundational to her and now you are helping her give affection. This affirms her, and tells her you approve of her and accept who she is.

But what do all those other sticky notes say? A lot of men have trouble figuring out what their wives need done. There are two obvious sources. If your wife gives you a "honey do" list, you just have been handed the responsibility to take care of a list of sticky notes. She may forget to thank you, but your cheerful help will not go unnoticed.

Newsflash to husbands: If your wife has not given you a list, try a radical idea: *Ask her.* Women typically are happy to tell their husbands what they believe needs to be done around the house.

BUT I DON'T WANT TO ...

What about husbands who simply "aren't the affectionate type"? This gets us to one of the hardest passages for husbands in all of Scripture, Ephesians 5:25:

> Husbands, love your wives, just as Christ loved the church and gave himself up for her ...

Christ came to serve. He came to give until there was nothing else to give. And He told us to love our wives, and everyone else, as He loved us. (John 13:34)

When a man says he is not the "affectionate type," he really is saying:
- I don't understand this;
- it doesn't do anything for me;
- I've never done this before; and
- it's uncomfortable for me to try something new.
- So, the bottom line is: I don't want to.

God's instruction to "love your wives" is a command, not a conditional suggestion. Scripture does *not* say, "Husbands love your wives as Christ loved the church *unless you're not the type*." It does *not* say, "Love others as I have loved you *unless you don't feel like it*." God tells husbands to love their wives in a way that *women* understand and appreciate. It makes no difference whether we as husbands understand or appreciate it.

For several years my wife and I lived within a mile and a half of my work in Adrian, Michigan. In "heavy" traffic I could drive home in less than five minutes. Sharron wanted me to call home when I was ready to leave the office. This made no sense to me. I could be home in almost the same time it took me to make the phone call. It took a long time for God to get through to me that it didn't matter whether it made "sense" *to me*. The only question was whether *my beloved* needed it. If she did, I had an obligation of love to satisfy that need.

I've had lots of husbands complain that they "don't understand" their wives. Frankly, I don't always understand my wife either.

Newsflash for husbands: Scripture commands us to *love* our wives. It does *not* tell us to *understand* them.[23] The Biblical principle is simple: "Each of you should look not only to your own interests, but also to the interests of others."[24] Men, this means looking out for your wife's needs.

WATCH OUT FOR LABELS

One of the mind tricks we all like to play is to "label" things we like and don't like in a way that will justify what we want to do.[25] If we want to do what our spouse asks, it is a "wonderful idea." If we don't want to, the idea is "silly" or a "waste of time." By labeling our wives' needs as only a "request" for something "silly" or a "waste of time," we automatically degrade the need into something we don't have to do. After all, no one should be required to do anything that is "silly" or a "waste of time."

The request may be "silly," but from *whose* point of view?

Newsflash for husbands: If your wife needs it, then it is not silly. Husbands are to love their wives "as Christ loved the church." But wasn't it "silly" for Christ to have to leave His throne in Heaven to come to earth to die for the Church? Wasn't it "silly" for Him to have to suffer six hours on the cross for sins He didn't commit? How *logical* is that? But mankind needed it, and *that* made it worthwhile.

Another newsflash for husbands: God made women and He made them in His own image. When men complain about their wives and the cut flowers and the soft fuzzies women like, they need to remember that God made them that way. If you don't like it, take up the argument with God, not your wife. She's only doing what God made her to do naturally.

BUT HOW DO I DO THIS ...?

If you're having trouble coming up with ways of giving affection to your wife in ways she will understand, first take care of her sticky notes and, second, try the following list. One way of doing this is to ask your wife to read the list out loud to you, and tell you which ones she would like you to do.

1. Hold hands when you walk together.
2. Find a time when you can walk through the woods together ... holding hands.
3. Bring her a fresh cup of coffee while she's still in bed first thing in the morning.

4. Ask whether she would like a cup of coffee, a soft drink, or a snack when you are relaxing together in the evening. (*Especially* if you're getting yourself something.)

5. Give her a back rub after she's had a hard day ... without expecting sex to follow.

6. Use pet names for each other for which ONLY the two of you know the meanings.

7. Have a "favorite song" ... and request the DJ to play it.

8. Leave a note on her pillow, saying "I miss you," if you're away for the night.

9. Put a sticky note on the mirror for her, saying, "I love you" or "I care for you."

10. Call her during the day just to tell her you love her.

11. Warm up her car for her before she leaves the house and scrape off the windows if there is any snow. (For an extra point, leave a note on her steering wheel, saying, "I love you." For five extra points have the note say, "My love for you melts the ice and warms your way.")

12. Warm up her side of the bed when she is going to be getting in after you.

13. Get a baby-sitter for the kids; "kidnap" your wife and take her to a bed and breakfast for an unexpected night.

14. Get a massage together as a gift.

15. Give her a sincere compliment when she looks really nice.

16. Open car doors for her.

17. In the evening offer to help with whatever needs doing, instead of plopping down in a chair ... she's had a long day, too.

18. Take her out to dinner as a surprise. (Even if she says "any-where" is fine, McDonald's won't hack it. Take her some place a little special. It doesn't have to be expensive, just special.)

19. Go shopping with her ... or do something else *she* likes to do. (Remember, when you're shopping, you are not necessarily there to "buy" anything. The object is to spend time with *her*, seeing what *she* likes, trying to learn who *she* is.)

20. Hug her and touch her, but NOT sexually and NOT expecting sex. Hug her and touch her just because you love her and want to be close to her.

Don't limit yourself to this list. *Ask* your wife what other things you could do that would

- make *her* feel appreciated, valued, loved;
- make her life easier, more significant, more meaningful;
- relieve her of some of the stresses she feels.

After all, *doing* what makes your wife feel loved is the action of the model husband described in the Song of Solomon. This is behavior which is the soft protection of the shade of an apple tree. It is putting a banner of love over your wife. In the end she will love you for it.

KEEPING THE MOTIVATION RIGHT

Men tend to be motivated by specific goals. Sex is one of the biggies.[26] But, this must not be the primary motivation for giving affection to your wife. Indeed, the more a husband associates affection with sex, or worse yet, begins to expect sex as the "payoff" for giving affection, the more likely his wife will begin to resent his actions. Your wife is not a vending machine. You cannot simply plug in the affection, then pull out the sex. The suggestion to give your wife a back rub specifically mentions "without expecting sex to follow." Realistically, *every* one of the suggestions should also be read "without expecting sex to follow."

If we love our wives "as Christ loved the church and gave himself up for her," there must be no motivation at all *EXCEPT* the desire to give love itself. Christ did not come to earth to negotiate a deal. Nowhere does Christ say, "Listen folks, I'll go ahead and die for you, but, I expect a payoff in return. Here's the list of things you're to do...."

Husbands are to give their wives unconditional love. As Dr. John Gray notes, women "idealize unconditional love."[27] That makes sense, since God does the same. That is why He commands husbands to give unconditional love, *agape*, to their wives. If our gift of affection is conditioned on sex, it is, by definition, not *agape*, and not a gift at all.

Scripture gives husbands the proper motivation. The husband is to love his wife:

> to make her holy, cleansing her by the washing with water through the word, and to present her to himself as a radiant church, without stain or wrinkle or any other blemish, but holy and blameless. In this same way, husbands ought to love their wives as their own bodies. He who loves his wife loves himself. After all, no one ever hated his own body, but he feeds and cares for it, just as Christ does the church ...[28]

As husbands, our efforts are to bring our wives closer to God by reflecting God's love to our wives as purely as possible, not to "get" sex.

Women who are committed to Christ understand the close connection between spiritual leadership by husbands and affectionate love to them. During a couples' retreat, a wife asked, "It seems like women always take the lead on nurturing relationships within the family. In what respect are husbands to take leadership in the area of nurturing relationships?"

I replied by asking, "How many women here would like their husbands to take a positive, loving lead in the spiritual life of the family by motivating everyone to worship regularly together, reading Scripture, leading devotions, and praying for the family? In other words, how many of you would like your husband to lead in *nurturing* the family's relationship with God?"

Every woman in the group raised her hand, then they gave me a standing ovation for asking the question.

Newsflash to husbands: Wives who are committed to Christ want you to take charge of the spiritual life of the family, to show your love of Christ in your dealings with them.

Those women understood that keeping a strong relationship with God inevitably will lead to strong relationships within the family. Any husband who works on giving his wife affection *and* leading the family in a strong spiritual life will be blessed with the joys of a close, loving family, and a wife who truly cares for him.

A CLOSING THOUGHT: WHEN MORE FLOWERS ARE NEEDED

The day I married Sharron my father and I were out tending to some last minute chores. He made a number of comments, all sound advice, about my upcoming change from bachelor to husband. One suggestion in particular stood out: "Be gentle." It was clear from the context he was talking about something other that sex. I didn't understand at first. It wasn't long before I did, however.

Men, if you haven't figured out by now, women are different from men. They have periods. We don't. They give birth to babies. We don't. They have hot flashes during menopause. We don't.

The emotional shifts and physical cramps associated with menstrual periods are very real. We can joke about PMS, but the feelings women experience are not at all funny. Women who are in the premenstrual and menstrual part of the monthly cycle make up only 18% of the female population of child-bearing age. Yet, as Dr. James Dobson has noted, this same group accounts for approximately 50% of suicides and about 75% of crimes committed by women in this age range. Also "clustered in the pre-menstrual period" are "accidents, a decline in the quality of school work, decline in intelligence test scores, visual acuity, and response speed."[29]

Most women know they are not behaving in a loving way when their hormones go on a rampage. (Indeed, I heard one woman quip that PMS actually means "Punish My Spouse.") It is beyond their control.[30]

My father's suggestion, "be gentle," actually was a paraphrase of Paul's statement, "Husbands love your wives, as Christ loved the church." "Be gentle" needs to be a guiding principle for husbands. When your wife is having a difficult time and takes it out on you, that is when she needs a hug. When she is going through PMS, and you feel like you're walking on egg shells, that is when she needs the flowers and hugs the most. As put in the Song of Solomon, she needs myrrh left on her door knob, a sign of constant, unchanging, unconditional love.

Childbirth and the adjustment to a newborn also is a time for special gentleness.

"The birth of a baby brings a challenging time for new parents who wish to resume intimate relations. Exhaustion usually sets in due to sleepless nights. Added duties and worries about parenting increase stress. Women experience dramatic physical changes after birth. Hormone levels (for women) plunge from a very high level within days after delivery. These levels remain low until breast feeding is completed.

"Most women experience some degree of discomfort or pain when intercourse does occur. Fear of pain leads to apprehension, which leads to tension. Tension leads to tightening of the vaginal wall muscles and decreased lubrication.

"The result ... The combination of exhaustion, stress, low hormones and apprehension about possible pain result in marked decrease in sexual desire in most women during the months following delivery."[31]

There are several important ways husbands can show affection to their wives after the birth of a child:[32]

- "Help with baby duties and household chores. Your wife will see it as a sign of affection and she will not be as tired.
- "Help her find time to nap. She will be more likely to be in the mood if she is not exhausted.
- "Give her a back rub. Most women love them, especially after giving birth.
- "A break helps. Send her out to do what she enjoys while you care for the baby.
- "Remember: You wouldn't be anxious to do something that might hurt you! So be patient, gentle and reassuring. This is one time that going slow will get you there much faster!
- "Talk with her about how you feel so she knows. It is not fair to her to be angry in silence, if you are feeling rejected or if your needs are not being met. Let her know in a loving way.

- "Women see sex and affection as very different issues. Affection can lead to sex, but not necessarily. Right now your wife needs lots of affection, but it should not be conditioned on leading to sexual intimacy. This is a long term investment of love she will remember with kindness for years to come.
- "Above all keep in mind when she says 'no' she is not rejecting you personally. She still loves you. She is only responding to a lack of hormones, exhaustion, stress and anxiety."

CLOSING COMMENTS TO MEN

Every woman is different. My wife, Sharron, does not like to receive cut flowers. To her, they are a waste of money. Give her a live plant, but not cut-flowers. However, countless women I have talked with would love their husbands to bring them even a single, long-stemmed red rose. Others like white roses. Still others prefer carnations. Some women like jewelry; others don't. You need to know *your* wife. Knowing what *most* women want is worthless information. Knowing what *your* woman wants is priceless.

Study your wife. Learn who she is. What types of clothes does she like to wear? What colors? What style of music does she enjoy? Is there any particular artist she seems to like the most? Does she like to go out to dinner? If so, what types of food does she like? These are the types of questions you need to answer about *your* wife. But, then you should go deeper. Ask her what she would like to be doing in five years? In 10 years? What would she like you to do to strengthen the spiritual life of the family? Does she have any personal aspirations to develop the unique talents God has given her? Are there any basic concerns that she has not shared with you before now? God commands us to learn this information, then to act on it. And, with our obedience comes God's blessing.

DISCUSSION QUESTIONS

1. Talk about the analogy brought out in this chapter, comparing affection to a room with many doors for women. Is this how women actually see affection? How does this affect their view of life? Their view of marriage?

2. How do women define affection? What is it? How does it look in real life? How would you describe the actions of a husband who truly is affectionate, based on how women see affection?

3. For a woman, what would the world be like with little affection...or, none at all?

4. If the husband is "not the affectionate type," what happens? What if the thing the wife wants is "silly" or "a waste of time" in his view? What do the passages in Scripture about obedience say about this view? What does Eph. 5:25 say about this view?

5. Go through the list of Showing Affection: Some Suggestions. Talk through the list, allowing time to talk about each of the suggestions. **Note for husbands:** This is a time to listen. Try to learn about *your* wife. What does *she* like? If you have a question, it should be to ask more details of *how* or *how often* she would like a particular thing done.

Suggestions for Couples:

Go back and read each of the **Newsflash** items. In this chapter *all* the **Newsflash** items are **Newsflash for husbands**, so have the husband read them out loud. Have the wife comment on each **Newsflash for husbands**. Does it apply to her? Would she like her husband to keep this **Newsflash** in mind and apply it to their relationship?

— 11 —

Men and Sexual Fulfillment:

A Quick Study for Women: Why Your Husband Wants You to Wear that Silly Sexy Stuff

S everal years ago our church's marriage enrichment group went through Dr. Willard Harley's book, *His Needs, Her Needs.*[1] The night we discussed the chapter about women's need for affection was a major revelation. The husbands were shocked to learn how women see affection and how it plays into their lives. The consensus among the women in the group seemed to be that it was "about time" the men finally understood what was so obvious to them. The next month, however, we covered the chapter on men and sex. It quickly became apparent that the women had as little understanding of men's need for sexual fulfillment as men had for women's need for affection.

Unquestionably, women know that the vast majority of men like sex...a lot! Instead of appreciating this information and using it in a loving way, however, many women either ignore it or complain about it. "Is that *all* men ever think about?," they demand, often with a tone of condescending self-righteousness. Before we get into specific issues of sex that women should understand, there is an initial question to address: Is there any evidence that the sex life of a couple plays into God's larger plan for strong relationships between husband and wife?

Primary and secondary goals of creatures in God's creation

One of the constants we find among the social creatures of God's creation is that when an activity takes much longer than appears reasonably necessary to get the job done, there is a deeper, more important reason for the behavior. Most people only need a few minutes to take a bath or shower, but can spend an hour relaxing while bathing. Rhesus monkeys take hours to groom. While humans need only 15 to 20 minutes to eat the typical fast food meal, they also can spend hours dining at a fine restaurant. Dogs typically gulp down their food, and if given a special treat, nearly inhale it. There is a constant at work here: Rhesus monkeys use the grooming process as part of the social interaction of the group and the bonding process. If humans are using a bath to relax, it takes a long time. If it is only to clean up, it can be done in minutes. When humans use eating solely for nourishment, they can "wolf down" food nearly as fast as dogs. But when we "dine," we can take hours because we are using meals for social interaction and bonding.[2] Indeed, time for conversation marks one of the prime differences between "eating" and "dining."

Sexual activities typically take husbands and wives anywhere from 10 minutes or less for a "quicky," to several hours for an evening of "romance and intimacy." The average is about 25 to 35 minutes. This is very inefficient, *if* procreation is the only reason for sex. Rhesus monkeys need only 12 seconds from the time the male says "HI" to when they roll over and say goodnight, ending the sexual contact.[3] The reason for this stark difference is that God created men and women in His image with marked differences from animals. God designed Rhesus monkeys to use sex only to make baby monkeys. However, God gave mankind sex and romance as a means of social interaction and bonding toward oneness between husbands and wives.

BUT, WHY IS SEX *SO* IMPORTANT TO MEN?

From a scientific perspective, the primary reason for men's apparent obsession with sex is the hormone testosterone. Both men and women produce testosterone as part of their hormone systems, but men average over three times as much as women.[4] The high level of testosterone makes men more aggressive and sexually driven.

Hormones may explain the reason for the sex drive men feel, but they do not explain the significance. Sexuality and sexual relations are both foundational to a man's ego structure and a physical event for which men feel an overwhelming drive, usually not shared by women.[5]

Men also see an equation between affection and sex.[6] Put bluntly, life without sexuality, for most men, is life without affection. If a wife deprives her husband of sexual teasing, flirting, touching, and intercourse, she is depriving him of affection. The world can seem just as cold and bleak to a man who has no sexual fulfillment as it is to a woman who goes without affection for long periods of time. A woman can learn how men feel simply by asking herself, "Would I like to live in a world without affection?" The answer is the same as if her husband were asked whether he would like to live in a world without sex. Men need affection just as much as do women. They also need affection continuously, just as do women. However, we must remember the oppositeness of men and women, the fact that each is the *ezer kenegdo* of the other. The oppositeness means that men *define* affection differently, in masculine terms of sex, not feminine terms of small acts of kindness.

> Men need affection just as much and just as continuously as women. However, men define affection in terms of sex.

In chapter 10 a room was used as a metaphor for how women see affection. Ladies, here is the male version of the same room. (Figure 7)

You will note that this room has only two doors. One for entering and one for exiting. Once you enter the room, it is a violation of the rules to leave by any door other than the one marked exit. The first section of the room is marked "Affection." By affection, men mean light touches, caresses, or hugs. The farther into the room you move, however, the more intense the physical contact becomes. This is one of the rules. There is a mystical, magical line in the room that divides one end

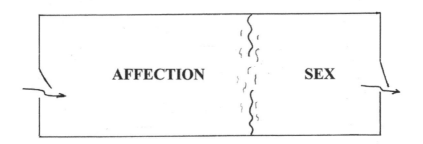

Figure 7.

from the other along the lines of a set of diaphanous, gossamer curtains. There is no clear, visible line anywhere in the room to let people know where it is. However, every male knows instinctively the moment it is reached. At that line, we are no longer in "Affection." We are in "Sex." And, sex must follow if the expectations of the male, which, from his perspective are most reasonable, are to be met.

If this sounds to the average female reader like most men think that once you start with affection that sex is inevitable, the average male's response is simple. "Well, of course. And, your point is what …?"

Women often consider this male equation between sexuality and affection as "proof" of how "shallow" men are. But this attitude needs to be followed by three questions: *Who* made men like this? In *Whose* image were men created? *Who* put all that testosterone in men at the time of creation? Any woman who wants to complain about men's need for sexual fulfillment needs to make her complaint to the Creator Who made men as they are.

Women may never understand completely the need for sexual fulfillment that men feel any more than men will understand completely women's need for affection. Part of the sacrifice of love is the willingness to give without ever totally understanding why.

Lots of wives have complained to me that they "don't understand" their husbands' constant desire for sex. Frankly, I doubt that my wife always understands mine, either.

Newsflash for wives: Scripture commands you to *love* your husbands. It does *not* tell you to understand them. The Biblical principle is simple, "Each of you should look not only to your own interests, but also to the interests of others."[7] Ladies, this means satisfying your husbands' needs.

We do this regularly with our children. We give them toys, games, music and clothes, which we never would buy for ourselves and don't truly understand. We do this because *they* want them and it brings *them* joy. Regardless of whether men completely understand why affection brings joy to their wives, they are to give it, nonetheless. Likewise, whether women completely understand why sexual fulfillment brings joy to their husbands, they are to give it, nonetheless. We are here to satisfy each other's needs. Holding back because *I* don't need it, or *I* don't want it, or *I* don't understand it, is pure selfishness. Love is selfless. Holding back is nothing less than sin.

I have talked with several husbands who have been married for years and are in a state of misery.[8] We have talked about the problem of the "unloved woman who is married."[9] The same fate can befall the man who feels unloved because of the lack of sexual fulfillment. The wives of these men feel totally satisfied and these husbands feel trapped in a hollow, meaningless relationship. Indeed, one husband who had sex only once or twice a year (when his wife "permitted it"), said he felt as if he had only a paper marriage, the license and nothing else. Dr. Linda Waite and Maggie Gallagher have noted, "A sexless marriage is apt to be viewed as a 'lie' or a 'pretense' or at best a divorce waiting to happen."[10]

Dr. Patricia Love and Jo Robinson report the comments from a group of men about what it was like to have their wives reject their advances time after time. Their pain and disappointment were palpable:

LENNY: When my wife shows no interest in sex, I feel empty, sad, discounted, left out, separate ...
TREVOR: I feel worthless. It has to do with my total being.
FRANK: I feel frustrated, angry, irritated.
MARK: I feel embarrassed.
JOHN: Rejected. It's castration.
TREVOR: Humiliation.

MARK: You know, the lack of response doesn't necessarily start in bed. I can read it about a mile and a half away when the no sign is up. I don't have to wait until I get in bed. I already know. So I feel depressed throughout the day.

DAN: There's a sign that says, "In case you wondered, the answer is no!" [Group laughter]

STUART: I feel helpless. When I know my wife is going to turn me down, there's nothing I can do. That's an awful feeling.

DAN: I truly desire my wife. I would like her to desire me. Is that too much to ask?"[11]

Life for a man without the male version of affection can be bleak, indeed.

Three Thoughts about Sex Every Woman Needs to Know.

First: The vow to remain sexually faithful in marriage applies equally, both to men and women. The effect of keeping that vow, however, can be very different. Women can receive affection from a multitude of sources, as we pointed out in chapter 10, although most women still want their primary source of affection to be their husbands. But husbands have one, and only one, source of the male version of affection: their wives. Because a woman can receive affection from many sources, she can have most of *her* needs met; while the husband, whose only source of sexual fulfillment is his wife, is left high and dry, living in a world totally void of any affection.

I have asked groups of wives whether they get some affection from people outside the marriage (coworkers, neighbors, etc.), and the answer always is an obvious, "Yes." When I ask whether there is any moral problem with that, the answer is an equally obvious, "No." Then I ask whether they would mind their husbands receiving some of the sexual satisfaction they need (the male form of affection) outside of marriage (coworkers, neighbors, etc.). The wives always are appalled that I even would ask. The question *is* appalling, but it underlines the male-dilemma when he wants to be sexually faithful and she refuses sex. It also underlines the wife's responsibility. Since both God[12] and she insist on her being the only source of the male style affection (i.e. sex) for her husband, then she needs to get busy doing it.

Second: Men spend so much time thinking about sex for the same reason women spend so much time thinking about giving and receiving affection. Women want men to spend time showing them affection because spending time on what *she* considers important means her husband thinks she is important. Men want women to spend time on sexuality for the same reason. Spending time on what *he* thinks is important means his wife thinks he is important.

Third: Attitude is everything. At a married couples' retreat I once asked a woman, who loved white roses, to consider this hypothetical situation:

Suppose your husband comes home one evening with a dozen perfect, long- stemmed white roses. He comes to you and with a soft voice says, "Honey, I love you more than you can know. The first three shops I went to didn't have flowers as perfect as you, so I drove across town to a shop I had heard about. I finally found these. I love you so much." He hands them to you, then hugs you.

As I was describing the event she got a faraway look in her eyes and her face flushed slightly. I asked her how she would react. She still had the dreamy look, then said in a soft, thick voice, "I'd do him right there on the kitchen floor." She instantly realized what she had said, straightened up in the chair, and quickly added, "Oh, I didn't mean that." However, her husband and everyone else in the group knew she had.

I then asked the same woman her thoughts about a second setting:

Suppose your husband came home with the same flowers, from the same shop. But, when he arrived home, he simply snarled, "Here are your darn flowers," threw them down on the kitchen counter, then stomped out of the room.

The woman looked at me in disbelief. "I'd either pitch them out or throw them at him."

I asked, "Why? They're the same flowers, aren't they?" Her answer was direct, "The flowers were the same, but the attitude is a slap in the face. He doesn't love me. It's all duty, no love."

I then turned to her husband who had been listening with interest. "Let me give you a hypothetical situation," I said.

Suppose you come home from work, and taped to the back door is a note in your wife's handwriting. It says, "Darling, the kids are spending the night with my folks. Come in and see if you can find me." You go into the house and there on the floor is one of your wife's shoes. A few feet further is the other shoe. Eight feet beyond that is her blouse. You follow the trail and find her skirt, followed by her slip. Next, you find her pantyhose at the foot of the stairs. At the head of the stairs you find her bra, and at your bedroom door are her panties. You open the bedroom door and inside you find soft music playing, scented candles burning, and your wife lying out on the bed, dressed in nothing more than a look of pure lust on her face.

I asked the husband, "What would be your response?" He was blushing crimson red and smiling ear to ear. "Are you kidding?" was all he could stammer.

I then asked the husband, "Well, let me change the situation slightly."

Suppose you're "engaged," on top of your wife "doing your thing." Your wife looks up at you and says, "Honey, can you move your shoulder a little? I'd really like to finish reading this magazine article."

He responded, "That would end the event for the night. I wouldn't even want to finish. It would probably be a week before I talked to her, I'd be so angry."

I asked, "But, why? It's the same sex, isn't it?" He glanced at his wife and paraphrased her words, "It's like she said. The attitude would be a slap, but a little lower than the face. She doesn't love me. It's all duty, no love."

Scripture tells us, "God loves a cheerful giver."[13] The same concept appears in Proverbs, "A generous man will prosper; he who refreshes others will himself be refreshed."[14] The context of these passages generally refers to financial giving. The principle is the same, however. Attitude is everything. Actions of either affection or sexual fulfillment given out of a sense of obligation, given grudgingly, or in anger are not affection at all.

I have talked with a number of clerks in stores specializing in "intimate apparel for women."[15] They all say that about 75% to 80% of the purchases are by men for their women. Not only is very little bought by women, worse yet, it appears from my discussion with men that most of the sexy stuff they buy for their wives somehow gets "lost" in the back of the bottom dresser drawer, never to be seen again. This is sad. Not only are a lot of women failing to act alluring toward their husbands as did Shulamite, who went to great lengths to prepare for a passionate sexual encounter,[16] but even when they are given the tools to do it (here the lingerie) they still miss the point.

I mentioned this in a conversation with a woman at a church gathering several years ago. Her response was an angry defense. "I would *never* humiliate myself by wearing stuff like *that*! I would look like a complete fool!" she insisted. This was a fascinating response, given the circumstances. The woman was decked out in a clown's costume, complete with oversized shoes, a bright orange wig, white make-up on her face with red paint making her lips look twice their normal size, and a set of fake buck teeth. She was on the floor playing with a couple of four-year olds. With children she was comfortable wearing a ridiculous costume, and humbling herself by getting on the floor to play at their level.

The woman was saying, "Yes, I can look foolish for kids, but when it comes to my husband, the person for whom I have vowed before God to humble myself, the person for whom I have vowed to sacrifice, the person that Scripture says owns part of my body, that I will *never* do. With these children, I can put their needs over my own. With my husband, *my* needs come first." Women who take this position through their actions are not following Scripture. Another word for this attitude is "Sin."

From Peek-A-Boo to Chase, Adult Style

Newsflash to wives: When your husband buys you that topless, bottomless, backless, see-through bit of nothing, an important event is taking place. To understand the event, think back to your experience with very young infants. What is the first game a child plays? Peek-a-boo. The game is simple: The infant covers his eyes and can't see you. Since he can't see you, he believes you cannot see him, either. He's hiding. He uncovers his eyes to discover you looking at him, with a big smile on your face saying, "Peek-a-boo!" The child is delighted.

What game does this turn into as the child gets older? Chase. Every child eventually tugs on his mom or dad's sleeve, and says, "Chase me," then runs off. Obviously, the child does not want to win. In fact, if you don't chase him, he will come back, tug on your sleeve again and say, "Mommy, you forgot to chase me." He *wants* you to chase him *and* catch him. Chasing the child means that he is of value, worth going after, something which should not be lost.

We never outgrow our desire to play chase. We *want* to have someone value us enough to go after us, chase us, take the time and energy to seek us. This, to a large degree, is what women want when they want their husbands to romance them. Romance is the adult *female* form of chase.

Newsflash to wives: When your husband buys you all that sexy stuff, he is asking you to chase him.

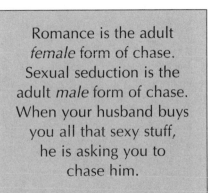

Romance is the adult *female* form of chase. Sexual seduction is the adult *male* form of chase. When your husband buys you all that sexy stuff, he is asking you to chase him.

Advertisers understand this. Look at all the bill boards and magazine ads showing a woman dressed in a provocative outfit, cut so low that half of her is falling out. What's the message? Men, if you use this product, the women will be chasing after you! You will be irresistible! Sure this is silly. But marketing executives spend millions upon millions of dollars on this type of ad every year because they know it works. Men want to be chased. Sexual seduction is the adult *male* form of chase.

Women who refuse to wear these outfits, or grudgingly wear them only once, then lose them in the back of the dresser drawer, are saying to their husbands, "I do not wish to chase you. You are not of enough value for me to chase you." Obviously, this probably is not the message women *intend* to send, but it is the message their husbands receive. That is not the message of love any wife should be communicating to her husband if she is following Scripture.

WHAT IS SEXUAL FULFILLMENT FOR MEN?

Sadly, most women confuse sexual fulfillment with sex. It's easy to do, because sexual fulfillment often involves sexual intercourse. But, not always, and not inevitably. And, that is where it gets tricky for many women.

Newsflash to wives: Sexual fulfillment includes sexual intercourse, but it encompasses much more. Sexual fulfillment is the larger context of showing your husband that he is of value as a sexual being and that he is sexually desirable. There definitely is a physical aspect to the process, but to be fulfilling, a man needs to feel wanted sexually. A survey of 5,000 men found that 77% of men listed "the intimacy" and "eroticism" as what they enjoyed "most about sex." Only 16% listed the orgasm.[17]

Sexual fulfillment for most men means being teased, flirted with, and seduced on a day-to-day basis. Sexually fulfilling behavior is made up of words and actions that tell husbands that they are sexually attractive and valued. Most husbands want their wives to be thinking of them in a sexual sense.[18] Women want their husbands to think of them regularly and value what they value. That is part of showing affection. Likewise, men want their wives to value them sexually and to show they are thinking of them by being sexually teasing on a regular basis. This can be done in a variety of ways, including giving a knowing look, making a sexy comment, taking a quick grope, wearing sexy lingerie, being seductive in bed, buying small gifts that have a sexual overtone (such as cologne), or occasionally setting up times to have sex in unusual situations as Shulamite did in the Song of Solomon.[19]

> Sexually fulfilling behavior is made up of words and actions that tell husbands that they are sexually attractive and valued.

How often do men want to be chased sexually by their wives? To answer this, ask another question. How often do women want to receive affection from their husbands? The answer to the second question is "all the time." The answer to the first question also is "all the time." Men do not want to *have sex* "all the time." But, they do want to be *valued sexually* all the time.

A word of caution is needed. While women want a constant stream of affection, there are other things to do in life. There is work to be done, which cannot be interrupted constantly by hearts and flowers. Even during work, however, a kind word of appreciation is valued. Men, also, want to be constantly thought of as sexually valued. But, they, too, have other work to do, which cannot be interrupted constantly by their wives parading around the house in a see-through teddy. Even during work, however, an occasional comment letting him know he "still has it" can do wonders.

"WAS IT AS GOOD FOR YOU AS IT WAS FOR ME?"

To be valued sexually, however, means a man must feel he is sexually competent. Imagine for a moment a couple that has just had sex. One of them asks the other, "Was it as good for you as it was for me?" It takes no genius to realize that the person asking the question is the husband. In fact, that question is so closely associated with male thinking that it is nearly a joke. What many wives fail to do, however, is ask why men would ask such a question? The answer is profoundly important. A great deal of sexual fulfillment for men is the feeling that they are competent as a sexual partner and, therefore, able to provide pleasure to their wives. It is not fulfilling for the typical husband if he has an orgasm and his wife is lying there bored and clearly not having a good time.

A *Men's Health* survey reported that for 99% of men sexual satisfaction for their partners was important to them. Indeed, fully 73% said their partners' orgasms were "priority number one" in sexual contact, while only 1% said they were of no importance. I have asked a number of men about this issue. Everyone of them agreed that if he had sex with his wife and only one of the two of them could have an orgasm, he would prefer it be his wife who has the orgasm, not himself. As marriage therapist and author, Michele Weiner Davis, has noted, "Women often underestimate how important it is to so many men to satisfy their wives sexually. To men, sex is not just about receiving; it's about giving."[20]

This should not be hard for women to understand if you think "woman" for a moment. How many women like to be thought of as competent home-makers? As affectionate people? Don't women believe they will be more respected as home-makers or as affectionate if others enjoy being in their homes or enjoy the signs of affection they demonstrate? Women tend to be nurturing by nature. God made them that way. As a result, a woman feels good when people talk about what a "kind, caring" person she is, or "what a nice home she has." Most women go out of their way to be caring when they invite someone into their home. It is more important that the guest have a good time than the hostess. That is why the hostess might say at the end of the evening, "I hope you had a good time."

Now, think "male" for a moment. Men want to be valued as sexually desirable. Most men believe that they cannot be sexually desirable if they are not sexually competent.

Newsflash to wives: When your husband invites you to have sex, he is inviting you into his world. For most men it is very important that you have a good time when you visit where he lives much of his life. That is why, afterward, he might say, "I hope it was as good for you as it was for me." It's his way of saying, "I hope you had a good time visiting where I live."

BUT, HOW DO I SHOW SEXUAL INTEREST TO MY HUSBAND ...?

Ladies, if you're having trouble coming up with ways of showing sexual interest in your husband in ways he will understand, try the following list. One way of doing this is to ask your husband to read this list to you and tell you which ones he would like you to do.

1. Wrap a "fantasy gift box" for your husband for a special occasion (Christmas, birthday, wedding anniversary, Ground Hog

Day, Johnnie Appleseed Day (March 11), St. Patrick's Day, etc.) In the box put a new, *VERY* sexy nightie for you to wear, and some scented candles.

2. For your next dinner party wear nothing under your dress. AFTER you arrive tell him what you are NOT wearing.

This suggestion comes from *The Sensuous Woman,* in which the author relays the story of "Janet, who is so respectable and ladylike in her looks and behavior she would make Emily Post seem like a wanton in comparison.

"One Saturday night recently Janet purposely delayed dressing until the very last minute for the dinner party she and her husband were attending. She was so short on time she had to finish applying her make-up in the car and, as they drove up their host's driveway, she was putting on her earrings and gloves. However, Janet stepped from the car bandbox-perfect in her appearance, beautifully groomed and elegantly gowned. She delivered her bombshell as they stood on the steps ringing their host's front bell.

"Just as the door started to open and it was too late to retreat, Janet grabbed her husband's arm and gasped, 'Oh, Dick, I was in such a hurry, I forgot to put on my panties!'

"All evening Dick kept picturing what his very ladylike wife looked like under her proper dress. He wouldn't let another man near her and by the time they started home he had become so excited by Janet's tantalizing and secret nakedness that he couldn't wait to make love to her. They stopped at a motel."[21]

3. Leave a note on his steering wheel for him to find as he leaves for work that you would like to make love that night ... and remind him to drive very carefully.

4. If you are going to have lunch at home with your husband, arrive a couple of minutes early. Leave a note on the door, "I'm waiting .....!" Then start undressing, leaving a trail of clothes to the bedroom. See whether he can find you and figure out what you have in mind.

This was suggested by a woman whose husband is a police officer. She said he had a great deal of fun "following the clues" and they had a wonderful time.

5. Give your husband a love pat on the rear end and tell him you love him.

6. Fix dinner at home <u>alone</u> with everything done prior to the meal and a minimum amount of clean up, soft music, candles and soft lights as a surprise. Wear your shortest skirt, heels ... and <u>NOTHING ELSE!</u>

The author of *The Sensuous Woman* notes, "A young housewife I know occasionally serves dinner to her husband wearing absolutely nothing above the waist. As a topless hostess she's a great success, for they haven't gotten as far as the dessert course yet."[22]

7. Fix the same meal with the same atmosphere and wear your nicest, most feminine blouse, high heels ... and <u>NOTHING</u> else. (... a garter belt, and hose are acceptable. If you are exceptionally modest, add a G-string.)

8. Send your husband a love letter at work, or leave it in his briefcase or lunch box. Mark it "personal." Tell him how much you enjoy making love with him and how sexy he is. Make it as explicit as you can.

9. Wrap up a nice box for a special occasion (Christmas, Glen Campbell's birthday, April 22, etc.). Put in a can of whipped cream and a note, "Use this <u>ANY</u> way you like ... I'd love it."

10. Give your husband a <u>full</u> body massage for a special occasion, like The Anniversary of Man's First Landing on the Moon, July 20, 1969, etc. Have soft music, low lights, a candle burning and a warm room. Talk softly, telling him how nice each part feels.

11. Buy some non-toxic paints. Wrap them up for a special occasion (International Left-Hander's Day, August 13) with a note, "We've painted the town. How'd you like to paint me? ... and then help wash it off when appropriate."

12. Invite your husband into the shower with you; ask him to wash you, and let you wash him. Make sure neither of you misses anything! If you have a small shower stall, all the better!

13. On your way home some night, or after you arrive, tell him you love him, that he's the sexiest guy in the world and you feel blessed that God sent him into your life ... in part because he's so sexy.

14. Keep yourself clean, neat and well-groomed, with hair done and make-up on to the extent possible and wear feminine lingerie as often as possible: lace, silk, sheer. Remember, men are visual creatures. Try to look good for your husband as much as possible.

15. At dinner hug your husband and whisper to him that you'd like to go to bed early. Then kiss him and pat him on the rear end. See whether he can figure out what you have in mind.

16. Wake him up early and make love before work. Send him off with a smile on his face.

17. Next dinner party or trip to the movies, make motel reservations, pack your sexiest nightie and a toothbrush in your purse, then tell him of your plan as you're leaving the party or movie. Make sure the babysitter knows where to find you!

18. On a warm summer night on the way home tell him to drive VERY carefully. Then take off your skirt or slacks ... and anything else you're brave enough to take off ... right in the car and tell him that you're ready when he gets you home ... then remind him to drive <u>VERY</u>, <u>VERY</u> carefully. This works best on lonely country roads.[23]

This suggestion came from an extremely conservative woman who teaches Bible studies and plays the organ for her church. When I expressed my surprise at the suggestion, since she always dresses very modestly, she added that it works best with a dress that buttons all the way from the neck to the hem.

I said, "You're kidding!"

She replied with a knowing grin, "Haven't you ever noticed the number of those kinds of dresses I wear," then turned and walked away without another comment.

19. If you ever realize you're both going to be free for an hour in the afternoon, call your husband and tell him to meet you at home ... or at a local motel.
20. Make a gift list of things you would like for a special occasion, like National Homemade Bread Day, November 17. Make sure it includes some really sexy things.

Don't limit yourself to this list. *Ask* your husband what would make *him* feel appreciated, valued, loved. Notice how this fits with the model wife from the Song of Solomon. This is behavior that shows outward confidence in your own beauty, and demonstrates a desire to be alluring and seductive toward your husband. Just like Shulamite in chapter 7 of the Song, you are planning your love-making and saying to him that he is worth the time involved in the planning. In the end, he will love you for it.

THE LAW OF SCREEN SAVERS

Husbands like sex. Husbands are visual. Wives like husbands. Wives want their husbands to think about them.

Newsflash to wives: This is not rocket science, so let's connect the dots. Use highly sexual, highly visual situations to keep your husband thinking of you.

This gets us to the Law of Screen Savers. Most computers have screen savers. If the computer is not being used for a short period of time, the screen saver automatically comes on. It usually is a set of repetitious pictures, or a blank screen with the same message slowly scrolling across it, over and over again. When men have nothing to think about, they often go into the "screen saver mode." It's not that they want to. It's automatic. They start thinking back to some event they really enjoyed or forward to some adventure they are anticipating with joy. If you want your husband to be thinking about you, make yourself the object of his "screen saver."

Creating a "screen saver" for your husband is easy. Just think male. Males like sex. Males are visual. (Yes, I know I just said that, but were you *really* paying attention?) What you need to do is provide your husband with highly sexually-charged visual images of you. It will keep him thinking of you for a long time.

Here are a few screen savers I have heard of from various couples. (All the names are fictional. They were picked simply to give alphabetical order.)

1. Anne met her husband for lunch in a bright yellow raincoat. She had nothing on under it. She drove him home for "a quickie" over the lunch hour.

2. Beth arranged to have their children gone for the evening. She met her husband at the door naked, stripped his clothes off and had sex with him right there on the floor. They then had a quiet dinner together without ever bothering to dress.

3. After dinner at a restaurant where Clair and her husband were celebrating a wedding anniversary, she excused herself after the meal to use the restroom. When she returned and sat down again, she reached her hand over to her husband, and put the very sexy pair of panties she had been wearing into his hand. She smiled and said, "I don't want these getting in the way later."

4. Late one night when it was storming, the lightning providing a major light show, Doris led her husband naked out to their screened-in back porch. With the wind occasionally blowing the mist from the rain on them they had sex.

These are events the husbands never will forget. When nothing is happening, even months later, these men have reported thinking of the situation and their wives. But then, isn't that what their wives wanted in the first place?

WHEN TO SAY "NO" TO SEX

Every woman will have a time when she simply is not interested in sex. It's the wrong time of the month. You are starting to come down with a cold and feel terrible. You have had a miserably hard day and are physically and emotionally exhausted. Now your husband wants to have sex and you don't. But you want to show love to your husband. There are at least three possible answers, two Biblical, one not.

#1. Just say "No."

This response is not Biblical. Love is sacrificial and understanding, and communicates in a way that "may impart grace to those who hear."[24] Simply saying "no" takes care of *your* needs, but totally trashes *your husband's* needs. Men and women use language differently. Men hear "no" in this setting as a rejection of them personally.[25] A woman once told me that in these settings wives are "not rejecting *him!* She is not receptive to the *activity.* Men are notorious for their bad timing." Unfortunately, she missed the point. Her statement is a correct reflection of how most *women* feel. It is completely wrong about how most *men* feel.

After conducting a workshop on marriage at a local church I was talking to one of the couples. The wife went through a long explanation that *her* husband does not feel "personally rejected" when she says "no" because "he understood."

When she was finished, I turned to her husband, who had stood patiently listening to the explanation. "So, how *do* you feel at those times?" I asked.

"Personally rejected," he answered in a very matter-of-fact tone.

The wife was shocked. "Why didn't you tell me?" she asked him.

He looked at her and answered, "Because it hurt too much to talk about."

Newsflash to wives: Sex is a man's expression of love and affection. If you say "no," *he* is *hearing* that you don't love *him.* If you do not want him to feel rejected, you need to say "no" in a way that *he* understands it is "no" to sex, but *not* "no" to *him* as a person.

#2. "No" with a rain check.

Saying "no" *and* adding a time when you will be available for sex, will be far more acceptable, and far less threatening to your relationship. For example, instead of "no," try:

- "Not tonight, honey. I'm really tired. How about tomorrow (Tuesday / Wednesday / this Friday, etc.) night. I really will be in the mood then."

- "Not tonight, honey. I'm coming down with a cold and feel terrible. I should be feeling better in a couple of days. Let's do something then. You plan the details and I'll look forward to the surprise."

- "This isn't a good night. My period started this morning and I'm suffering with cramps. You're such a sexy guy. You just get some rest. You're going to need it on Friday night when I make this up to you."

The Rain Check Rules

There are three rules about giving sexual rain checks. These rules cannot be over-emphasized, and they must *never* be broken.

• **First, *ALWAYS* keep the rain check.** If you "forget," not only do you lose credibility, but your husband will take it to mean that remembering things important to him is not important to you. Most women would feel hurt if their husbands "forgot" their birthdays or wedding anniversaries. "Forgetting" to follow up on a rain check means the same thing to your husband.

• **Second, *you* should be the initiator when that day arrives.** Indeed, at least once, preferably on the morning of the day the rain check is due, *remind* him of it, and make sure he knows you'll be ready. Don't worry; he does *NOT* need reminding. The purpose of the reminder has nothing to do with your husband's memory. It is a powerful statement to him that he is sexually attractive and that you will be acting on the rain check. Moreover, this will become a "screen saver" for him all day, which means he will be thinking of you all day.

• **Third, hug your husband and kiss him,** assuming you don't have a communicable disease, in a way that tells him you would really like to be in the mood and that you find him sexually attractive.

#3. Mercy Sex

Whenever I mention mercy sex to a group, I am always greeted with laughter. The phrase itself sounds a bit silly. Yet it makes sense, and is Biblically sound.

We all do things we don't want to do. We do them for different reasons. With those we love we often do things we normally would not do, but we do them simply because the person we love needs it at that moment. Our children, parents, and friends all call upon us to do things we really would prefer not to do. But, we do them because that's what love does. It sacrifices joyfully.

All believers are called upon to show mercy. God tells us that He "desires mercy"[26] in our dealings with others, indeed, that we are to "love mercy."[27] Mercy is "a kindly abatement of what we might justly demand, and a hearty desire to do good to others."[28] Jesus emphasizes mercy by saying in the Sermon on the Mount that it is one of the primary characteristics of members of His kingdom.[29]

One marriage counselor I know explains men's sense of urgency in sex as the result of DSB, i.e., "Deadly Sperm Backup." According to this counselor, if the male does not release his sperm he will suffer terrible, debilitating physical consequences. The counselor is kidding, of course. But, as with all humor, there is a large element of truth to it. Men often feel that if they don't have sexual release they will experience total turmoil inside. Mercy deals with that need. There are times when wives need to show that mercy.

Here again, attitude is everything. If you give your husband mercy sex with a sense of love, and feel the joy of the intimacy of the moment, he will love your gift. It will be like a perfect flower presented with love. If you do it grudgingly and with a sense of resentment, he will resent your every move.

A CLOSING THOUGHT: WHEN SEX IS *REALLY* IMPORTANT

There is an old saying about men. As men, all we do in our lives is provide, protect and procreate. Men, as women, like to think they are competent at what they do. Every man likes to think he's a good provider, a true protector of his wife and family, and a great lover. When a man believes that he has failed in one of these areas, his ego is under serious attack. If he has lost his job, even if it is through no fault of his own, in his eyes he no longer is the "good provider." He has failed in one of his prime purposes in life. Just as women need an extra hug when their hormones go on a rampage, men need an extra hug when their sense of self-worth gets shot down.

Newsflash to wives: A man takes it as a real boost to his ego when his wife gently makes sure he knows he still is sexually attractive to her.

A husband also can experience a profound sense of isolation around the time of the birth of a child. His wife is exhausted and busy with the baby. She is showering affection on the baby and has little time for him. She has no sense of sexual interest at this time and he's wondering what has happened to their relationship. The lack of sexual intimacy following the birth of a child contributes to a stressful period in any marriage.

Within the context of marriage, men and women see sex and affection as mirror images: exactly the opposite. Here is what it looks like.

Women: **Relationship gives meaning to the sex.**
Without a relationship there can be no real sex life. The sex that exists is hollow and meaningless.

Men: **Sex gives meaning to the relationship.**
Without sex there can be no real relationship. What does exist is hollow and meaningless.

After a child is born, the lack of sexual intimacy can undermine a husband's confidence in the existence of the relationship. Men understand that there will be a time during which their wives will be out of commission. But it is important to keep that time to what actually is needed for the physical health of the wife.

There are several important things a wife should do after the birth of a child to help her relationship with her husband:

- "Remember! Even though your hormone levels are at an all time low, his are just as high as ever. While he needs to understand your feelings, you also need to understand his.
- "Let your spouse know that he is still important. Men often feel they have been displaced by the baby as the main object of your affection.
- "Make time to be a couple at least on a weekly basis, even if it is only an hour of uninterrupted time together.
- "Ask your husband to install a good lock on your bedroom door to insure privacy when the baby gets a little older.
- "Do your best to let him know that you find him sexually attractive and important, even if you are not in the mood for sex at that time.
- "And above all, keep in mind when you say 'no' to your husband, he likely will take it as a personal rejection. To avoid this:
  - "Suggest things he can do to make it easier for you to say 'yes.'
  - "Only say 'no,' if you really need to. If possible, suggest ways to help him get you in the mood.
  - "If you say 'no,' tell him you still love him and give a rain-check. Then always act on the rain-check."[30]

Newsflash for wives: You can send a powerful message to your husband that you love him, and that your relationship is secure, and can also provide him with sexual release even when you are not able to have vaginal intercourse due to childbirth. Manual stimulation and oral sex are very acceptable alternatives in these circumstances.

From a man's point of view, sex always is important. It may be more or less at different times, but it always is there. Some men have told me that sexual fulfillment is so important that on those rare occasions when they do not feel it is important, they begin to get really worried that there is something wrong with them.

For many women, providing sexual fulfillment can be a real challenge. However, God will bless the marriage and the wife who joyfully meets this need of her husband. We can see ths blessing with Janet, the wife who "forgot" her panties before going to the formal dinner party with her husband. The author continued the story, "Janet confessed to me the next day that Dick had outdone himself as a lover that night and that she had never felt so wicked and sensual–and desirable."[31] The feeling of being "wicked" in this setting comes from having acted contrary to what society says how a "proper" wife should behave. She was acting as an alluring wife, however, like Shulamite, and God blessed her with a stronger marriage and a stronger sense of her own beauty.

DISCUSSION QUESTIONS

1. We tend to think of sex as something couples "do." Is it surprising that God would use sex not only for procreation, but also as a way to keep us physically and emotionally healthy, and to further bond us in our relationships with our spouses?

2. What are the implications for women that men *need* regular sexual relations, not that they simply "want" it? Does this start answering the question, "Is that all you guys ever think about?"

3. What is the similarity between men's view of sex compared to women's view of affection?

4. When men talk about sexual fulfillment, are they talking only about the frequency of sexual intercourse? If not, what more is involved?

5. What does sexual fulfillment look like on a day-to-day basis for most men? What do men want their wives to do? Should wives consciously work on initiating sex with their husbands? Why would this be important to husbands?

6. This chapter talks about how most men equate being accepted as a sexual being and being accepted as a person. Rejection of one is rejection of the other. What do you think about this view?

7. What is your response to the idea that a wife never should say simply "No" to her husband if he initiates sexual relations? Is saying "No" consistent with Scripture? Is saying "No" with a rain check consistent with Scripture?

8. Go through the list of suggestions for showing sexual interest. Talk through the list, allowing time to talk about each suggestion.

Note for wives: This is a time to listen. Try to learn about *your* husband. What does *he* like? If you have a question, it should be to ask more details of *how* or *how often* he would like the particular thing done. Avoid asking *why* your husband might like a particular sexual activity.

Suggestions for Couples:

Go back and read each of the **Newsflash** items. In this chapter *all* the **Newsflash** items are **Newsflash for wives**, so have the wife read them out loud. Have the husband comment on each **Newsflash for wives**. Does it apply to him? Would he like his wife to keep this **Newsflash** in mind and apply it to their relationship?

— 12 —

A Final Sendoff:

To Moonlight and Roses...
and the Bedroom

The spark plug of any engine is relatively small, but if it is corroded or completely absent, the engine will run roughly or not at all. The romance and sex life of a married couple is not the biggest part of the marriage ... unless it is going poorly. Then, like a corroded spark plug, it seems to cause the rest of the marriage to cough and chug at every turn.[1] Men and women have other needs. Women need meaningful conversation, honesty and openness, financial support, and commitment to the family, in addition to affection. Men need companionship in their recreation, an attractive spouse, domestic support and admiration, along with sexual fulfillment.[2] Both need respect.

We do 3,000 mile checkups for automobiles. We change the oil, check the plugs and points, and rotate the tires. With marriage, however, we keep chugging along, often ignoring even the gasoline level. Everything seems to get in the way. Work, community projects, the kids, home fix-up projects, and problems with the retirement account all take priority. As long as the marriage is intact, not healthy, but at least alive, we tend to assume it always will be there to work on later,...some other day,...maybe,...when we get around to it.

Steven Covey once said, "The main thing is to keep the main thing the main thing."[3] He noted that when people are on their death beds, they never regret not having spent more time at work. What they do regret is not having spent more time with their spouses and families. The romance and sex life of marriage is a major part of your relationship with your spouse and the foundation of your marriage. Ignore it and it will turn into a mountain of regret as the years go by.

Taking your car in for the 3,000 mile checkup takes time and costs money. Keeping the intimate part of marriage healthy also takes time and costs money. The difference is it will cost a lot less and be much more fun than maintaining a car.

GETTING DOWN TO WORK

The entire subject of this book actually is submission to God's beautiful plan for your intimate life. When you want to know something about your car, you look in the manufacturer's manual. If you want to keep the car running smoothly, you follow the maker's recommendations. You might say, you "submit to them." When you want to know about people, you also look to the Maker's manual, the Bible. If you want your relationships to run smoothly, you have to follow the Maker's recommendations. But, are you ready to submit to God's word? That is the "cost" of moving toward the beautiful intimacy He has in mind for your marriage.

God intended marriage to be a source of joy and fulfillment. While the Bible records a number of prominent individuals who remained single, and there were historical instances in which remaining single was encouraged,[4] the single life was "not the normal and expected biblical pattern."[5] Indeed, "it is not surprising that biblical Hebrew has no word for 'bachelor.'"[6] On only one occasion in the story of creation does God describe something as "not good" prior to the fall. The "not good" thing was that "it is *not good* that the man should be alone."[7] God is a God of love. He wants us to have a mate in most instances because He wants us to experience the full range of love in our lives. It is not good to have anything less than that.

The picture of marriage God gives in Scripture is absolutely consistent from Genesis through the New Testament. He wants husbands and wives to have no restraints, no reluctance, no inhibitions, no fears, and no selfishness in their intimate lives. God describes the "oneness" of husband and wife with the same word He uses to describe the "oneness" of Himself.[8] If there is to be "oneness" in marriage, there cannot be anything dividing the halves.

AN EXERCISE TO GET THINGS GOING

In chapter 10 we listed 20 ways husbands could show affection for their wives. In chapter 11 we listed 20 ways for wives to show sexual interest in their husbands. These lists are reproduced in the Appendix at the end of this book, with the addition of #21 for "OTHER." Copy them. The wife should take the list of ways of showing affection. The husband should take the list of ways of showing sexual interest. Each of you can go through the list and circle six you really like. (NO! You may *not* circle an entire page as "one" item.)

If you think of things that are not on the list, feel free to add them as #21 OTHER. (If you can think of 14, or 279 ideas not on the list, add them all. Don't feel limited by the list.) After you both have six marked, exchange lists.

Now, each of you has a list of six things your spouse would like you to do. Read through it. Take a few minutes to talk about it. First one, then the other, can take a marked item and talk a little about what makes it appealing. (Remember, this is not a time to ask "why" your spouse finds the idea attractive.)

Now that you have this information, what can you do with it?

- Remember, these are *not* demands. This is *information* about the person you love.
- Treat this information as a sacred trust. It is *not* something to share with *anyone* other than your spouse and God.
- Pray. Get God involved. He is the center of your marriage anyway. He already knows more than you do about any issue you

have. He also has a better idea than you can think of for resolving any difficulty.

- Over the next six months, try to add one item per month to the list of things you regularly do for your spouse. Do your best. But, *TRY!* Your marriage is too important to let it drift. TRY your utmost. Start with the easiest items first. Only add the more difficult requests after you feel comfortable with the simpler ones.
- If you only do part, and fall short of the entire request, pray and try again.

If you see your spouse trying to meet your requests, appreciate the effort. Even if the effort falls short, praise the attempt. And accept what is offered as a gift of love.

SO...? WHAT'S THE DIFFERENCE?

Biblical marriage is a covenant. It is not based on how we *feel* at any given moment. It is centered in God's word and founded on the concept of love. Once you enter into a covenant, you are obligated to fulfill your promise *no matter* what the other person does and regardless of any change of circumstances. This goes beyond the modern concept of contract, by which I promise to do something in return for your promise also to do something. In a contract, if *you* fail to act, then *I* no longer have to, either, because *you* breached the agreement. A covenant requires me to fulfill my promise *no matter what.* Contracts are based on rights. Indeed, my "rights under the contract" is a common phrase in contract law. Covenants are based on a promised obligation. In Scripture, the covenant is based on the obligation to love.

This is radically different from what the modern world teaches about relationships. Today, we concentrate on "rights." People demand their rights; fight for their rights; sue for their rights; march, shout and petition for their rights. We do this while ignoring the reality that every "right" I have creates a corresponding responsibility for you. If *I* have a right to something, *you* have a responsibility to provide it.

Whether we control our behavior based on rights or on covenant-love makes a world of difference in marriage. Consider the primary focus of each of the two models.

Rights Model

Theoretical Basis: Based on legalism and technicalities of language. The classic language of contract law is a "meeting of the minds" so I am sure of my benefits and obligations.

Central Focus: What *I* am entitled to have, *you* give me.

Motivation: *Self*-fulfillment; *you* meet *my* needs and desires.

Goal: Get the most *I* can for as little as possible, as soon as possible, since *my* rights are the most important things.

Primary Element: Taking for *my*self.

Covenant-Love Model

Theoretical Basis: Based on love and compassion. The classic language of love is a meeting of the hearts and a desire to give life to the other heart.

Central Focus: What I desire to give you.

Motivation: *Other*-fulfillment; *me* meeting *your* needs and desires.

Goal: *Give* the most I can to make *you* the best person *you* can be, so *you* can fulfill the potential God gave *you*.

Primary Element: Sacrificing for others.

The two models play out very differently in practice because of the priorities they represent.

Priorities in a Rights Model:

#1 Me | The Rights Model makes *me* the most important person. *My* needs always come first. After all, *I* have *my* rights!

#2 The Marriage | Since I get something out of the relationship that meets *my* needs and desires, the relationship will come second.

#3 My Spouse | My spouse is simply a provider, a source, as it were, of what I need. If my spouse fails to meet my needs, I have a right to find someone who can, since my rights are paramount.

Priorities in a Covenant-Love Model:

#1 The Marriage | I have made a covenant with God and with my spouse to do all that is necessary to maintain the relationship. No issue is more important than safeguarding the relationship. Covenants always define the primary obligation.

#2 My Spouse | My spouse's needs come second because love gives sacrificially and my spouse is the one I have vowed to love.

#3 Me | Sacrificial love always puts my own interests last. Such love gives without counting the cost or keeping records of who has received the most.

God is love and love gives. When He saw it was not good that the man should be alone, He gave woman to man. When He saw that mankind was hopelessly sinking ever deeper into sin, He "gave His only begotten Son" to mankind.[9] The form of love that describes God best, *agape*, is an all-giving, all-forgiving, inexhaustible love. It also is the love He wants us to give our spouses. The model of relationships He describes in His Word for husbands and wives is the Covenant-Love Model.[10]

God tells us a great deal about the Covenant-Love Model by spelling out in detail how men and women are to love each other in marriage. This is spread out from Genesis 2:24–25 through Proverbs, the entire Song of Solomon, into the New Testament in 1 Corinthians 7:3–5, Ephesians 5:21–33, and the epistles of Peter. Over and over we are told that we are to "love one another."[11] As Paul says, "Therefore love is the fulfillment of the law."[12]

AND, IN CONCLUSION...

God created man and woman, and established the institution of marriage. He blessed man, woman, and marriage, and declared them to be "very good."[13] Now, here you are, just the two of you, husband and wife. What do you need to do in your intimate life to be in step with God's will? Here it is in a nut shell:

As a husband, you should:

1. **Give compliments...lots of them.** Your wife needs to hear words that lift her up and show her that you respect her as a woman and a wife, that God values her and so do you. Never criticize her to others.

2. **Be protective of your wife and of your marriage relationship.** A woman needs a sense of security. She needs to know you'll always be a safe haven for her when she's having a rough time. She needs to know with certainty that your marriage is a top priority in your life. One of the greatest fears a woman can have is to worry that she will wake up five, 10, 20 years from now, and her husband won't be there. A husband's job is to do everything necessary to give his wife security.

3. **Be concerned about her needs.** Your wife needs to know that what she needs is important to you, something you will not trivialize. Having and showing this concern makes her feel valued and loved.

4. **Be patient.** Your wife needs a man who is stable, even through stressful times. Every woman knows she goes through emotional highs and lows. She wants you to recognize this part of her, accept it as who she is, and be patient with her at those times.

5. **Be romantic and give her lots of affection.** Affection is the life blood of most women. It comes in a hundred little things you can do to make sure she knows you're thinking of her, and find important what she considers important. Affection includes helping her...a lot. Helping her makes her feel accepted and significant.

6. **Demonstrate integrity, strong character and high ethical standards in everything you do.** Your wife wants to be intimate with you, but with intimacy comes vulnerability. Before she can relax to intimacy she needs to trust you completely.

7. **Pray with her and for her; say a blessing for her.** Your wife will love you for caring enough to petition God on her behalf. This is part of leading her, and the entire family, in a closer walk with God. Everything you do should demonstrate God's love in action.

As a wife, you should:

1. **Give compliments...lots of them.** Your husband needs to hear words that lift him up and show him that you respect him as a man and a husband, that God values him, and so do you. Never criticize him to others.

2. **Be self-confident and accepting of who you are.** Your husband needs you to be a woman who is not afraid of being a woman, who accepts herself as a beautiful creation of God's own making.

3. **Be alluring.** Men tend to be visual creatures. Your husband likes to see you looking beautiful and acting seductively, which includes often being nude in the privacy of your marriage.

4. **Be forthright in your desires.** Men like to seduce their wives, but every man also likes to know he is sexually attractive to the woman he loves the most. The woman who lets her husband know he is attractive to her instantly becomes an uplifting force in his life.

5. **Have a strong character and high ethical standards.** Most men want to share the little secrets of their hearts with their wives. Every husband needs to trust his wife implicitly. This requires unwavering character on your part. Character includes *not* telling others the innermost secrets of your husband's heart to others. You should never, ever make your husband the subject of gossip.

6. **Pray for him.** This is part of your role as wife and nurturer. Your husband will appreciate you for caring enough to petition God on his behalf. Your husband needs the help. Give it to him. Make it easy for your husband to be a spiritual leader.

However, these need to be more than "shoulds." God's word tells us that these are the actions that husbands and wives *are to do.* Now, it's up to you. Are you going to do what He wants or not? It's that simple. If you do, God promises that you will have His blessing. If you do not, then your marriage will suffer as you fail to receive God's blessings. If you do not, you also should quit calling Jesus "Lord" of your life.[14] Don't bother calling Him "Lord," if He has no say in what you do. And, don't complain if you don't get His blessing.

Neither God nor your spouse is a vending machine

God tells us what to do. It is by faith that we do it, knowing that He knows more than we do, and that He loves us. Keep in mind, however, that God is not a vending machine: Do what He says and out pops the prize from God. Instead, God promises a blessing for your family, your marriage, and your life. God will provide what you *need,* not necessarily

> Neither God nor your spouse is a vending machine.

what you *want*. He promises to be with you through the tough times. The blessing will be part of God's plan, not necessarily yours. Wait and watch. He will provide.

Your spouse also is not a vending machine: You cannot just put in a compliment (or any of the other things we are to do) and expect your spouse suddenly to become the most caring, affectionate husband in the world or the most seductive, loving wife you could ask for.

We all are sinners, including you and your spouse. People also suffer from physical and emotional illnesses. However, that does not change the nature of our covenant with God. We are to love our spouses no matter what. Scripture gives no exceptions.

The information in this book is analogous to tending a garden. When we marry we have the seeds of love that have started to absorb warmth and water. Although there are no guarantees that the seeds will germinate and produce a bountiful crop, it still is a good idea to water the seeds, keep the weeds from growing around them, and add fertilizer as needed. Creating an environment that encourages growth will produce a much larger crop than ignoring the seeds. The same is true of your marriage and your spouse. If *you* do everything possible, you create an environment of love and acceptance that will encourage your mate to grow in the direction God has in mind.

I have seen marriages turn around completely through the application of God's Word. No matter where you *think* your marriage is (on the verge of divorce or one step short of heaven) the application of God's word will improve your life, including the intimate areas of your life.

If you have doubts about the suggestions in this book, you should do four things.

First, be like the Bereans, who "received the message with great eagerness and examined the Scriptures every day to see if what [this book] said was true."[15] If it doesn't pass the scriptural test, forget the idea.

Second, pray. Pray a lot. God invites us to "pray continually,"[16] so why not take Him up on the invitation.

Third, start *doing* God's Word. God blesses those who do His will, instead of just talk about it. As you are doing, keep praying continually.

Fourth, watch and see whether God blesses what you are doing. If the suggestions in this book are in accordance with God's plan, and you follow them, you will receive a blessing. If these suggestions are not His will, there will be no blessing.

While you are going through all this, keep in mind that love is the central point of what God wants for us...and wants us to give to others. Now, go and love your spouse...intimately, passionately, emotionally, romantically, and sexually. Seek oneness with your spouse and pray continually. You and your spouse will be *doing* God's will in your marriage, and you and your marriage will reflect His love to others more often and in more ways than you ever could imagine. And, by the way, your love life, both in and out of the bedroom (or wherever else you wish to make love in the privacy of your marriage) will be better than it's ever been. Love much, love sincerely, love often, love romantically, love passionately, love always. That is God's plan.

DISCUSSION QUESTIONS

1. In your relationship with your spouse, have you ever found yourself putting off until later something you really should have done that would have helped your relationship? How can you put into action Steven Covey's statement, "the main thing is to keep the main thing the main thing"?

2. Go through the exercise suggested in this chapter. Were you surprised by any of the things your spouse would like you to do? Are you going to find any of them difficult? Have you taken this difficulty to God?

3. How do you see the difference between the Rights Model and the Covenant-Love Model as it affects your marriage on a day-to-day basis?

4. As you read about the things husbands and wives should be doing, which will provide you, as an individual, with the greatest challenge? Talk about strategies for doing what God has in mind for you in your marriage.

Appendix

SHOWING AFFECTION –
SOME SUGGESTIONS FOR HUSBANDS

1. Hold hands when you walk together.
2. Find a time when you can walk through the woods together ... holding hands.
3. Bring her a fresh cup of coffee while she's still in bed first thing in the morning.
4. Ask whether she would like a cup of coffee, a soft drink, or a snack when you are relaxing in the evening together. (Especially if you're getting yourself something.)
5. Give her a back rub after she's had a hard day ... without expecting sex to follow.
6. Use pet names for each other for which ONLY the two of you know the meanings.
7. Have a "favorite song" ... and request the DJ to play it.
8. Leave a note on her pillow, saying, "I miss you," if you're away for the night.
9. Put a sticky note on the mirror for her, saying, "I love you" or "I care for you."
10. Call her during the day just to tell her you love her.
11. Warm up her car for her before she leaves the house for the day and scrape off the windows if there is any snow. (For an extra point, leave a note on her steering wheel, saying "I love you." For five extra points, have the note say, "My love for you melts the ice and warms your way.")

12. Warm up her side of the bed when she is going to be getting in after you.
13. Get a baby-sitter for the kids; "kidnap" your wife, then take her to a bed and breakfast for an unexpected night.
14. Get a massage together as a gift.
15. Give her a sincere compliment when she looks really nice.
16. Open car doors for her.
17. In the evening offer to help with whatever needs doing instead of plopping down in a chair ... she had a long day, too.
18. Take her out to dinner as a surprise. (Even if she says "anywhere" is fine, McDonald's won't hack it. Take her some place a little special. It doesn't have to be expensive, just special.)
19. Go shopping with her ... or do something else *she* likes to do. (Remember: when you're shopping, you are not necessarily there to "buy" anything. The object is to spend time with *her*, discovering what *she* likes, trying to learn who *she* is.)
20. Hug her and touch her again, but NOT sexually and NOT expecting sex. Hug her and touch her just because you love her and want to be close to her.
21. Other. _____

_____

_____

_____

_____

SHOWING SEXUAL INTEREST – SOME SUGGESTIONS FOR WIVES

1. Wrap a "fantasy gift box" for your husband for a special occasion (Christmas, birthday, wedding anniversary, Ground Hog Day, Johnnie Appleseed Day, March 11, St. Patrick's Day, etc.) In the box put a new, *VERY* sexy nightie for you to wear, and some scented candles.
2. For your next dinner party wear nothing under your dress. *AFTER* you arrive, tell him what you are NOT wearing.

3. Leave a note on his steering wheel for him to find as he leaves for work that you would like to make love that night ... and reminding him to drive very carefully.

4. If you are going to have lunch at home with your husband, arrive a couple of minutes early. Leave a note on the door: "I'm waiting .....!" Then start undressing, leaving a trail of clothes to the bedroom. See whether he can find you and figure out what you have in mind.

5. Give your husband a love pat on the rear end and tell him you love him.

6. Fix dinner at home *alone* with everything done prior to the meal and minimum clean up, soft music, candles and soft lights as a surprise. Wear your shortest skirt, heels ... and *NOTHING ELSE!*

7. Fix the same meal with the same atmosphere and wear your nicest, most feminine blouse, high heels ... and *NOTHING* else. (... a garter belt, and hose are acceptable. If you are exceptionally modest, add a G-string.)

8. Send your husband a love letter at work (or leave it in his briefcase or lunch box). Mark it "personal." Tell him how much you enjoy making love with him and how sexy he is. (Make it as explicit as you can.)

9. Wrap up a nice box for a special occasion (Christmas, Glen Campbell's birthday, April 22, etc.). Put in a can of whipped cream and a note: "Use this *ANY* way you like ... I'd love it."

10. Give your husband a *full* body massage for a special occasion, like The Anniversary of Man's First Landing on the Moon, July 20, 1969, etc. Have soft music, low lights, a candle burning and a warm room. Talk softly, telling him how nice each part feels.

11. Buy some non-toxic paints. Wrap them up for a special occasion (International Left-Hander's Day, August 13) with a note: "We've painted the town. How'd you like to paint me? ... and then help wash it off when appropriate."

12. Invite your husband into the shower with you and ask him to wash you and let you wash him. (Make sure neither of you miss anything! If you have a small shower stall, all the better!)

13. On your way home some night, or after you arrive, tell him you love him, that he's the sexiest guy in the world, and you feel blessed that God sent him into your life ... in part because he's so sexy.

14. Keep yourself clean, neat and well-groomed, with hair done, and makeup on to the extent possible and wear feminine lingerie as often as possible: lace, silk, sheer. (Remember, men are visual creatures. Try to look good for your husband as often as possible.)

15. At dinner, hug your husband and whisper to him that you'd like to go to bed early that night. Then kiss him and pat him on the rear end. (See whether he can figure out what you have in mind.)

16. Wake him up early and make love before work; send him off with a smile on his face.

17. Next dinner party or trip to the movies, make motel reservations, pack your sexiest nightie and a toothbrush in your purse and tell him of your plan as you're leaving the party or movie. (Make sure the babysitter knows of this plan!)

18. On a warm summer night on the way home tell him to drive VERY carefully. Then take off your skirt (or slacks) ... and anything else you're brave enough to take off ... right in the car and tell him that you're ready when he gets you home ... then remind him to drive *VERY, VERY* carefully. (This works best on lonely country roads.)[1]

19. If you ever realize you're both going to be free for an hour in the afternoon, call your husband and tell him to meet you at home ... or a local motel.

20. Make a gift list of things you would like for a special occasion like National Homemade Bread Day, November 17. Make sure it includes some really sexy things.

21. Other. _____

_____

_____

_____

_____

Bibliography

Articles, Lectures & Pamphlets

Brooks, J.K., K.A Hoper, M.A Reynolds, "Formation of Mucogingival Defects Associated With Intraoral and Perioral Piercing: Case Reports," *JADA The Journal of the American Dental Association*, vol. 134, no. 7, p. 837 – 843, July 2003.

Chapell, Brian, *The Submissive Wife*, Alliance of Confessing Evangelicals, Mar/Apr 1995.

Covey, Steven, Smart Marriage Conference, Arlington, VA, July 11, 2002.

Declaire, Joan, "Your Marriage, Getting Better All The Time," *Reader's Digest*, p. 69, February, 2003.

Dothan, Trude, "Philistine Fashion," *Biblical Archaeology Review*, November / December 2003, Vol. 29, No. 6.

Fagan, Patrick F. and Robert Rector, "The Effects of Divorce on America," *Backgrounder, The Heritage Foundation*, No. 1373, p. 5, June 5, 2000.

Gardner, Michelle, MD, Ob. Gyn.; Dennis Shelle, MD, Pediatrician; and James E. Sheridan, (District Court Judge), "We've Had Our Baby ... Now What About Sex," Marriages That Work of Lenawee County, MI.

Gray, John, Smart Marriage Conference, Orlando, FL, July, 2001.

O'Neill, Hugh, "Get a Wife!", *Men's Health*, Rodale, Inc., Vol 16, No.5, June 2001.

Rochelle, Riley, "Dear People: The sexiest man alive is …," *Detroit Free Press*, Section J, p. 1, Dec. 7, 2003.

Turner, Megan, "Why Models Got So Skinny," *Cosmopolitan Magazine*, p. 167, August, 2001.

Bureau of Justice Statistics, "Violence Against Women," U.S. Department of Justice, January, 1994.

U.S. Department of Justice, "Violence by Intimates: Analysis of Data on Crimes by Current or Former Spouses, Boyfriends, and Girlfriends," March, 1998.

Waite, Linda, Ph D, "Does Marriage Matter," *Demography*, Vol. 32, No. 4, Nov. , 1995.

Wilson, James Q., "What To Do About Crime," *Commentary*, pp. 25-34, September 1994.

Audio Tapes

History and Customs of Marriage, Parish Leadership Seminars, Inc., Indianapolis, IN, 1982.

Pryor, Dwight A., *In His Image, Biblical Insights Into Love, Marriage, and the Family,* Center For Judaic-Christian Studies, Dayton, OH

Books

Bannon, Race, *Learning the Ropes*, Los Angeles, CA: Daedalus Publishing Commpany, 1992.

Barclay, William, *The Gospel of John, Vol I, Revised Edition*, Louisville, KY: Westminster John Knox Press, 1975.

Buttrick, George Arthur, ed., *The Interpreter's Bible, in Twelve Volumes*, Vol. 1, New York, NY: Abingdon-Cokesbury Press, 1952.

Buttrick, George Arthur, ed., *The Interpreter's Bible, in Twelve Volumes*, Vol. 5, Nashville, TN: Abingdon Press, 1956.

Canfield, Jack, Mark Victor Hansen, *Chicken Soup For The Soul*, Deerfield Beach, FL: Health Communications, Inc, 1993.

Cohen, Abraham, *Everyman's Talmud*, New York, NY: Shocken Books, 1995.

Dickens, Charles, *Oliver Twist*, New York, NY: Heritage Club, 1939.

Dillow, Linda, Lorraine Pintus, *Intimate Issues*, Waterbook Press: Colorado Springs, CO, 1999.

Dobson, James C., Ph.D., *Love for a Lifetime, Building a Marriage That Will Go the Distance,*, Portland, Oregon: Mutnomah Press, 1987.

Edersheim, Alfred, *Sketches of Jewish Social Life*, Peabody, MA: Hendrickson Publishers, Inc., 1995.

Ehlke, Ronald Cap, *People's Bible Commentary, Ecclesiastes, Song of Solomon*, St. Louis, MO: Concordia Publishing House, 1992.

Flowers, Karen and Ron, *Love Aflame*, Hagerstown, MD Review and Herald® Publishing Association, 1992.

Gagnon, Robert A. J., *The Bible And Homosexual Practice, Text and Hermeneutics*, Nashville, TN: Abingdon Press, 2001.

Garascia, Anthony J., *Rekindle the Passion While Raising Your Kids*, Notre Dame, IN: Sorin Books, 2001.

Gardner, Tim Alan, *Sacred Sex*, Colorado Springs, CO: Waterbrook Press, 2002.

Gottman John M., Ph.D., and Nan Silver, *The Seven Principles For Making Marriage Work*, New York, NY: Three Rivers Press,1999.

Graham, Billy, *The Holy Spirit*, Dallas, TX: Word Publishing, 1988.

Gray, John, Ph.D., *Men are From Mars, Women are From Venus,* New York, NY: Harper Collins Publishers, 1992.

Handford, Elizabeth Rice, *Me? Obey Him?*, Murfreesboro, TN: Sword of the Lord Publishers, 1972.

Harley, Willard, Jr., Ph.D., *His Needs, Her Needs*, Grand Rapids, MI: Fleming H. Revel, 1994.

Hocking, David & Carole, *Romantic Lovers, the Intimate Marriage*, Eugene, OR: Harvest House Publishers, 1986.

"J", *The Sensuous Woman*, New York, NY: Dell Publishing Company, Inc., 1969.

Jenkins, Natalie, *The Christian PREP® One Day Workshop Leader Manual*, Version 1, p. 55 – 58, based on the book by Howard Markman, Scott Stanley, and Susan Blumberg, *Fighting for Your Marriage*, San Francisco, CA: Jossey-Bass Publishers, 1994.

Joannides, Paul, *Guide To Getting It On*, Waldport, OR: Goofy Foot Press, 2000.

Kreidman, Ellen, *How Can We Light A Fire When The Kids Are Driving Us Crazy?*, New York, NY: Villard Books, 1993.

LaHaye, Tim and Beverly, *The Act of Marriage*, Grand Rapids, MI: Zondervan Publishing House, 1976.

Lamm, Maurice, *The Jewish Way in Love & Marriage*, Middle Village, NY: Johathan David Publishers, Inc., 1980.

Leman, Kevin, Ph.D., *Sex Begins in the Kitchen*, Ventura, CA: Regal Books, 1983.

Lenski, R. C. H., *The Interpretation of St. Matthew's Gospel*, Columbus, OH: The Wartburg Press, 1943.

Love, Patricia and Jo Robinson, *Hot Monogamy*, New York, NY: A Plume Book, the Penguin Group, Penguin Group, USA, Inc., 1995.

The Merck Manual of Diagnosis and Therapy, Robert Berkow, M.D., Editor, Rahway, NJ: Merck Sharp & Dohme Research Laboratories, Division of Merck & Co., Inc. 1977.

McManus, Michael J., *Marriage Savers*, Revised Edition, Grand Rapids, MI: Zondervan Publishing House, 1995.

Miller, Philip and Molly Devon, *Screw the Roses, Send Me the Thorns*, Fairfield, CN: Mystic Rose Press, 1995.

Morin, Jack, Ph.D., *Anal Pleasure & Health*, San Francisco, CA: Down There Press, 1998.

Morris, Desmond, *Intimate Behavior*, New York, NY: Kodansha International, Reprint edition, 1997.

Nee, Watchman, *Song of Song*, trans. Elizabeth K. Mei and Daniel Smith, Fort Washington, PA: Christian Literature Crusade, 1965.

Nelson, Tommy, *The Book of Romance*, Nashville, TN: Thomas Nelson Publishers, 1998.

Nelson's Illustrated Bible Dictionary, Nashville, TN: Thomas Nelson Publishers, 1986.

New Webster's Dictionary and Thesaurus of the English Language, Danbury, CT: Lexicon Publications, Inc., 1992.

Penny, Alexandra, *How To Keep Your Man Monogamous*, New York, NY: Bantam Books, 1989.

Penny, Alexandra, *How To Make Love To A Man*, New York, NY: Dell Publishing, 1982.

Rainey, Dennis, *Lonely Husbands, Lonely Wives,* Dallas, TX: Word Publishing, 1989.

Richards, Lawrence O., *The Teacher's Commentary*, Wheaton, IL: Scripture Press Publications, 1988.

Robinson, Julian, *A Guide to Human Sexual Display, Body Packaging*, Los Angeles, CA: Elysium Growth Press, 1988.

Shedd, Charlie and Martha, *Celebration in the Bedroom,* Word Publishing, Dallas, TX, 1985.

Tenney, Merrill C., ed., *The Zondervan Pictorial Bible Dictionary*, Grand Rapids, MI: Zondervan Publishing House, 1967.

The New Unger's Bible Dictionary, Chicago, IL: Moody Press, 1988.

Tingley, Judith, *Genderflex*, New York, NY.: AMACOM, a division of American Management Association, 1994.

Trent, John, Ph.D. *Love For All Seasons*, Chicago, IL: Moody Press, 1996.

Waite, Linda, Ph.D., and Maggie Gallagher, *The Case For Marriage*, New York, NY: Doubleday, 2000.

Warner-Davis, Michelle, *Changing Her Man, Without His Even Knowing It*, New York, NY: Golden Books, 1998.

Warner-Davis, Michelle, *The Sex Starved Marriage*, New York, NY: Simon & Schuster, 2003.

Warren, Rick, *The Purpose Driven Life*, Grand Rapids, MI: Zondervan, 2002.

Wheat, Ed and Gloria Okes Perkins, *Love Life For Every Married Couple*, New York, NY: Harper Paperbacks, 1980.

Whitehead, Barbara Dafoe, *The Divorce Culture*, New York, NY: Alfred A. Knopf, 1997.

Wilson, Marvin R., *Our Father Abraham, Jewish Root of the Christian Faith*, Grand Rapids, MI: Willaim B. Eerdmans Publishing Company, and Dayton, OH: Center for Judaic-Christian Studies, 1989.

Wilson, P.B., *Liberated Through Submission, The Ultimate Paradox*, Eugene, OR: Harvest House Publishers, 1990.

Wiseman, Jay, *SM 101*, San Francisco, CA: Greenery Press, 1992.

Zacharias, Ravi, *Can Man Live Without God*, Dallas, TX: Word Publishing, 1994.

Computer Programs and Web Sites

Barnes' Notes, Seattle, WA: Electronic Database, Biblesoft, 1997.

Biblesoft's New Exhaustive Strong's Numbers and Concordance, with Expanded Greek-Hebrew Dictionary, Seattle, WA: Biblesoft and International Bible Translators, Inc., 1994.

www.bmezine.com and www.bmezine.com/risk/index/html.

Interlinear Transliterated Bible, Seattle, WA: Biblesoft, 1994.

Jamieson, Fausset, and Brown Commentary, Electronic Database, Seattle, WA: Biblesoft, 1997.

Keil & Delitzsch, *Commentary on the Old Testament: New Updated Edition,* Electronic Database, Hendrickson Publishers, Inc., 1996.

Matthew Henry's Commentary on the Whole Bible: New Modern Edition, Electronic Database, Hendrickson Publishers, Inc., 1991.

The Wycliffe Bible Commentary, Electronic Database, Moody Press, 1962.

Song Lyrics

Lerner, Alan Jay and Frederick Loewe, *My Fair Lady,* New York, NY: Columbia Records, CBS Inc.

Statutes

Michigan Public Acts 1974, No. 266.

Michigan Public Acts 1988, No. 138.

End Notes

Introduction

[1] 2 Tim. 3:16.

[2] For example: David & Carole Hocking, *Romantic Lovers, the Intimate Marriage,* and Tommy Nelson, *The Book of Romance.*

[3] Gen. 2:18-25.

[4] Gen 1:28.

[5] The Rabbinic Period was about 400 B.C. through about 200 A.D. It might be noted that when Christ was asked what was the greatest commandment He did not quote any of the Ten Commandments, but rather referred to Lev. 19:18 and Deut. 6:4, which were among the 613 laws identified by the Rabbis. See Matt. 22:36–40.

[6] John 2.

[7] Cf: Isaiah 62:5, Jer. 2:2, John 3:28–29, Eph. 5:31–32, Rev 19:7, Rev 21:2, 9.

[8] King James Version (KJV).

[9] Dr. Linda Waite, "Does Marriage Matter," *Demography.* The article also notes that men have substantially more trouble with alcohol than women. Therefore, although the increase in problems is greater for women than men following divorce, the total number of problems remains larger for men as a group.

[10] Linda Waite and Maggie Gallagher, *The Case For Marriage*, p. 54 – 55.

[11] James Q. Wilson, "What To Do About Crime," *Commentary*, pp. 25-34, September 1994.

[12] Patrick F. Fagan and Robert Rector, "The Effects of Divorce on America," *Backgrounder*, p. 5.

[13] Part of the "political incorrectness" will be the use of traditional rules of English relating to pronouns. God will be referred to as "He" and "Him," since the Bible uses masculine pronouns. Keep in mind, however, the Biblical use of the masculine pronoun when referring to God is not meant to suggest that God, who is pure spirit, is "male." Also, unless the context implies otherwise, the use of "he" or "him" is not gender specific. The politically correct use of "he or she" and "him or her" makes awkward phrases which are difficult to read.

[14] Deut. 4:2, 12:32; Prov. 30:5–6; Rev. 22:18–19.

[15] By "romance life" I am referring to the feelings of affection and emotional connection between husband and wife.

[16] God will give us what we *need*, not necessarily what we *desire*. Our desires flow from the same human condition, flawed and sinful that it is, that got us into the messes we have made in our relationships in the first place.

[17] Acts 17:11-12.

Chapter One

[1] Actually, *all* marriages are "Biblical marriages." God created man, woman and the institution of marriage. All marriages are covenants before God, whether performed by a minister in a church or by the local judge at the court house. Cf: Prov. 2:17 and Mal. 2:14.

[2] Revised Standard Version (RSV).

[3] John Eldridge, *Wild at Heart*, p. 51.

[4] John Eldridge, *Wild at Heart*, p. 51.

[5] Maurice Lamm, *The Jewish Way in Love & Marriage*, p. 126.

[6] KJV. God is also described as an "ezer" in Psalm 30:10, 33:20, 40:17, 54:4, and 63:7.

[7] The word *ezer* (OT 5828) appears 21 times in the Old Testament. With the exception of Ezek 12:14, it is used only to describe God in His role as helper to mankind and woman in her role as helper to man.

[8] Dennis Rainey, *Lonely Husbands, Lonely Wives*, explains in reference to Genesis 2:18, "In the original text, the Hebrew word for 'helper' means *wholeness*," p. 119.

[9] Ibid, page 125. The Interlinear Bible transliterates it "Kanegadow" (OT:5048). Strong's defines it as: "a front, i.e. part opposite; specifically a counterpart, or mate."

[10] Dwight A. Pryor, *In His Image, Biblical Insights Into Love, Marriage, and the Family*, an audio tape set.

[11] We are still living in "Biblical times" since the Bible is as relevant and applicable today as ever. However, in this book, by referring to "Biblical times," I mean the time period when the Bible was written (i.e., the approximately 1,500 years from about 1,400 B.C. to about 100 A.D.). This is meant to be an estimated time period. This book does not address the subject of when the Bible was actually written.

[12] Pryor, op. cit., *In His Image, Biblical Insights Into Love, Marriage, and the Family*.

[13] Judith Tingley, *Genderflex*, p. 21 – 38.

[14] The differences between men and women described in this quote and in the remainder of the paragraph were taken from: Dr. James C. Dobson, *Love for a Lifetime*, p. 42.

[15] Gen 1:27, KJV.

[16] Genesis 1:4, 10, 12, 18, 25.

[17] Genesis 1:31.

[18] RSV.

[19] RSV.

[20] John Eldridge, *Wild at Heart*, p. 211-212. Italics are in the original text.

[21] RSV.

[22] KJV.

[23] Among them are Deuteronomy 10:20, 11:22, 13:4, 30:20; Joshua 22:5, 23:8; Psalm 119:31; Isaiah 56:4 and 6.

[24] Gen. 24:67.

[25] KJV.

[26] Deut. 6:4, "Hear, O Israel: The LORD our God, the LORD is one."

[27] John 10:30 (KJV)

[28] The following list is taken from: Natalie Jenkins, *The Christian PREP® One Day Workshop Leader Manual*, Version 1, p. 55 – 58, based on the book by Howard Markman, Scott Stanley, and Susan Blumberg, *Fighting for Your Marriage*.

[29] James 1:19. Cf: Prov. 19:20.

[30] Dr. John Gottman and Nan Silver spend an entire chapter on the subject "Let Your Partner Influence You" in their book, John M. Gottman, Ph.D. and Nan Silver, *The Seven Principles For Making Marriage Work*, Chapter 6.

[31] In Chapter 9 we will address the problem of dealing with differences as they relate to issues involving sex and romance.

[32] Alan Jay Lerner and Fredrick Loewe, *My Fair Lady*.

[33] Alfred Edersheim, *Sketches of Jewish Social Life*, p. 131.

[34] References to the "rabbis of Biblical times" in this book refer to the teachings of the rabbis in the Talmud and other Jewish writings of the period. Most of the teachings of the Jews were fully accepted by Jesus. See Matt. 5:17–18, 23:2–3. The profoundly important issue that Jesus *did* disagree with the rabbis was the identity of the Messiah.

[35] 1 John 4:8.

[36] Maurice Lamm, *The Jewish Way in Love & Marriage*, p. 119.

[37] Couples in this setting should consider Rev 3:20.

[38] There are situations in which divorce is the lesser of two evils. Domestic violence, unrepentant adultery, addiction to drugs or alcohol, or compulsive gambling may create situations in which remaining in the marriage is dangerous either physically or spiritually. Even in these instances, however, I never have seen anyone "enjoy" the divorce and describe it as a "good" event. It remains the lesser of two very bad options. Not every marriage is "put together" by God. But, every marriage is a covenant, which God has witnessed. (Mal. 2:14) Any time a covenant is broken, bad things will happen. They may be "less bad" than some alternatives, but they are bad, nonetheless.

[39] One last reminder to the reader. This is a use of the masculine pronoun, which is gender neutral. Christ died for the sins of both men and women.

[40] Peter uses a different word for respect than does Paul. Peter used *timao* (tim-ah'-o) NT:5091; Paul used *phobeo* (fob-eh'-o) NT:5399. *Timao* means to hold in the highest degree of esteem, to honor, to value highly or to hold precious. *Phobeo* means to be in awe of; i.e., revere, to hold in reverence. (See generally: Biblesoft's New Exhaustive Strong's Numbers and Concordance with Expanded Greek-Hebrew Dictionary.) I do not find any real difference between the two concepts any more than I understand the difference between defendants who were "intoxicated" and those who were "drunk."

41 Dr. Linda Waite, "Does Marriage Matter," *Demography*, Vol. 32, No. 4, 1995, p. 483.

42 The following citations are, respectively: Num. 14:18; Lam. 3:22 - 23; 1 John 4:8; Lev. 19:18; John 13:34-35; 1 John 4:7-8. In these and subsequent Bible quotations from the NIV, which use a pronoun to refer to God, the lower case will be used (i.e, he, his or him). This is to keep the quote faithful to the source. The general pattern of capitalizing these pronouns in the text will continue.

43 See also Exodus 34:6 - 7 and John 3:16.

44 See also Is. 1:17, Mic 6:8, Matt 22:36-40, Rom. 13:9-10, Gal 5:14.

45 Luke 10:29-37.

46 Another Greek word, *eros*, which can be translated as love, is the source of the word "erotic." *Eros* does not appear in the New Testament, but the concept of *eros* is apparent in the Old Testament in the Song of Solomon.

47 *Agape* appears 319 times in the New Testament in one of three forms: *agapao, agape* and *agapetos.* It is how God loves us (John 3:16) and how He commands us to love others (John 13:34–35). It is also the way husbands are to love their wives (Eph. 5:25).

Phileo appears 25 times in the New Testament. See, for example, Matt. 10:37 (love between parents and children), John 11:34–36, 20:2 (love between very close friends), and Matt. 6:5, Luke 20:46 (the love of symbols of status). The name for the city of Philadelphia, which means city of brotherly love, comes from the word *phileo.*

Epithumia is used 54 times in the New Testament in one of two forms, *epithumia* or *epithumeo.* See, for example, Luke 22:15 (Jesus eagerly "desired" to eat the Passover Meal with his disciples) and Romans 1:24 (which refers to "the sinful desires" of the heart.)

48 John 3:16.

49 John 13:34.

50 Eph. 5:25; Proverbs 5:19.

51 Eph. 4:29, 32.

52 Natalie Jenkins, *The Christian PREP® One Day Workshop Leader Manual,* p. 49.

53 In Abraham Cohen, *Everyman's Talmud*, referring to the word "torah," the author observes, "This Hebrew word, incorrectly translated 'law,' means 'teaching, direction.'" Introduction, p. xxxiv.

54 Psalm 1:2-3 and Psalm 119:105, respectively.

55 Cf: Matt. 19:17, 23:3, 28:20; Luke 6:46–49, 8:21, 11:28; John 8:31-32,15:10, 14, 15, and 17.

56 It goes without saying that over the centuries a great deal of evil has been done in the name of Christianity. Jesus defines a person who is a member of His Kingdom in the Sermon on the Mount. (See: Matt 5 – 7) It is apparent that many who *call* themselves "Christian" are not following His word and, as mentioned in the text, are patronizing and insulting Him. Jesus tells us of the final judgement on those people in Luke 13: 23–30.

57 Exodus 19:5.

58 See, for example, Gen. 26:5, Gen. 27:8, 13; Gen. 27:43; Gen. 28:7; Ex. 19:5; Josh. 5:6; Judges 2:17, and 1 Samuel 8:19.

59 The word "said," *'amar* (aw-mar'), can be translated as "command," "declare," or "demand." OT:559.

Biblesoft's New Exhaustive Strong's Numbers and Concordance with Expanded Greek-Hebrew Dictionary.

60 Gen. 3:12 TLB.

61 Clearly, there are situations involving emotional problems or mental illness in which this will not apply. However, it is good advice in the vast majority of situations.

Chapter Two

1 The idea that "all you need is love" is referred to as "Myth 1" by Barbara Chesser, in "21 Myths That Can Wreck Your Marriage." She also notes, "Erroneously, we believe that after we 'tie the knot,' we will automatically, effortlessly live in marital bliss 'till death do us part.' This is a dangerous myth, and anyone who lives by this fanciful notion is likely to live instead in marital blahs." P. 1.

2 1 Kings 4:32.

3 Like all great poetry, the Song is written in rich, picture language, presenting a panorama of events and feelings. Thus, a number of valid views of the Song are pos-

sible, which are completely consistent with Scripture. Many commentators have treated the Song as an allegory. (Watchman Nee, *Song of Song*, translated by Elizabeth K. Mei and Daniel Smith) *The Interpreter's Bible*, Vol. 5, p. 98, points out that the Song has been seen as an allegory, a drama, a series of secular love songs, a Syrian wedding ritual, and a Hebrew poem. It continues by noting, "Sermons preached from this book, in early, medieval, and modern times, have been based in the main upon the allegorical method, which in our day has been discarded as out of keeping with reality and good scholarship." Indeed, some modern authors refer to explaining the Song as a "theological metaphor" as "just nonsense." (John Eldridge, *Wild at Heart*, p. 33.) This book will treat the Song as the inspired word of God to men and women about marriage.

4 Song 6:13.

5 From Jamieson, Fausset, and Brown Commentary, Electronic Database. Some commentators, however, believe her name is a reference to where she was from, the town of Shunem. (*The Wycliffe Commentary*, Electronic Database.) Some writers prefer to call her "Shulamith," which has a more personal and feminine sound. (Karen and Ron Flowers, *Love Aflame*.)

6 Today, when we compare a woman to a fox, it is a wonderful compliment. But in Luke 13:31–32, after some Pharisees told Jesus that King Herod wanted to kill him, He began His reply, "Go tell that fox..." At that time "a fox" was contemptuous term, connoting both slyness and cowardice. (*The Wycliffe Bible Commentary*, Electronic Database.)

7 As mentioned above, Shulamite is the feminine form of Solomon. The Hebrew word for Solomon is Shelomoh (shel-o-mo'), OT:8010, which comes from the root word shalom (shaw-lome'), OT:7965, which means peace or prosperity. *Biblesoft's New Exhaustive Strong's Numbers and Concordance* with Expanded Greek-Hebrew Dictionary.

8 Song 5:1 - 15, 6:4 -9, and 7:1– 9a.

9 David and Carole Hocking, *Romantic Lovers*, p. 99.

10 At that time in history, and even until the last century, many people, including young men and women, had teeth missing.

11 The symbol of the neck in relation to character will be explained in detail in Chapter 7.

12 Song 2:1.

13 Linda Dillow & Lorraine Pintus, *Intimate Issues*, p. 183.

[14] Jer. 2:13, 17:13.

[15] John 4:10-11, 7:38.

[16] Rev.7:17.

[17] Keep in mind that what should be learned often should be limited to the subject and the tone. Many women's magazines, just as many men's magazines, give advice based on values that are not Biblically sound and can be harmful to marriage.

[18] Ex. 3:13-14.

[19] *Barnes' Notes*, Electronic Database, explains Ex. 3:14: " 'I am what I am.' The words express absolute, and therefore unchanging and eternal Being." The significance of the name, in this case God's name, can be seen in that sense throughout the Old Testament (Lev. 18:21, 19:12, 21, 6, 22:2, 22:32; Ezek. 20:39; Amos 2:7; Mal. 1:11-12). God tells His people not to "profane" His Holy name. *Profaning* means to make something common or ordinary. God is anything but ordinary. By "profaning God's name" a person says that the essence of God is simply ordinary; nothing to get excited about; common; don't worry about it; it will go away soon. God will not tolerate such treatment of His *name*.

[20] Gen. 17:5.

[21] Matt. 1:21.

[22] See: *Barnes' Notes*, Electronic Database, which notes, "The name Jesus is the same as Saviour." It can also be translated as: "Jehovah saves" (The Wycliffe Bible Commentary, Electronic Database.) or "Yahweh saves" (R. C. H. Lenski, *The Interpretation of St. Matthew's Gospel*, p. 49.)

[23] Song 2:9

[24] "His cheeks are like such a soft raised bed, and the impression their appearance makes is like the fragrance which flows from such a bed planted with sweet-scented flowers." Song 5:13. Keil & Delitzsch, *Commentary on the Old Testament: New Updated Edition*, Electronic Database.

[25] Ibid.

[26] Eph. 4:29.

[27] The issue of men's feelings about sexual issues will be discussed in much greater detail in chapter 11.

[28] Dr. Kevin Leman, *Sex Begins in the Kitchen*, p. 8.

Chapter Three

[1] John Gray, *Men are From Mars, Women are From Venus*, pp. 135-136.

[2] Alexandra Penny, *How To Keep Your Man Monogamous*, p. 82.

[3] Song 1:5-6

[4] "Why Models Got So Skinny," by Megan Turner, *Cosmopolitan Magazine*, August, 2001, p. 172.

[5] The process of making the model look better than life can be fairly elaborate. Before she arrives for the photo shoot, she has to spend hours sunbathing nude. (We can't have any strap lines from some other bathing suit.) Of course, they have to radically shave their pubic hairs. (We don't want any of those curly little devils sneaking out from under the suit line.) And the models need to wear loose clothing and no underwear on the way to the shoot. (We can't have any strap marks left from bras or panties to mess up the picture.) Then the model has to arrive early to make sure there is time for the make-up. Time of day is also important, since many photographers like the soft light of early morning, right after sunrise or just before sunset, rather than the harsh light of noon. When the photo shoot starts, the photographer is careful to pick just the right background, and the perfect lighting. If the lighting is not perfect, backlights or reflectors will be put in place to get rid of any shadows which might detract from the photo. We see one picture on the magazine cover. However, it is not unusual to shoot an entire roll of film at the same location to make certain at least one shot is perfect. The model often is told to move gracefully or to dance as a series of shots are taken, with the hope that one is just "right." After the film is shot and developed and the best photo is picked, it is sent to a touch-up lab, where the rest of the magic is done.

[6] "Kedar was a son of Ishmael (Gen 25:13). The tents of the nomadic tribe descended from him (Jer 2:10; Ps 120:5) were of black or dark brown goatskin. The hyperbolic reference to these tents emphasizes the darkness of the complexion of the girl. The curtains of Solomon must have been very beautiful; and notwithstanding her dark complexion, the bride is still lovely like them." *The Wycliffe Bible Commentary.*

[7] His enormous wealth is described in 1 Kings 10:14-15; 23-29.

[8] The results are (in centimeters): Bust: 14.00, Waist: 7.25, Hips: 12.75.

[9] Needless to say, many women are overweight, just as are many men. Indeed, obesity has been recognized as a major health concern in the United States. For health purposes, people who are overweight should lose the extra pounds. Heart disease, bad knees and adult-onset sugar diabetes are among the many problems associated with

excess weight. The body is the temple of the soul (1 Cor 6:19) and a gift of God. It is our obligation to try to maintain it as best we can, and that includes issues of weight. Recognizing a weight problem, however, is different from refusing to see the beauty God has given to each of us as a special gift.

[10] Song 2:1 KJV.

[11] "A literal translation of the Hebrew word *havatstseleth* indicates a bulbous plant instead of a woody vine or shrub belonging to genus *Rosa*." *The Zondervan Pictorial Bible Dictionary*, by Merrill C. Tenney, p. 667. See also *Jamieson, Fausset, and Brown Commentary*, Electronic Database, by Biblesoft, commentary on Song 2:1.

[12] *Nelson's Illustrated Bible Dictionary*.

[13] *The New Unger's Bible Dictionary* states, "'The fear of the Lord' is used for the worship of God, e.g., 'I will teach you the fear of the Lord' (34:11) and for the law of God (19:8-9)." (NOTE: these references are to Psalm 34:11 and Psalm 19:8–9.)

[14] Tim and Beverly LaHaye, *The Act of Marriage*, p. 104.

[15] Ibid.

[16] The issue of appropriate modesty will be addressed in more detail in Chapter 8. While women are to be "modest" in their dress (1 Tim 2:9–10), that is for outside the marital bedroom. Inside the sanctity of the marital bedroom "modest" dress includes being completely nude.

[17] Song 2:2 KJV.

[18] It is also a good idea, ladies, to remember that there are lots of women who enjoy the view of a nice set of buns on men. Women simply tend to be more subtle and less verbal about their observations.

[19] Ps. 34:1, Eph. 5:20, 1 Thess. 5:16–18.

[20] Song 2:3.

[21] David & Carole Hocking, *Romantic Lovers, The Intimate Marriage*, p. 49.

[22] RSV.

[23] In chapter 5 we will return to the early verses of the Song in which Solomon first demonstrated his concern for her concerns.

[24] In Chapter 12 we will be outlining in detail the difference between a "rights model" of behavior and a "love model."

25 Romans 13:8.

26 Don't worry, ladies; men have their own sets of insecurities which will be addressed later.

Chapter Four

1 Song 1:7.

2 "It was the custom of harlots to veil themselves (Gen. 38:14). True love wishes to avoid every appearance of unfaithfulness and impurity." Song 1:7-8. From *The Wycliffe Bible Commentary.*

3 It is unlikely that Solomon would have been out working as a common shepherd. However, the passage does not say he was working in that capacity. It simply indicates that he was with the flock for one reason or another.

4 Song 1:8.

5 Song 1:5–7.

6 1 Sam 16:7. See also 1 Peter 3:3–4.

7 *Matthew Henry's Commentary on the Whole Bible: New Modern Edition,* Electronic Database. See specifically, comments on 1 Sam. 16:6-13.

8 Ruth 3:11; Prov. 12:4, 31:10; Song 1:2–3, 7, 4:4, 8:10; Acts 17:11; and 1 Cor. 15:33.

9 We will be touching on the issue of character again in chapter 6.

10 Song 2:6.

11 In Scripture the right hand and arm are generally associated with power. See Ex. 15:6, Ps. 17:7, Ps. 20:6, Is. 41:10.

12 *Biblesoft's New Exhaustive Strong's Numbers and Concordance with Expanded Greek-Hebrew Dictionary.* OT:2263.

13 Eph. 5:25.

14 Mark 10:45.

15 Eph. 5:27.

16 See Eph. 5:22 and Eph. 5:21, respectively.

[17] See Matt. 7:3–5.

[18] As a group, women tend to like "fixing" their husbands. Dr. John Gray, *Men are From Mars, Women are from Venus,* addresses this inclination directly in a chapter 2, entitled "Mr. Fixit and the Home Improvement Committee."

[19] Song of Solomon 4:9, 10, 12 and 5:1.

[20] Song 2:14.

[21] Dr. Willard Harley, Jr. *His Needs, Her Needs,* chapter 5.

[22] Ibid, p. 60.

[23] From a lecture presented by John Gray at the Smart Marriage Conference, July, 2001, Orlando, Florida.

[24] Natalie Jenkins, *The Christian PREP® One Day Workshop Leader* Manual, Version 1, p. 52, based on Howard Markman, Scott Stanley, and Susan Blumberg, *Fighting for Your Marriage,* p. 42.

[25] For a straightforward discussion of this point see Dr. John Gray, *Men Are From Mars, Women Are From Venus,* p. 16–18.

[26] Song 1:2 KJV.

[27] Rom. 16:16, 1 Thess. 5:26, 1 Peter 5:14.

[28] Keil & Delitzsch, *Commentary on the Old Testament: New Updated Edition,* Electronic Database, commentary on Song 1:2.

[29] Song 4:16.

[30] Song 6:2-3.

[31] Song 7:2.

[32] Andrew Fletcher, quoted in Harold A. Bosley, *Sermons on the Pslams* (New York: Harper & Brothers, 1956), 40, as quoted in Ravi Zacharias, *Can Man Live Without God,* p. 3.

[33] 1 Cor. 13:5.

[34] Scripture does speak of the "rights" of the bride (Ex. 21:9-10), but that is in the context of an arranged marriage and the need to protect the wife if the husband did not fulfill his obligation of love to her.

35 For more detail on the differences between a "rights" model of relationships and a "love" model, see chapter 12.

36 This is alluded to in John 1:26-27 when John the Baptist told the Pharisees who had come to question him, "... among you stands one you do not know. He is the one who comes after me, the thongs of whose sandals I am not worthy to untie" NIV. The lowest slave untied the sandals. John was saying that compared to the Christ, he was not even worthy to be the lowest slave. See also William Barclay, *The Gospel of John, Vol I, Revised Edition,* p. 79–80.

37 John 13:14-15.

38 Luke 6:40.

39 Eph. 5:21. Some translations have verse Eph. 5:21 as a part of the preceding paragraph and Eph. 5:22 as the beginning of the new paragraph. The oldest manuscripts available, however, show verse 21 to be actually part of the same sentence as verse 22. Indeed, the word "submit" does not actually appear in verse 22. Paul clearly is talking to both husbands and wives when he speaks of mutual submission. This same pattern is followed in 1 Peter 3:1 (referring to wives) and 3:7 (referring to husbands), which both refer back to 1 Peter 2:13 and 2:18.

40 See John 13:34 and Luke 6:46.

41 Is. 1:19-20.

42 Ps. 1:2-3.

43 Alfred Edersheim, *Sketches of Jewish Social Life* (Updated Edition), p. 130.

44 Paul Joannides, *Guide To Getting It On,* p. 283.

Chapter Five

1 See 1 Kings 4:21– 28.

2 Song 3:6 – 11.

3 Comedian Red Green plays on this attitude with what he calls *The Man's Prayer,* "I'm a man, but I can change, if I have to, I guess." Using a play on an old philosophy question, another comedian asked, "If a man is alone in the woods and says something and a woman is not there to correct him, is he still wrong?" The answer from the comedian's point of view was, "Of course."

[4] Phil. 2:6-8 and Mark 10:45, See also James 3:13; 1 Peter 5:5.

[5] Keil & Delitzsch, *Commentary on the Old Testament: New Updated Edition*, Electronic Database.

[6] Song 2:10-13.

[7] David & Carole Hocking, *Romantic Lovers*, p. 65. Also, see Keil & Delitzsch *Commentary on the Old Testament: New Updated Edition*, Electronic Database, which notes with regard to Song 2:10, "Solomon again once more passes, perhaps on a hunting expedition into the northern mountains after the winter with its rains, which made them inaccessible, is over; and after long waiting, Shulamith at length again sees him, and he invites her to enjoy with him the spring season." (Note: there are a number of ways Shulamite is spelled in English. Keil & Delitzsch use "Shulamith." Old Testament Hebrew has 22 consonants and no vowels, which makes transliteration difficult. The two spellings are of the same name, however.)

[8] 2 Kings 18:31, Micah 4:4, Zechariah 3:10. Compare for bad times: Joel 1:12 and Hag. 2:19.

[9] Song 3:6-11.

[10] This will be discussed in much more detail in Chapter 10.

[11] Song 2:5.

[12] Keil & Delitzsch, *Commentary on the Old Testament: New Updated Edition*, Electronic Database.

[13] Song 2:17.

[14] The first time Solomon referred to Shulamite as his "bride" was Song 4:8. Then he referred to her with this term in five successive verses. In Song 4:12 he described her: "You are a garden locked up, my sister, my bride; you are a spring enclosed, a sealed fountain." This was a reference to her virginity as they are about to marry. In verse 16 she invited him into her garden. They were married, and this was their wedding night. The passage that is quoted, Song 7:12-13, is long after the wedding.

[15] Alexandra Penny, *How To Make Love To A Man*, p. 36.

[16] Gen 1:26 and Song of Solomon 5:1b.

[17] See generally 1 John 4: 8 and John 10: 10.

[18] The word "servanthood" is being used here intentionally, although it does not appear in the dictionaries available to me. Servanthood is used here to mean an atti-

tude of wanting to serve another, motivated by love. It is a desire to do things for, build up, look after, care for and meet the needs of another with a feeling of joy. The word "servitude" has too much of an implication of blind obedience to commands and a sense of drudgery while serving. Servanthood involves actions we *want* to do, choose to do, rather than are *required* to do.

[19] Even the word "holy," with which we describe God, refers to a separateness. As *The New Unger's Bible Dictionary*, notes regarding the word HOLINESS: "Heb. qodesh; Gk. hagiosune; in both cases "separation," or "setting apart...""

[20] One of the best descriptions of servanthood and the motivation behind it are contained in Chapters 33 and 34 of *The Purpose Driven Life*, by Rev. Rick Warren. On page 257, he points out that "Jesus ... measured greatness in terms of service, not status. God determines your greatness by how many people you serve, not by how many people serve you."

[21] Song 4:16 - 5:1.

[22] Song 4:12.

[23] Shulamite had twice warned against the untimely arousal and awakening of love in Song of Solomon 2:7 and 3:5. Later, she reprises this warning as advice to unmarried women in 8:4. This issue will be discussed in detail in Chapter 6.

[24] Song 4:16.

[25] One of the individuals who edited this book asked, "Is this appropriate for high school aged students?" In other words, is the subject of sexuality in marriage, and what Scripture says about it, appropriate for high school seniors? The answer is clearly *yes*. One of the reasons for this book is that we are not teaching proper Biblical principles about sexuality. Young men and women in their late teens need this information. They will be considering marriage in the next few years. They need to be fully prepared with God's word, not simply the misguided messages the world sends. Clearly the best *place* for this subject to be taught to high school students, however, is in the home and the church.

[26] Song 5:1.

[27] Verse 5:1 has a second sentence, which will be addressed in Chapter 8.

[28] Some commentators see this scene as a dream. (See Keil & Delitzsch *Commentary on the Old Testament: New Updated Edition*, Electronic Database; and *The Wycliffe Bible Commentary*, Electronic Database.) Others see it as a real event. (See *Jamieson, Fausset, and Brown Commentary*, Electronic Database.) The entire context appears to

better support the argument that this is a real event, not a dream. Whether this is a dream or reality, the lesson to be learned is the same and equally valuable.

[29] When I mentioned this passage, one woman replied, "She was not rejecting *him*. She was not accepting to the activity at this time. Maybe it was midnight or 4 a.m. Men are notorious for bad timing." This is an important observation since it underlines many of the differences between men and women when it comes to sexual matters. It will be covered in detail in Chapter 11. For now, however, ladies, keep this in mind. Even if your husband is "notorious for bad timing," he will consider rejecting sex as the equivalent of rejecting him. This, too, will be explained in greater detail in Chapter 11.

[30] From Keil & Delitzsch, *Commentary on the Old Testament: New Updated Edition*, Electronic Database.

[31] Cf: Matthew 2:1.

[32] From *Barnes' Notes*, Electronic Database.

[33] Song 5:9.

[34] Song 5:10 - 16.

[35] Eph. 5:33.

Chapter Six

[1] If this sounds "unforgiving" on my part, keep in mind that *forgiveness* and *trust*, while somewhat related, are actually two different issues. For a wonderful discussion of forgiveness and its relationship to trust, see Rev. Rick Warren, *The Purpose Driven Life*, p. 142 – 143.

[2] For an excellent discussion of this issue, see John Trent, Ph.D., *Love For All Seasons*, p. 33 - 63.

[3] Song 1:3.

[4] Song 1:7.

[5] Song 3:5 and 8:4.

[6] From Keil & Delitzsch, *Commentary on the Old Testament: New Updated Edition*, Electronic Database.

7 This point will be explained in much greater detail in chapter 8 when the Biblical limits of sex are described.

8 Song 8:8 – 9 with Shulamite responding in verse 10.

9 The word *shalom* (shaw-lome') OT:7965, which the NIV translates as "contentment" can also be translated as "peace." *(Biblesoft's New Exhaustive Strong's Numbers and Concordance with Expanded Greek-Hebrew Dictionary.)* See also, NKJ, ASV, NAS, NASU, and RSV.

10 The simplistic attitude that "kids will do it anyway" ignores the reality that the wide-spread involvement in sex before marriage is largely a modern Western phenomenon. If "kids will engage in sex anyway," one must wonder why they did not do so at such a rate for the 2,000 years preceding the late 20th century.

11 See: Song 4:4 and Song 7:4a, respectively.

12 See Deut. 31:27 and Jer. 17:23 for "stiff-necked." Also see how "outstretched neck" is used to describe people in Ps. 75:5 and Is. 3:16.

13 Cf: Ezek. 27:10-11.

14 Prov. 31:25-26.

15 This was one of the major problems of the Pharisees. Jesus was not the only person to attack the Pharisees in this regard. The rabbis regularly poked fun at the Pharisees for their extreme self-righteousness. See, for example, Abraham Cohen, *Everyman's Talmud,* p. 100 – 101.

16 Many commentators believe Solomon wrote this poem early in his life. There is little doubt that, as he went along in his political career, some of the women he married for purposes of state led him away from his original high ideals. However, that does not diminish the significance of what he was writing in this Song. The fact that he was led astray also stands as a warning to those who are proud of their own morality.

17 Song 2:16, 6:3 and 7:10, respectively.

18 See also Matthew 19:5-6.

19 Ecclesiastes 4:9-12.

20 Genesis 2:18.

21 Mal. 2:15.

[22] Prov. 2:16-17.

[23] Jesus directly addressed this issue when he was asked by the Pharisees about divorce. Matt 19:3 – 8.

[24] The nature of covenant is alluded to in Genesis 15:9-21 with the cutting of the animals in half and the fire pot passing between the pieces. In Jeremiah 34:18, God warns, "The men who have violated my covenant and have not fulfilled the terms of the covenant they made before me, I will treat like the calf they cut in two and then walked between its pieces." A covenant was made by walking between the halves of the calf which was cut in two. Indeed, it was said that people "cut" covenants; they did not "make" them. Breaching the covenant meant you would be treated like the calf, i.e., you too would be cut in half. Thus, breaching the covenant resulted in a death sentence. The marriage vows were a very serious covenant, indeed.

[25] Ecc. 4:12 and Mal. 2:14, respectively.

[26] The actual speaker of the second sentence in Song 5:1 is a subject of controversy among scholars. Some Bibles identify the speakers as "friends" (NIV), others as "the women" (Today's English Version), still others as "Young Women of Jerusalem" (New Living Translation). Commentators also are divided. Barnes' Notes and Adam Clarke's Commentary describe this as a statement by the husband to the guests. The Wycliffe Bible Commentary says it is "Someone (possibly more than one), we do not know who, is speaking here and exhorting the two lovers to delight fully in each other's presence." (*The Wycliffe Bible Commentary*, Electronic Database.) Regardless of who the speaker is, it is apparent that these are inspired words (2 Tim. 3:16), and, therefore, God's view of marital sex. David and Carole Hocking, (*Romantic Lovers, The Intimate Marriage*, p.119*)*, conclude simply that these words are "Spoken by God Himself." Since Sharron and I do not have a bunch of friends or a group of women in the bedroom with us when we are making love, but God is present, and because the words are inspired, I join the Hockings in their conclusion that God is the speaker.

[27] Michael J. McManus, *Marriage Savers*, Revised Edition, p. 50, points out that about 73% of all first marriages take place in a church, synagogue, mosque or other religious setting. That means that the remaining 27% do not. Of these a measurable percentage would be civil weddings.

[28] "The objection that nothing is known of any religious benediction at the marriage, or any mutual vow of fidelity, is merely an *argumentum a silentio*, which proves nothing." Keil & Delitzsch, *Commentary on the Old Testament: New Updated Edition*, Electronic Database. Comments regarding Mal. 2:10-16. (Emphasis added.)

[29] See *History and Customs of Marriage*, Parish Leadership Seminars, Inc., (an audio tape series.)

[30] Obviously, the only exception is a professional counselor in a counseling setting, who is controlled by rules of confidentiality .

[31] 1 John 4:18.

[32] Matt. 7:3-5.

[33] 1 John 1:8-10. (As on prior occasions, the personal pronoun for God is left in the lower case to keep the quote from the NIV accurate.)

[34] Rom. 3:23.

[35] Song 2:15.

[36] From *The Wycliffe Bible Commentary*, Electronic Database.

Chapter Seven

[1] Song 8:6-7. As *The Wycliffe Bible Commentary*, Electronic Database, notes: "These words, uttered by the bride, sum up the theme of the entire Song and constitute its climax."

[2] "Verse 6. The key-note of the poem. It forms the Old Testament counterpart to Paul's panegyric (1 Cor. 13) under the New." *Barnes' Notes*, Electronic Database, Song 8:6-7.

[3] Solomon uses the Hebrew word 'ahabah (a-hab-aw) for "love." *Biblesoft's New Exhaustive Strong's Numbers and Concordance with Expanded Greek-Hebrew Dictionary*. OT:160 *Ahabah* is the Hebrew equivalent to the Greek word *agape*, which Paul used in his epistle to the Corinthians. However, *ahabah* also adds the Greek concepts of the warm feelings of friendship *(philios)* and may include sexual attraction *(eros)*.

[4] *The Wycliffe Commentary*, Electronic Database, for 1 Corinthians 13:4–7, notes: "Charity suffereth long, and is kind may be a summary statement of the section, with the next eight qualities related to longsuffering and the next four to kindness." Wycliff uses the phrase "longsuffering," which is another translation for *makrothumia (mak-roth-oo-mee-ah)*, which we translate as "patience."

[5] 'Arak (aw-rak), in Hebrew, and *makrothumia (mak-roth-oo-mee-ah)*, in Greek. OT:750, NT:3114 *Biblesoft's New Exhaustive Strong's Numbers and Concordance with Expanded Greek-Hebrew Dictionary*.

[6] Billy Graham, *The Holy Spirit*, p. 195.

[7] John 13:34-35.

[8] Jesus prayed that the cup of suffering on the cross be taken from Him (Mark 14:36; Luke 22:42). Only a masochist would *want* to die such a horrible death. Christ clearly was doing something He did not want to do.

[9] John 15:13.

[10] The expectation that we will forgive is so important that Christ considers forgiveness to be the starting point of obedience, not even worthy of praise. In Luke 17:3 – 10, He explains that the servant who shows a forgiving heart still says to the master, "We are unworthy servants; we have only done our duty."

[11] Matt. 6:12, 14 –15.

[12] Matt. 18:22 NKJV.

[13] Our sinfulness is a constant theme in Scripture: 2 Chron. 6:36: "there is no one who does not sin." Jer. 17:9: "The heart is deceitful above all things and beyond cure. Who can understand it?" Rom. 3:23: "For all have sinned and fall short of the glory of God." Eph. 2:3: "All of us also lived among them at one time, gratifying the cravings of our sinful nature and following its desires and thoughts." 1 John 1:8: "If we claim to be without sin, we deceive ourselves and the truth is not in us."

[14] See Matt. 18:25 in which Jesus tells His followers that they will not be forgiven "unless you forgive your brother from your heart."

[15] See also Jer. 15:19, Luke 13:3, and Acts 3:19 for the same concept expressed.

[16] 2 Cor. 7:10.

[17] Acts 26:20.

[18] See also Solomon's Prayer at the dedication of the Temple, 1 Kings 8:33–36, along with Ezek. 18:21–22; 27–28, 30–32, and Rev. 2:5 for the same concept.

[19] Luke 19:8–10.

[20] Needless to say, even if there is no forgiveness (by our fellow human beings) God still wants us to repent. In those instances, He can provide the ultimate forgiveness, since, in an ultimate sense, we sinned against Him. Cf. Psalm 51, especially verse 4.

[21] Rev. Rick Warren, *The Purpose Driven Life*, p. 143. This quotation is correct, although it there is a grammatically incorrect mixing of singular and plural pronouns.

[22] 1 Cor. 13:7.

23 *New Webster's Dictionary and Thesaurus of the English Language*, p. 540.

24 *Barnes' Notes*, Electronic Database.

25 Cf: "Finally, all of you, live in harmony with one another; be sympathetic, love as brothers, be compassionate and humble." (1 Peter 3:8) Indeed, the fruits of the Spirit listed in Gal. 5:22–23 in large measure constitute the "kindness" side of love.

26 James 3:17.

27 "Chresteuomai (khraste-yoo'-om-ahee); middle voice from NT:5543; to show one-self useful, i.e. act benevolently NT:5541." *Biblesoft's New Exhaustive Strong's Numbers and Concordance*, with Expanded Greek-Hebrew Dictionary.

28 The word used in 1 Cor 13:7 can be translated as "protects" (NIV) or "bears all things" (NKJV, RSV, and NAS). As *Barnes' Notes* observes, however, "The "real" sense of the passage is not materially varied, whichever interpretation is adopted. It means, that in regard to the errors and faults of others, there is a disposition "not" to notice or to revenge them. There is a willingness to conceal, or to bear with them patiently." From *Barnes' Notes*, Electronic Database.

29 In court I have seen "supporters" (typically parents, a spouse or close friends) who keep insisting on the innocence of the defendant despite overwhelming evidence. They deny eyewitnesses, taped confessions, written confessions, photographs, finger-prints and other physical evidence. This is all in the name of "loyalty" and being a "trusting" friend. Unfortunately, these actions ignore that kindness rejoices in the truth. In the end, these individuals do not help the defendant. Instead, they enable the defendant to remain in a state of self-destructive sin. Mental health counselors call this a state of denial.

30 "Agape" (Strong's Numbers 25) is used to describe God's love for us (John 3:16) and for how we are to love God and mankind (Matt. 22:36-40). Paul tells husbands they are to show agape love toward their wives. Eph. 5:25. "Philo" (Strong's Numbers 5368) refers to the close affection or love between friends. Wives are told to learn this form of love toward their husbands in Titus 2:4.

31 Both Lev. 19:18 and Deut. 6:4, the two verses Jesus quotes in Matt. 22:36-40 use *ahab*. *Ahab* includes the concept of the deep love of a close friend. In 1 Sam. 18:1 we are told, "Jonathan became one in spirit with David, and he loved him as himself." The word used to describe Jonathan's love is *ahab*.

32 Song 8:6-7.

33 There are other driving forces that cause people to do things they otherwise would not consider, including guilt, resentment, anger, fear, materialism, lust and the need

for approval. (See Rev. Rick Warren, *The Purpose Driven Life*, p. 27–29) But, God wants *love* to be the only driving force in our lives. Unlike the others, it will lead to positive results.

34 Linda Waite and Maggie Gallagher, *The Case For Marriage*. See generally chapter 7, especially pp. 54–55.

35 Song 8:6.

36 The Scriptural basis for these points are Gen. 2:24, 24:67; Prov. 5:18–19; Song 8:6–7.

37 Eph. 5:18.

38 Song 4:16–5:1.

39 Song 5:1.

40 *Ravah* (OT 7301) and *shagah* (OT 7686), respectively, both refer to being drunk or to reel as from intoxication. See, generally, *Strong's Definitions*.

41 Song 1:2.

42 Ellen Kreidman, *How Can We Light A Fire When The Kids Are Driving Us Crazy?*, p. 47.

43 My wife and I owned a timeshare in a cottage near Traverse City, MI, for several years. We loaned it out to our married friends during the fall and spring with only two conditions: They could take no one with them, no kids, no friends, no parents. And they could take no underwear. Every couple reported having a great time. We jokingly called these weekends "Love and Lust" weekends. The idea, however, was serious. This was to be a time of renewal and rejoicing as a couple.

44 For some excellent ideas on how to love as if there is no tomorrow two resources are: Ellen Kreidman, *How Can We Light A Fire When The Kids Are Driving Us Crazy?*, and Anthony J. Garascia, *Rekindle the Passion While Raising Your Kids*.

Chapter Eight

1 Rev. Tim Gardner begins his book, *Sacred Sex*, with much the same observation: "*Holy sex?* ... How can I mention holiness and sex in the same phrase?" He continued with the answer, "Well, for one thing, because God does." *Sacred Sex*, Tim Alan Gardner, p.1.

[2]The original title for this book was to be "*Sex and Romance in the Biblical Marriage.*" The idea was quickly squelched, however, since the very notion of sex and romance existing in a biblically-based marriage was deemed to be offensive, and certainly not a title that would attract potential readers.

[3] Gen. 2:17. Emphasis added.

[4] Gen. 3:3. Emphasis added.

[5] I have had many discussions with atheists who have a remarkable knowledge of the Bible. In virtually every instance they use archaic translations or take passages out of context to make God's word appear arbitrary and unreasonable. Even when Scripture agrees with the basic social stance the atheist is taking, he will often twist the words to make it appear that Scripture disagrees. They use this to justify ignoring God's word.

[6] Every one of us has this tendency, including me. That is one of the reasons I start every Bible study by praying, "God lead us in the direction You would like us to go, not the direction *we* want to go."

[7] Unfortunately, this desire also moves us to justify our own lusts and perversions.

[8] Cf: Gen. 24:22-47 and Ezek. 16:12.

[9] The following four references are taken from Deut. 4:2, 12:32; Prov. 30:5–6; and Rev. 22:18–19, respectively. See also, Matt. 5:18–19.

[10] The mere existence of what appears to be a pleasure, however, does not mean God approves of it. Someone once told me that God would not have put cocaine in the world if He did not intend us to use it! Not only did God invent sexual intimacy in marriage, but it also is clear that He commands us to enjoy it. Such passages as Gen. 1:27; Prov. 5:18-19 and the entire Song of Solomon urge us to partake of this pleasure God has set before us.

[11] A rabbi once told me that the rabbis of Biblical times taught that sin not only included doing the things God told us not to do, and failing to do the things He commanded us to do, but also included failing (or refusing) to participate in the pleasures God gave us to enjoy. Their reasoning makes sense.

[12] See, generally, Gen. 1:28 and Gen. 2:18–25.

[13] Gen. 2:24, and the meaning of "cleave" or "be united to" (*davaq*) as explained in chapter 1.

[14] See, generally, Gen. 1:28, Prov. 5:18–19, Song 4:16–5:1, and 1 Cor. 7:3–5.

[15] See, generally, such passages as Ex. 20:14, Deut. 5:18, Matt. 19:18, Luke 18:20, and Rom. 13:9.

[16] Scripture generally equates fornication with uncleanliness and adultery. (Cf: 2 Cor. 12:21, Gal. 5:19, Eph. 5:3, and Col. 3:5.) Moreover, where the term "fornication" is used it always is in a derogatory way, indicating that a serious sin has been committed. (For example: Is. 23:17, John 8:41, Rev. 17:1-4, 19:2.)

[17] Lev. 18:22 specifically prohibits homosexuality. Other passages refer to the act in ways which clearly indicate that it is sinful. (Gen. 19:5, Lev. 20:13, Judges 19:22, 1 Kings 14:24, Rom. 1:26-27, 1 Cor. 6:9, and Jude 7). This is an issue that has generated a great deal of controversy recently. This book is not intended to be a discussion of homosexuality. It is meant to address heterosexual couples. Therefore, we will not take a side-trip into this subject. For a complete discussion of the issue, see Robert A. J. Gagnon, *The Bible And Homosexual Practice, Text and Hermeneutics.*

[18] Gen. 1:28 and 1 Cor. 7:3–5.

[19] An excellent resource on the extent of the celebration is Charlie Shedd and Martha Shedd, *Celebration in the Bedroom.*

[20] Mal. 2:15.

[21] Indeed, as Shulamite puts it in Song 8:7, "If one were to give all the wealth of his house for love, it would be utterly scorned."

[22] 1 Cor. 3:16-17, 6:19.

[23] See, for example, "Formation of Mucogingival Defects Associated With Intraoral and Perioral Piercing: Case Reports," by Brooks J.K., Hoper K.A., Reynolds M.A., *JADA The Journal of the American Dental Association,* July 2003, vol. 134, no. 7, p.p. 837 – 843.

[24] Rom. 13:1-2.

[25] A number of authors also have given lists of sexual practices prohibited in Scripture, for example, Linda Dillow and Lorraine Pintus, *Intimate Issues,* p. 199– 201, list 10 prohibited activities. However, a review of the 10 items listed as prohibited shows that all 10 would be covered by the five principles set out here.

[26] Lawrence O. Richards, *The Teacher's Commentary,* p. 356.

[27] Gen. 3:7.

[28] Gen. 3:21.

29 See also Song 2:16, 6:3, and 7:10. The passage from 1 Cor 7:4 continues, "In the same way, the husband's body does not belong to him alone but also to his wife." Inappropriate modesty by a husband, therefore, also cannot be justified.

30 Gen. 2:24, Matt. 19:5, Eph. 5:31.

31 Genesis 4:1 NKJV.

32 See 1Tim. 2:15 in RSV and TEV.

33 Sophrosune [so-fros-oo'-nay].

34 *Biblesoft's New Exhaustive Strong's Numbers and Concordance with Expanded Greek-Hebrew Dictionary.*

35 "SIN: Heb. hatta'a; Grk. hamartia, a falling away from or missing the right path." *The New Unger's Bible Dictionary.*

36 Marvin R. Wilson, *Our Father Abraham, Jewish Root of the Christian Faith*, p. 126. The author adds by way of footnote, "Note the verb form of *het* is *hata.* In addition to this Hebrew verb being translated 'to sin' (see Deut. 1:41), it may be rendered 'miss (the mark)' as in Judg. 20:16."

37 Tim Alan Gardner, *Sacred Sex*, p. 48.

38 Ibid, p. 49.

39 Lev. 19:17. Husbands should not become too self-righteous, however. Not only are there men who are inappropriately modest in the presence of their wives, but we men have at least our share of faults for which our wives need to "rebuke" us.

40 Shulamite invited Solomon to get a "little wild" in Song 7:12.

41 See, for example, Ezek. 3:1– 3, where God has the prophet "eat" the scroll, which contains His word.

42 Julian Robinson, *A Guide to Human Sexual Display, Body Packaging*, p. 38.

43 "In fact, one writer of the period states that fresh flowers were also used, as were many precious and semi-precious jewels that were neatly tied into position in a random pattern with the flowers. Some ladies used perfume that was discreetly located and they also plucked out the fringe areas of the pubic region, somewhat in the oriental manner, to achieve a more aesthetically decorative shape, whilst others preferred small plaits adorned with baroque pearl droplets – suggesting that such a fashion gave rise to the term 'a woman's treasure chest' and 'to obtain the favour of a lady' was an expression to be taken in a literal sense" Ibid, p. 64.

[44] Be aware that there can be a definite "itch" factor when the hair starts to grow back, however. If you wish to try shaving, make sure to use a good safety razor, not a cheap disposable, lots of soap and very warm water. Afterwards, use a skin cream with aloe, which will avoid the initial itch.

[45] The Kama Sutra is the Indian book on sexual relations. Modern English versions of the book, some illustrated, can be found in any good bookstore.

[46] Technically, masturbation is an act which one performs on one's self. Here I am using the word in a broader sense and including manual stimulation of one spouse by the other.

[47] Eccl. 9:9.

[48] John 10:10 RSV.

[49] Song 5:1.

Chapter Nine

[1] Song 4:16.

[2] Song 8:12.

[3] Ronald Cap Ehlke, *People's Bible Commentary, Ecclesiastes, Song of Solomon*, p. 219.

[4] John 3:16.

[5] Mark 10:45.

[6] The difference between a "rights" model and "love" model will be explained in detail in Chapter 12.

[7] This, at least, is the popular view of traditional values. Whether it was ever completely true in practice, however, is another matter. As Mr. Bumble put it in *Oliver Twist*, by Charles Dickens, (Ch. 51), after being told that the law assumed that he was in control of his wife and, therefore, responsible for her actions: "If the law supposes that, the law is an ass – an idiot."

[8] In Michigan, which has been a leader in the legal development of rape law, a man could not rape his wife. This was changed somewhat in 1974 when Public Acts 1974, No. 266, was adopted, which provided: "A person does not commit sexual assault under this act if the victim is his or her legal spouse, unless the couple are living apart and one of them has filed for separate maintenance or divorce." It was not until 1988 when Public Acts 1988, No. 138, was adopted that marriage ceased to be a defense to

a rape charge. The new language states: "A person may be charged and convicted ... [of criminal sexual conduct] ... even though the victim is his or her legal spouse." MCLA 750.520a et seq.

[9] See, generally, the concepts in 1 Cor 13:4–7. Also, cf: Hosea 2:16.

[10] In court, I have had defendants with as many as six drunk driving and a dozen other alcohol-related convictions take "offense" when I suggested they are alcoholics and need to address the issue.

[11] Lev. 19:18, Matt. 22: 37–40, John 13:34-35, Rom. 13:9, Gal. 5:14, and James 2:8.

[12] This is based on a complete word search of *The King James Version, New King James Version, New International Version, Revised Standard Version, The Living Bible, Today's English Version, American Standard Version, New American Standard Version* and the *New American Standard Bible – Updated Edition.* Variations of "compromise," such as "compromised," "compromises" and "compromising," also were checked, and not found in any of these translations.

[13] For example, the concept of Trinity can be found in such passages as Matt. 28:19 and 2 Corinthians 13:14. The Old Testament refers to the Father and the Holy Spirit in Joel 2:28 – 29.

[14] Of course, there is the famous "negotiation" between Abraham and God over the fate of Sodom and Gomorrah in Gen. 18: 20–33. A fair reading of the event, however, demonstrates that it was not a compromise. Abraham petitioned God six times, constantly reducing the number of righteous people needed for the cities to be saved. God granted all six requests. God never asked for anything in return nor set a limit on what He was ready to give.

[15] Gen. 4:1.

[16] Dennis Rainey, *Lonely Husbands, Lonely Wives,* p. 122.

[17] Gary Chapman, *The Five Languages of Love,* p. 93.

[18] "A new command I give you: Love one another. As I have loved you, so you must love one another." John 13:34-35.

[19] Zachariah and Elizabeth are names taken from the Gospel of Luke, the parents of John the Baptizer. The names do not represent any real couple, since I seriously doubt that the hypothetical situation presented here was one that ever crossed the minds of either the original Zachariah or Elizabeth.

[20] I have a framed drawing in my office which my daughter made when she was six. It is glorified stick figures (they have clothes on) of her and her brother, both with big

smiles. In the background are a dozen bright yellow "suns." When she first gave it to me, I asked her why there would be more than one sun in the sky. She said, with the perfect logic of a six year old, "Daddy, if it can rain rain, it should be able to rain sunshine." That was over 25 years ago. I will keep it always. For the same reason, I also have art work from my son in the office.

21 Since the entire world belongs to God (Ex. 19:5) there really is nothing we can "give" God that He doesn't own already.

22 John 13:34.

23 Trial lawyers often talk about the "perfect compromise" being one in which both parties feel "equally unhappy" because of what they had to give up. Unfortunately, in marriage it often can be the same, with both husband and wife feeling "equally unhappy" at what they "had to give up." God created marriage to bring joy and intimate oneness, not a sense of equal unhappiness.

24 Eph. 5:25.

25 One of the best communications skills programs available that can be used in conjunction with the model described in this chapter is PREP® developed by Drs. Howard Markman and Scott Stanley of the University of Denver, with the help of Drs. Susan Blumberg and Savanna McCain.

Chapter Ten

1 Willard F. Harley, Jr., *His Needs, Her Needs*, chapter 2. Dr. Harley uses the metaphor of a "love bank" which needs regular deposits if there are to be regular withdrawals. *His Needs, Her Needs*. Here I am using the metaphor of "love tank," which Gary Chapman uses in *The Five Love Languages*, p. 21.

2 *kephale* (kef-al-ay') Biblesoft's *New Exhaustive Strong's Numbers and Concordance with Expanded Greek-Hebrew Dictionary.* Strong's Number NT:2776.

3 Cf: Matt. 6:17, 8:20, 10:30.

4 Matt. 21:42, Mk. 12:10, Luke 20:17. See also 1 Cor. 11:3, 1 Peter 2:7.

5 ro'sh (roshe) Biblesoft's *New Exhaustive Strong's Numbers and Concordance with Expanded Greek-Hebrew Dictionary.* Strongs Number OT:7218.

6 Ro'sh is often translated as "the beginning," for example in Ex. 12:2 (NKJV; NASU); Numbers 10:10; Deut. 32:42 (KJV); Judges 7:19; Is. 40:21, 41:4, 26.

[7] Dwight A. Pryor of The Center for Judaic-Christian Studies, in his tape series, *In His Image: Biblical Insights into Love, Marriage and the Family,* (Tape 2, Side A), points out that *kephale* can also be translated as "a source," as in the head waters of a river.

[8] Joan Declaire, "Your Marriage, Getting Better All The Time," *Reader's Digest,* February, 2003, P.p. 69.

[9] Riley Rochelle, "Dear People: The sexiest man alive is ...," *Detroit Free Press,* Section J, Dec. 7, 2003.

[10] Dr. James C. Dobson, *Love For A Lifetime.* p. 93.

[11] Dr. John Gray, *Men are from Mars, Women are from Venus,* (chapter 10). Dr. John Gray makes a wonderful point of this in his chapter "Scoring Points With The Opposite Sex."

[12] In addition to those quoted below, see Dennis Rainey, *Lonely Husbands, Lonely Wives,* p. 255; and, Ed Wheat and Gloria Okes Perkins, *Love Life For Every Married Couple.*

[13] Dr. Willard F. Harley *His Needs, Her Needs,* p. 27.

[14] Ibid. p. 40.

[15] Op cit, p. 41.

[16] Alexandra Penney, *How To Keep Your Man Monogamous,* p. 88.

[17] Ibid. p. 91.

[18] 1 Cor. 7:3-5.

[19] Dr. Willard F. Harley, Jr., *His Needs, Her Needs,* p. 32.

[20] Proverbs 30:21–23. The other three are, "a servant who becomes king, a fool who is full of food, ... and a maidservant who displaces her mistress."

[21] See *His Needs, Her Needs,* by Dr. Willard Harley, p. 34, which notes that the typical male "sees showing affection as part of sexual foreplay, and he is normally aroused in a flash."

[22] As one author bluntly puts it in basic terms, "Studies show that the guy who helps out around the house gets laid more often than guys who don't, causing speculation that Windex and 409 are better aphrodisiacs than oysters, expensive cars and a medicine chest full of Viagra." Paul Joannides, *Guide to Getting It On!, Third Edition,* p. 283.

23 Ladies, don't get too smug about this. Wives also are to love their husbands, not necessarily understand them.

24 Phil. 2:4.

25 We see this in all aspects of life. If we like a person in public office, the person is a "public servant." If we don't like him, he is simply a "self-serving politician."

26 As I was writing this, I asked about the spelling of "biggies" in this context. As soon as I read the sentence, every man in the room quickly corrected me by saying it was not "one" of the biggies, it is "the" biggie!

27 Dr. John Gray, *Men are from Mars, Women are from Venus*, p. 193.

28 Eph. 5:26-29.

29 Dr. James C. Dobson, *Love For A Lifetime, Building a Marriage That Will Go the Distance*, p. 41.

30 Don't become too self-righteous about this, men. We can be less than loving when *our* hormones take over and we push the issue of sex or our tendency to dominate more than we should.

31 "We've Had Our Baby ... Now What About Sex," Marriages That Work of Lenawee County, MI. The following list of suggestions also is quoted from this source.

32 Ibid.

Chapter Eleven

1 Dr. Willard Harley, *His Needs, Her Needs*, Chapter 4.

2 This is the basis of the complaints about Jesus by the Pharisees in Luke 15:2.

3 Desmond Morris, *Intimate Behavior*, p. 97–98.

4 The normal level for an adult male is >0.30 micrograms / 100 ml, while an adult female has only <0.10 micrograms/100 ml. *The Merck Manual of Diagnosis and Therapy*, Robert Berkow, M.D., Editor, p. 2071, Table 24-5.

5 See, generally, Dr. Willard F. Harley, Jr., *His Needs, Her Needs,* p. 43–44.

6 Ibid, p. 34.

7 Phil. 2:2-4.

[8] Most often it appears to be the wife who feels unhappy and disconnected, but husbands also feel this way more often than God intends.

[9] Proverbs 30:23.

[10] Waite, Linda, and Maggie Gallagher, *The Case for Marriage*, p. 94.

[11] Dr. Patricia Love and Jo Robinson, *Hot Monogamy*, pp. 81–82.

[12] See, generally, Ex. 20:14; Lev. 20:10; Deut. 5:18.

[13] 2 Cor. 9:7.

[14] Prov. 11:25.

[15] Fredericks of Hollywood, The Sleazy Lingerie Shop of Los Angeles and similar stores.

[16] See Song 7:11–13.

[17] Men's Health, June 2001, Vol. 16, No.5, p. 128.

[18] Men also want to be thought of as good providers and competent protectors. They want to be respected for whom they are. This book is about the intimate aspects of marriage, however, and, therefore, is focused on how men want to be understood in *this* area of their lives. John Gray provides a wonderful outline of a more complete list of men's needs in *Men are from Mars, Women are from Venus*, p. 140–141. Willard Harley, Jr., also provides an outline of men's needs from a different perspective in *His Needs, Her Needs*.

[19] Song 7:12-13.

[20] Weiner Davis, Michele, *The Sex Starved Marriage*, p. 58.

[21] "J", *The Sensuous Woman*, p. 88–89.

[22] "J", *The Sensuous Woman*, p. 90.

[23] Remember, letting others see you would be inviting them into your marriage, which is inappropriate. It also would take a great deal of the spark out of the evening if you ended up in jail for indecent exposure.

[24] Eph. 4:29. RSV.

[25] Michelle Weiner Davis makes the same observation, quoting one man as saying, "I always have to initiate. When I get rejected it feels like a rejection of *me*, not the activity. The rejection hurts." *The Sex Starved Marriage*, p. 58.

26 Hos. 6:6.

27 Mic. 6:8.

28 From *Jamieson, Fausset, and Brown Commentary Electronic Database*, on Micah 6:8.

29 Matt. 5:7.

30 These suggestions for wives are taken from "We Had Our Baby ... Now What About Sex?", a brochure by Marriages That Work, Inc., of Lenawee County, Michigan. A few minor grammatical changes were made that do not in any way affect the meaning of the text.

31 "J", *The Sensuous Woman*, p. 90.

Chapter Twelve

1 There are couples who have medical problems from accidents or illnesses, which can greatly interfere with their sex lives or the ability to provide romance. Indeed, in some instances accidents or illness may bring a complete end to a couple's sex life. Couples in these situations need to work out alternative methods of maintaining oneness in their relationship. However, that would be the subject of a completely different book.

2 This list of needs for men and women is taken from *His Needs, Her Needs*, by Dr. Willard Harley. Note, also: These needs are not meant to be gender exclusive. Men and women share all the needs on both lists. The level of need and the prioritizing are different, however. Dr. John Gray, in *Men are from Mars, Women are from Venus*, p.p. 134–138, adds that women need caring, understanding, respect, devotion, validation, and reassurance. Men need trust, acceptance, appreciation, admiration, approval, and encouragement.

3 Steven Covey, Smart Marriage Conference, Arlington, VA, July 11, 2002.

4 See Jer. 16:1–2 and 1 Cor. 7:1. Both Jeremiah and Paul remained single.

5 Marvin R. Wilson, *Our Father Abraham, Jewish Roots of the Christian Faith*, p. 198.

6 Ibid, p. 199.

7 Gen. 2:18.

8 Gen. 2:24; Deut. 6:4. Both passages use the word *'echad* (ekh-awd') for "one." OT:259 *Biblesoft's New Exhaustive Strong's Numbers and Concordance with Expanded Greek-Hebrew Dictionary.*

9 John 3:16.

10 The concept of "rights" in relation to marriage appears only once in Scripture. (Ex 21:9 – 10)   It is in regard to a slave who has a covenant relationship with her master, who is not to "break faith." When the covenant is broken, she then has "rights" at the very least. The "right" God described was to protect married women in these settings by requiring they be treated like daughters of their new households and not be denied food, shelter, or marital privileges by husbands who took second wives. A closer look at even this "right," however, shows that it is little more than the "right" to receive the minimum of what love would give.

11 See, for example, Lev. 19:18, Matt. 19:19, John 13:34 – 35, Rom. 13:9, Gal. 5:14, and James 2:8. There are numerous other references to loving others, although different wording is used. Cf: Hosea 6:6 and Micah 6:8.

12 Rom. 13:10.

13 Gen. 1: 31.

14 Luke 6:46.

15 Acts 17:11. So, OK, you caught me. The original has the Bereans checking the Scripture every day to see if what *Paul* said was true. But, the same principle applies.

16 1 Thess. 5:17.

Appendix

1 Remember, letting others see you would be inviting them into your marriage, which is inappropriate. It would also take a great deal of the spark out of the evening if you ended up in jail for indecent exposure.

Marriage Done Right
10864 Burton Rd.
Adrian, MI 49221-9432
(517) 547-4905
www.marriagedoneright.com

Other marriage support resources by James E. Sheridan brought to you
by **Marriage Done Right.**

Sex and Romance in the Biblical Marriage $125.00

This 6-hour videotape series is a presentation of the basic material found in *A Blessing for
the Heart.* James Sheridan employs his usual dynamic, energetic style to present a comprehensive review of how Scripture depicts sexual intimacy and romance in marriage.
You will laugh while you learn detailed suggestions on how to apply Biblical principles to
your marriage. Church groups have used it successfully across the country in Sunday
morning couples' Bible study, small group couples' studies, and marriage enrichment
gatherings.

The set includes a discussion leader's guide and a participants' guide. All participants'
materials may be copied for use by couples working with the videos without prior permission from **Marriage Done Right.**

Domestic Violence: The Biblical View $12.50
By: James E. Sheridan, © 1997 LCMS

One of the most perverse crutches used by abusive men to "justify" physical violence
against women is Scripture. In this video James Sheridan directly faces the "wives be subject" passages (Eph. 5:22–24) and other verses which appear to authorize men to dominate women. Sheridan paints a broader picture of the Biblical vision of how husbands
and wives are to see each other. He also puts these and many other passages into proper
historic, cultural, linguistic and Biblical context.

This video is a must for counselors or church professionals who deal with abusive men. It
is also an excellent review of the subject for Bible study groups interested in the issue of
domestic violence. You will never again have to sit quietly by when an abusive male tells
you, "I don't care what *you* say... *God* tells me I can physically discipline my wife!"

This video was produced by the Lutheran Church Missouri Synod.

A Handbook for Implementing a Community Marriage Policy™
$12.50

This handbook is based on the Lenawee County, Michigan, experience in establishing a
Community Marriage Policy™ following the Marriage Saver® model. This is a step by
step description of how to organize and implement a policy of support in your community.

Marriage Done Right Order Form

	No. Ordered	Total Price

Sex and Romance in the Biblical Marriage
Videotape set plus leader and participant materials   @ $125.00   _____ _____

**A Handbook for Implementing
a Community Marriage Policy™**   @ $12.50   _____ _____

Domestic Violence: The Biblical View
Videotape   @ $12.50   _____ _____

A Blessing for the Heart   Single issue price   @ $14.50   _____ _____
                             Orders of 10 or more @ $12.50 each   _____ _____
                             Orders of 50 or more @ $10.00 each   _____ _____

SUBTOTAL

Sales tax: 6% for non-tax exempt purchasers   _____

Shipping and Handling:
          Sex & Romance Video set $7.50   _____
          Handbook $1.50   _____
          Domestic Violence Video $3.50   _____
          A Blessing for the Heart: add $3.00 for first copy
          and .50 for each additional copy   _____

Total Shipping and Handling: _____

TOTAL   _____

Mastercard and Visa accepted for mail, phone and fax orders.

Orders by telephone: (517) 547-4905

Mail orders: Marriage Done Right   **Enclose check or credit card information**
                   10864 Burton Rd.   Name of card holder: ———————————————
                   Adrian, MI 49221   Expiration date: ———————————————————
                                           Card no.: ——————————————————————————

Fax orders: (517) 547-5744   **Fill out credit card information above**

Shipping information: Name: ——————————————————————————————————
(Print clearly or type)   Address: ———————————————————————————————
                                      ————————————————————————————————————
                                      ————————————————————————————————————

Phone number in case of problems with the order: ————————————————————

(Note: All prices are subject to change without notice. In the event of a price change,
the order will not be filled without the purchaser's consent to the change in price.
Books shipped USPS, book rate, unless otherwise requested.)

Marriage Done Right
10864 Burton Rd.
Adrian, MI 49221-9432
(517) 547-4905
www.marriagedoneright.com

Other marriage support resources by James E. Sheridan brought to you
by **Marriage Done Right.**

Sex and Romance in the Biblical Marriage $125.00

This 6-hour videotape series is a presentation of the basic material found in *A Blessing for
the Heart.* James Sheridan employs his usual dynamic, energetic style to present a comprehensive review of how Scripture depicts sexual intimacy and romance in marriage.
You will laugh while you learn detailed suggestions on how to apply Biblical principles to
your marriage. Church groups have used it successfully across the country in Sunday
morning couples' Bible study, small group couples' studies, and marriage enrichment
gatherings.

The set includes a discussion leader's guide and a participants' guide. All participants'
materials may be copied for use by couples working with the videos without prior permission from **Marriage Done Right.**

Domestic Violence: The Biblical View $12.50
By: James E. Sheridan, © 1997 LCMS

One of the most perverse crutches used by abusive men to "justify" physical violence
against women is Scripture. In this video James Sheridan directly faces the "wives be subject" passages (Eph. 5:22–24) and other verses which appear to authorize men to dominate women. Sheridan paints a broader picture of the Biblical vision of how husbands
and wives are to see each other. He also puts these and many other passages into proper
historic, cultural, linguistic and Biblical context.

This video is a must for counselors or church professionals who deal with abusive men. It
is also an excellent review of the subject for Bible study groups interested in the issue of
domestic violence. You will never again have to sit quietly by when an abusive male tells
you, "I don't care what *you* say…*God* tells me I can physically discipline my wife!"

This video was produced by the Lutheran Church Missouri Synod.

A Handbook for Implementing a Community Marriage Policy™
$12.50

This handbook is based on the Lenawee County, Michigan, experience in establishing a
Community Marriage Policy™ following the Marriage Saver® model. This is a step by
step description of how to organize and implement a policy of support in your community.

Marriage Done Right Order Form

	No. Ordered	Total Price

Sex and Romance in the Biblical Marriage
Videotape set plus leader and participant materials   @ $125.00   _____ _____

**A Handbook for Implementing
a Community Marriage Policy™**   @ $12.50   _____ _____

Domestic Violence: The Biblical View
Videotape   @ $12.50   _____ _____

A Blessing for the Heart   Single issue price   @ $14.50   _____ _____
Orders of 10 or more @ $12.50 each   _____ _____
Orders of 50 or more @ $10.00 each   _____ _____

SUBTOTAL

Sales tax: 6% for non-tax exempt purchasers   _____

Shipping and Handling:
Sex & Romance Video set $7.50   _____
Handbook $1.50   _____
Domestic Violence Video $3.50   _____
A Blessing for the Heart: add $3.00 for first copy
and .50 for each additional copy   _____

Total Shipping and Handling: _____

TOTAL   _____

Mastercard and Visa accepted for mail, phone and fax orders.

Orders by telephone: (517) 547-4905

Mail orders: Marriage Done Right   **Enclose check or credit card information**
10864 Burton Rd.   Name of card holder: ——————————
Adrian, MI 49221   Expiration date: ————————————
Card no.: ——————————————

Fax orders: (517) 547-5744   **Fill out credit card information above**

Shipping information: Name: ——————————————————————
(Print clearly or type)   Address: —————————————————————
——————————————————————
——————————————————————

Phone number in case of problems with the order: ——————————————————

(Note: All prices are subject to change without notice. In the event of a price change,
the order will not be filled without the purchaser's consent to the change in price.
Books shipped USPS, book rate, unless otherwise requested.)